BUSINESS MATH BASICS

FOURTH EDITION

Robert E. Swindle, M.B.A., Ph.D.

Glendale Community College

PWS-KENT Publishing Company
Boston

PWS–KENT
Publishing Company

20 Park Plaza
Boston, Massachusetts 02116

Sponsoring Editor: Timothy L. Anderson
Production Coordinator: Wanda K. Wilking
Production: Linda Belamarich
Interior Designer: Wanda K. Wilking
Cover Designer: Jean Hammond
Manufacturing Coordinator: Marcia A. Locke
Typesetter: Beacon Graphics
Cover Printer: John P. Pow Company, Inc.
Text Printer and Binder: The Murray Printing Company

PWS-KENT Publishing Company is a division of Wadsworth, Inc.

Printed in the United States of America
1 2 3 4 5 6 7 8 9—94 93 92 91 90

Library of Congress Cataloging-in-Publication Data

Swindle, Robert E.
    Business math basics/Robert E. Swindle—4th ed.
      p. cm.
    ISBN 0-534-91995-2
    1. Business mathematics. I. Title.
HF5691.S84   1989
650'.01'513—dc20   89-36804
                             CIP

Contents

PART 2: Foundational Math of Business

PART 3: Mathematics of Banking

PART 4: Mathematics of Marketing

PART 5: Mathematics of Accounting

PART 6: Mathematics of Finance

APPENDIX

A Note to You, the Student

This book is designed to increase your effectiveness in:

1. Performing the math that is required in other business courses, such as accounting, finance, and marketing.
2. Taking the preemployment tests that most businesses now administer to applicants.
3. Performing the math calculations needed in your present work and in the jobs you will eventually hold.
4. Completing everyday transactions as a citizen and consumer.

Systematic Approach

Each section of the book begins with a clear **explanation of a business math concept**—not only to acquaint you with the materials, but also to tell you how every concept is applied to actual business transactions. All instructions are followed by **self-check questions** (answers at the end of each chapter) to help ensure that you understand what you have just read before you continue.

Then, after having completed either or both of the end-of-chapter assignments, as directed by your instructor, you may check the **answers to odd-numbered problems** in the Appendix beginning on page 412. Additionally, you may preview a test before you take it, with use of special **practice tests** at the end of each of the six parts of the book.

Real-World Orientation

All materials are designed to prepare you for success in class and to familiarize you with typical business transactions. Relevance is enhanced through the use of authentic invoices, tax tables, bank statements, stock and bond quotations, and other documents used in actual business situations.

Comprehensive Coverage

Following a review of basic mathematics, you will build a solid foundation in measures and percents in preparation for the sections that follow. You will then encounter subjects that are present in an applied setting, including the mathematics of banking, marketing, accounting, and finance. Key terms are highlighted throughout the chapters for easy review, and a complete index is provided near the front of the book. *Business Math Basics* will serve you well as a valuable reference source long after you have completed this course.

Acknowledgments

Many talented people helped with this edition. Tim Anderson, Sponsoring Editor, provided marketing expertise. Maureen Brooks, Editorial Assistant, provided support. Wanda Wilking, Production Coordinator, managed the production of this text. In creating a computerized test bank, I worked with Andrew Dunlap, Vicki Roberts, and Valary Cruz of Wadsworth Corporate Testing Services. Credit for coordinating and taping twelve hours of lectures goes to Scott Kozakiewicz and Wayne Bruno of Glendale Community College. Finally, the input provided by the following educators was of critical importance to the creation of an effective textbook:

Professor Darlene Appel
University of Alaska

Professor James Carey
Onondaga Community College

Professor Charles Cooper
San Antonio College

Professor Charles F. Dye
York College

Professor Aurelia Gomez
Glendale Community College

Professor Nancy Spillman
LA Trade-Technical College

Credit is also due those people who helped with earlier editions:

Professor James F. Carey
Onondaga Community College

Professor John Chestnutt
Allan Hancock College

Professor Helen M. Etherington
Onondaga Community College

Professor Carleton S. Everett
Des Moines Area Community College

Professor Russell L. Gentry
Mount San Antonio College

Professor Don Isenhart
Wenatchee Valley College

Professor Bernard Karne
Laney College

Professor Murray Krieger
Bronx Community College

Professor John Kroencke
Victor Valley College

Professor Gwen Loftis
Oscar Rose Junior College

Professor William J. Matechak
Broome Community College

Professor James O'Donovan
Cayuga County Community College

Professor Sandra Philips
Central City Business Institute

Professor Lora Todesco
Canada College

Professor Warren C. Weber
California State Polytechnic University

Professor William B. Williams
Columbia State Community College

A final word of appreciation goes to our students, those men and women who form the classroom settings that are so essential to the creation and testing of effective learning materials. My sincere thanks to all of you!

R.E.S.

Index

Review of Math Basics

PART

1

Review of Math Basics

1. Review of Basic Operations

Decimals
Addition with Decimals
Subtraction with Decimals
Multiplication with Decimals
Division with Decimals
Rounding Numbers
Estimating Answers

2. Review of Fractions

Converting Fractions
Adding Fractions
Subtracting Fractions
Multiplying Fractions
Dividing Fractions

3. Review of Percents and Decimals

Changing Percents to Decimals
Changing Decimals to Percents
Changing Fractions to Decimals
Changing Decimals to Fractions
Common Relationships

4. Review of Equations

Working with Signed Numbers
Gathering Terms
Finding an Unknown Number
Using Simple Equations
Proportional Problems

Review of Basic Operations

After reading Chapter 1, you will be able to

- Distinguish between thousands, millions, billions, and trillions, as well as between 10ths, 100ths, and 1,000ths.
- Add, subtract, multiply, and divide numbers with and without decimals.
- Round numbers according to standard business guidelines.
- Estimate answers for those times when it is impractical to manipulate exact figures.

Key Terms

units	dividend
sum	product
minuend	divisor
subtrahend	quotient
difference	remainder
multiplicand	round
multiplier	

Although the materials in Chapter 1 are based on the assumption that you are already familiar with the fundamental operations of addition, subtraction, multiplication, and division, this review of decimal notation will enable you to (1) improve your speed and accuracy in basic calculations and (2) identify such mathematical terms as multiplier, multiplicand, divisor, quotient, dividend, and difference.

Decimals

Decimals are used to separate whole numbers from fractional numbers. If Line B in Figure 1.1 were dollars, the decimal separates the whole dollars (287) from the fractional dollars (a little more than one-half dollar). Rather than list 100 twice, the two in the hundreds position denotes $200. The eight (in the tens position) reflects $80, and the seven (in the **units** position) is for $7. In Line C, 120 thousand is added; Line D, 346 million; Line E, 973 billion; and Line F, 2 trillion. Line F is read as follows:

2 trillion, 973 billion, 346 million, 120 thousand, 287 dollars, and $51\frac{1}{2}$ cents,

or $\$2{,}973{,}346{,}120{,}287.51\frac{1}{2}$

You must be able to distinguish between thousands, millions, and billions because such large figures are widely used. We will learn more about fractional values in Chapters 2 and 3.

	Trillions	Billions	Millions	Thousands	Hundreds Tens Units		10ths	100ths	1000ths
A						•	5	1	5
B					287	•	5	1	5
C				120	287	•	5	1	5
D			346	120	287	•	5	1	5
E		973	346	120	287	•	5	1	5
F	2	973	346	120	287	•	5	1	5

Figure 1.1   Numerical Positions

Self-Check 1A   Decimals

1.   How many millions are included in one billion?

2. Enter in figures the number two million, six hundred fifteen thousand, one hundred sixty-five, and twenty-three hundredths.

3. Describe the following number in words: $1,212,563.12.

4. Enter in figures the number one thousand seventy dollars and fifty-one cents.

5. Enter in figures the number one hundred thousand, eighty dollars.

Addition with Decimals

When adding numbers with decimals, you should always place the decimals in a vertical line and then bring the decimal straight down into the sum. The numbers 26.1, 34.45, 0.045, and 92 would be placed in a column so that the decimals are in line with each other.

$$
\begin{array}{r}
26.1 \\
34.45 \\
0.045 \\
+\ 92. \\
\hline
152.595
\end{array}
$$

For a number that doesn't show a decimal, such as the 92 in the preceding problem, the decimal is assumed to follow the number (92 is the same as 92.). Notice also that the decimal in the sum is directly below the decimals in the numbers being added.

Addition is the simplest type of mathematical operation, and you probably have noticed that some people can add faster than others. Such differences in speed usually result from the use of combinations in adding. For example, people who add fast generally rely on combinations of numbers totaling ten. Consider the numbers 2, 6, 2, 9, 1, 7, and 4. Observe that the first three numbers (2, 6, and 2) equal 10 — to which you add 10 (9 + 1), giving you 20, to which you add 11 (7 + 4), totaling 31. The **sum** (31) is the total of the numbers that have been added.

Also consider the following example in adding 26, 44, 28, 29, 59, and 99. In adding the column at the right (units), you should view 6 and 4 as 10, to which you add 8, giving you 18. The addition then becomes easier because each 9 may be added as "10 less 1," giving you 27, 36, and 45. The 5 in the total 45 is placed in the units column of the answer line, and the 4 is carried to the top of the left column (tens). You should then see the first three numbers in the left column as 10 (4 + 2 + 4), to which you add 9 (2 + 2 + 5), giving you 19, to which you add "10 less 1," resulting in a sum of 28.

$$+10 \left\{ \begin{array}{c} \overset{4}{26} \\ 44 \end{array} \right\} + 10$$

$$\begin{array}{rlll} & 28 & +8 & = 18 \\ +9 = \quad 19 \left\{ \begin{array}{r} 29 \\ 59 \end{array} \right. & +9 & = 27 \\ & +9 & = 36 \\ +9 = \quad 28 \quad \underline{99} & +9 & = 45 \end{array}$$

285 (the sum)

To double-check your answers in addition, you may add the numbers in reverse. If you added from top to bottom to begin with, you may add the numbers a second time, proceeding from the bottom number to the top number.

Self-Check 1B   Addition with Decimals
---

1.   16.10
31.41
26.51
<u>18.91</u>

2.   18.1 + 1.18 + 181 =

3.   279.15 + 15.279 =

4.   If your boss instructs you to buy three items costing $2.17, $5, and 83¢ from an office supply company, what is the total amount that you must pay, including 40¢ tax?

5.   If weekly sales during March were $16,321.12, $17,945.40, $15,915.23, and $18,111.25, what were the total sales for the month?

Subtraction with Decimals

Subtracting one number from another is also an easy operation. Consider the following problem:

21 (minuend)
<u>−14</u> (subtrahend)
7 (difference)

The **minuend** is the number from which the **subtrahend** is being subtracted, and the **difference** between the two numbers is the answer. You may check your answer by adding the subtrahend and difference (14 + 7) to make sure they total the minuend (21). Such double-checks are especially useful in recording calculations in your checkbook.

As in addition, the decimals in the minuend and the subtrahend are placed in a vertical line, and the decimal is brought straight down into the difference (the answer). To subtract 26.74 from 75.28, we therefore place the numbers as follows:

$$
\begin{array}{r}
\overset{6\ 4}{7\cancel{5}.28} \\
-\ 26.74 \\
\hline
48.54
\end{array}
$$

To solve this problem, first subtract the 4 from the 8, resulting in a 4 in the answer. Because 7 cannot be subtracted from 2, you borrow from the 5, reducing the 5 to 4 and increasing the 2 to 12. The 7 is then subtracted from the 12, resulting in 5. Because 6 cannot be subtracted from 4 (remember that the 5 is now a 4), you borrow from the 7, reducing the 7 to 6 and increasing the 4 to 14. You then subtract the 6 from 14, resulting in an answer of 8, and you finish by subtracting the 2 from the 6 (remember that the 6 was a 7 before you borrowed from it). Notice, finally, that the decimal in the answer is directly below the decimals in the numbers being subtracted.

In the following example, the subtrahend is greater than the minuend, resulting in a negative number.

$$
\begin{array}{r}
45.56 \\
-\ 72.18 \\
\hline
-\ 26.62
\end{array}
$$

When subtracting manually, move the larger number to the top, switch the smaller number to the bottom, and then subtract. To show that it is a negative number, either place a minus sign in front of the answer or enclose the answer with parentheses.

Self-Check 1C   Subtraction with Decimals

---

1. $\begin{array}{r} 182 \\ -\ 73 \\ \hline \end{array}$

2. $\begin{array}{r} 300.27 \\ -\ 117.31 \\ \hline \end{array}$

3. Find the difference between 72.61 and 98.805.

4. If you pay $317.25 to a supplier for materials, and later find that the total cost should have been $295.96, how much money should the supplier refund to you?

5. If the sales receipts at Abco Rentals for June were $7,632 and costs and expenses totaled $8,616, what amount of profit was realized for the month?

Multiplication with Decimals

Multiplication is a shortcut for addition. If a small business sells five television sets at $650 each, the easier calculation for the owner to determine total sales is through multiplication.

Addition	*Multiplication*	
$ 650	$ 650	(multiplicand)
650	× 5	(multiplier)
650	$3,250	(product)
650		
650		
$3,250		

The **multiplicand** is the number at the top of a multiplication problem, the **multiplier** is the second listed number, and the **product** is the resulting answer. It is easier to place the larger number at the top and the smaller at the bottom, as shown in the following example:

$$
\begin{array}{r}
315 \\
\times\ 25 \\
\hline
1\ 575 \quad (315 \times 5) \\
6\ 30 \quad\ \ (315 \times 2) \\
\hline
7,875
\end{array}
$$

You begin solving this problem by multiplying 315 by 5:

$5 \times 5 = 25$, with the 5 in the answer being placed in the first answer row and the 2 being carried to the tens column.

$5 \times 1 = 5 +$ the 2 that was carried forward $= 7$, which is also placed in the first answer row.

$5 \times 3 = 15$, which is placed to the left side of the first answer row.

Then multiply 315 by 2 in the same fashion, beginning the answer in the tens column, immediately below the 7 in the first answer line. As a final step, you add the two answer rows to find the product.

When the multiplier contains zeros, some people include unnecessary rows of zeros, as shown in Example 1. This extra step can be avoided by simply moving the next answer line an extra place to the left, as shown in Example 2.

Example 1 (extra step)

```
       4251
     × 1303
      12753
       0000
      12753
      4251
    5539053
```

Example 2 (faster)

```
     4251
   × 1303
    12753
    12753  ←——— Begin an extra place to the left
    4251          to allow for the zero.
  5539053
```

When the numbers being multiplied end in zero, you may simplify the problem by leaving off the zeros and then replacing them in the answer.

$$90 \times 30 = 9 \times 3 = 27 + 00 = 2,700$$

$$2,700 \times 20 = 27 \times 2 = 54 + 000 = 54,000$$

$$4,444 \times 2,000 = 4,444 \times 2 = 8,888 + 000 = 8,888,000$$

When multiplication problems involve decimals, the decimal in the answer (product) is moved one place to the left for every digit to the right of the decimal in both the multiplicand and the multiplier. For example, in the problem 317×1.5, there is only one digit to the right of the decimal: the number 5. Therefore, the decimal in the answer is moved one place to the left:

$$317 \times 1.5 = 475.5$$

Also consider the following examples:

$$3.25 \times 0.25 = 0.8125 \quad \text{decimal moved four places to the left}$$

$$32.12 \times 0.05 = 1.6060 \quad \text{decimal moved four places to the left}$$

$$94 \times 0.005 = 0.470 \quad \text{decimal moved three places to the left}$$

Zeros to the right of decimals that are not followed by numbers greater than zero may be ignored. The preceding 1.6060 is 1.606 because the second 0 is dropped; 0.470 is 0.47 because the 0 is dropped.

When multiplying by 10, 100, 1000, and so on, you simply move the decimal in the multiplicand one place to the right for every zero in the multiplier:

18.32 × 10 = 183.2   decimal moved one place to the right

18.32 × 100 = 1832.   decimal moved two places to the right

18.32 × 1,000 = 18320.   decimal moved three places to the right

To move the decimal three places to the right as in the final example, it is necessary to add a zero to the answer.

The most practical method for proving answers in multiplication is to reverse the positions of the multiplicand and the multiplier and remultiply. If you have multiplied 23 times 47, double-check the answer by multiplying 47 times 23.

Self-Check 1D   Multiplication with Decimals

---

1. 25 × 329 =

2. 940 × 400 =

3. 12.53 × 1.02 =

4. 99 × 0.150 =

5. If you are shipping 150 packages that weigh 1.5 pounds each, what is the total weight of the shipment?

6. Multiply 173.456 by 100.

7. One member of the sales staff sold 128 items priced at $23.12 each and 109 items priced at $51.50 each. What was the total value of the sales made by this one person?

Division with Decimals

Division is the inverse relationship to multiplication. In the problem 2 × 3 = 6, for example, we can check the answer 6 by dividing 6 by 3 to find 2, or we can divide 6 by 2 to find 3. Division is more time-consuming than multiplication because it involves a certain amount of trial and error. To help us with our discussion, let's first consider the parts of a division problem. The **dividend** is the number being divided, the **divisor** is the number being divided into the dividend, and the **quotient** is the answer.

$$\text{Divisor}\overline{)\,\text{Dividend}}^{\,\text{Quotient}}$$

When the divisor contains two or more digits, you generally should use long division. To illustrate, let's divide 605,330 by 55:

$$
\begin{array}{r}
11006 \\
55\overline{)605330} \\
55 \\
\overline{55} \\
55 \\
\overline{330} \\
330 \\
\overline{}
\end{array}
$$

The divisor 55 will not divide into 6, but it will go into 60 one time. The 1 is placed in the quotient above the 60 in the dividend, and 1 times 55 is placed below the 60. The 55 is then subtracted from 60, leaving a remainder of 5, and one number (the number 5) is brought down from the dividend. The divisor 55 goes into 55 one time, adding a second 1 to the answer. The first 3 is brought down, but since 55 does not divide into 3, a 0 is added to the answer and the second 3 is brought down. Because 55 will not divide into 33, a second 0 is added to the answer and the 0 in the dividend is brought down. The divisor 55 will divide into 330 six times, so a 6 is added to the answer (the quotient).

When the divisor is a single-digit number, you should use short division, performing the calculations in your head:

$$
\begin{array}{r}
1632 \\
5\overline{)8160}
\end{array}
$$

The 5 goes into 8 one time, with 3 remaining. The 3 is placed before the 1 in the dividend, making it 31; then 5 goes into 31 six times with a remainder of 1. The remainder of 1 is placed before the 6, making it 16, and the 5 goes into 16 three times with a remainder of 1. The remainder 1 is placed before the 0 making it 10, and 5 goes into 10 two times.

When only the dividend contains a decimal, the decimal is moved straight up into the quotient:

Short division	*Long division*

$$
\begin{array}{r}
5.26 \\
3\overline{)15.78}
\end{array}
\qquad\qquad
\begin{array}{r}
0.526 \\
33\overline{)17.358} \\
16\,5 \\
\overline{85} \\
66 \\
\overline{198} \\
198
\end{array}
$$

When the divisor contains a decimal, begin the problem by moving the decimal to the extreme right of the divisor. And when you move the decimal in the divisor, also move the decimal in the dividend the same number of places. Consider the following examples:

Example 3	*Example 4*	*Example 5*
43.35	433.5	$43350.$
$0.5 \overline{)21.6\ 75}$	$0.05 \overline{)21.67\ 5}$	$0.0005 \overline{)21.6750}$

In Example 3, you move the decimal one place to the right of the divisor 5, and you move the decimal in the dividend just one place to the right of the 6. After dividing by 5 (using short division), you move the newly positioned decimal in the dividend straight up into the quotient. In Example 4, the decimals in both the divisor and the dividend are moved two places to the right, and both decimals in Example 5 are moved four places to the right. It is necessary to add a zero to the dividend in Example 5 to move the decimal four places to the right.

To prove answers in division problems, multiply the divisor by the quotient. To prove that 8,160 divided by 5 equals 1,632, for example, multiply 5 (the divisor) by 1,632 (the quotient). The answer 8,160 confirms that our division was accurate because it equals the dividend of 8,160.

When dividing by 10, 100, 1,000, and so on, simply move the decimal in the dividend one place to the left for every zero in the divisor—just the opposite as when multiplying by 10, 100, and 1,000.

$$19.65 \div 10 = 1.965$$
$$19.65 \div 100 = 0.1965$$
$$19.65 \div 1,000 = 0.01965$$

We may add as many zeros at the left as necessary to accommodate the newly placed decimal.

Self-Check 1E   Division with Decimals

1. $5 \overline{)16,205}$ 2. $11 \overline{)57,838}$ 3. $7 \overline{)227.465}$ 4. $0.025 \overline{)0.8036}$

5. If four investors decide to buy a factory for $275,250, with each person owning an equal share, how much money must each person invest?

6. If 120-pound bags of peanuts are to be placed in individual packages weighing 2.5 pounds each, how many packages will twenty-eight 120-pound bags make?

7. Divide 165.22 by 10.

Rounding Numbers

The **remainder** in a division problem is the amount left over when a divisor does not divide evenly into a dividend. When dividing 138 by 15, for example, we derive a quotient of 9 with a remainder of 3.

$$
\begin{array}{r}
9 \\
15\overline{)138} \\
135 \\
\hline
3
\end{array}
$$

The answer, therefore, is $9\frac{3}{15}$ or $9\frac{1}{5}$. These relationships are explained further in Chapter 2, "Reviews of Fractions."

Divisors that do not divide evenly into dividends sometimes result in repeating numbers. Repeating numbers occur when 2 is divided by 3:

$$
\begin{array}{r}
.666666666 \\
3\overline{)2.000000000}
\end{array}
$$

We **round** the number by cutting off (truncating) the unnecessary digits of this endless string of sixes. We may round to one place to the right of the decimal (10ths position); two places (100ths or cents position), which is most commonly used in business transactions; three places (1,000ths position); or more, depending on the degree of accuracy needed.

	One place (10ths)	Two places (100ths)	Three places (1,000ths)
.6666	.7	.67	.667

To round to the tenths position, we round upward, changing the first 6 to a 7 because the digit immediately to the right of it is 5 or greater. To round to the hundredths position (two places to the right of the decimal), we change the second 6 to a 7 because the digit to its immediate right is 5 or greater. To round to the thousandths position (three places to the right of the decimal), we change the third 6 to a 7 because the fourth digit (the one to its immediate right) is 5 or greater. We must sometimes round down, as illustrated with another repeating number:

	10ths	100ths	1,000ths
.3333	.3	.33	.333

With each of these numbers, we disregard the digit to the right, because it is less than 5. When rounding to the tenths position, we ignore the digit at the hundredths position because it is less than 5; when rounding to the hundredths position, we ignore the third 3 because it is less than 5; and so on. For further clarification, consider the following numbers:

	10ths	100ths	1,000ths	10,000ths
67.37035	67.4	67.37	67.370	67.3704
1.24761	1.2	1.25	1.248	1.2476

The general rule is as follows: Round up if the following number is 5 or greater, and round down if the following number is less than 5.

───── **Self-Check 1F**   Rounding Numbers ─────

Round the following numbers as specified.

	10ths	100ths	1,000ths
1. 163.4280			
2. 0.46915			
3. 5.99999			
4. 0.11111			
5. 9.85714			

Estimating Answers

We often find it expedient to estimate answers—when a sales clerk is ringing up our purchases, when pricing the cost of carpeting, when checking payroll deductions, and during many other business transactions. If you are picking up the check for yourself and two business acquaintances, for instance, involving three lunches costing $6.95, $8.50, and $9.25, plus two desserts costing $2.25 and $2.15, and two coffees at 75¢ each, think of the meals as costing $25.00 ($7.00, $9.00, $9.00), with the two desserts adding $4.50 (bringing the total to $29.50) and the two coffees as $1.50 (resulting in an estimated total of $31.00). Your estimated figure of $31.00 is pretty close to the actual sum of $30.60, close enough to be certain that you have not been overcharged and without having to analyze the check in the presence of your guests. If the applicable sales tax is 5 percent, you know that 10 percent is about $3.00 and that half of that amount is $1.50. It is obvious, therefore, that a tax of $1.50 on the $30.60 check is a close approximation.

Now assume the role as a buyer of canned goods for a large grocery chain. Also assume that a salesperson on the opposite side of your desk has just offered you an opportunity to buy 3,000 cases of peaches at $12.10 per case. You need not resort to a calculator to know that the purchase will cost about $36,000, because you have mentally multiplied 3 times 12 to get 36 and then added back the three zeros.

You might wish to compare the $12.10 price with an earlier $12.00 offer from another vendor, on which you must pay transportation costs of $450. You know that $450 equals 15¢ a case ($450 divided by 3, with the decimal being moved three places to the left because you are dealing with 3,000 cases). This makes the earlier offer an actual $12.15 per case ($12.00 plus 15¢), or 5¢ per case higher than the current offer on which you do not have to pay transportation costs.

Even when using a calculator, you should not stop thinking. Instead, you should undertake some mental estimates to be absolutely certain that you have entered the numbers and decimals correctly. Miscalculating the cost of a $36,000 shipment of peaches at $3,600 (off just one decimal place) would eventually result in a $32,400 surprise (the difference) for both you and your boss.

Self-Check 1G   Estimating Answers

Mentally estimate answers to the following problems:

1. $25.10 + $16.32 + $3.85 + $22.50 =

2. $78.25 × 29 =

3. $160 ÷ 42 =

4. If you have an opportunity to purchase 2,100 units of a product at $25 per unit, what is the approximate total cost?

5. If sales for the four weeks in June were $5,206, $4,305, $6,718, and $5,312, what is a close estimate of total monthly sales?

Answers to Self-Checks

Self-Check 1A

1. 1,000
2. 2,615,165.23
3. One million, two hundred twelve thousand, five hundred sixty-three dollars, and twelve cents
4. $1,070.51
5. $100,080

Self-Check 1B

1. 92.93
2. 200.28
3. 294.429
4. $8.40
5. $68,293

Self-Check 1C

1. 109
2. 182.96
3. 26.195
4. $21.29
5. ($984)

Self-Check 1D

1. 8,225
2. 376,000
3. 12.7806
4. 14.85
5. 225 pounds
6. 17,345.6
7. $8,572.86

Self-Check 1E

1. 3,241
2. 5,258
3. 32.494
4. 32.144
5. 68,812.50
6. 1,344
7. 16.522

Self-Check 1F

1. 163.4   163.43   163.428
2. 0.5   0.47   0.469
3. 6.0   6.00   6.000
4. 0.1   0.11   0.111
5. 9.9   9.86   9.857

Self-Check 1G

1. $67.77 (about 25 + 16 + 4 + 22 = 67)
2. $2,269.25 (less than 80 × 30 = 24 + 00 = 2,400)
3. $3.81 (about 16 ÷ 4 = 4)
4. $52,500
5. $21,541 (about 20,000 + 1,500 = 21,500)

Name _____

Addition and Subtraction

Score _____

1. Addition (2 points each)

2,751	8,227	3,821	3,298	5,256	3,456	1,989
9,026	1,052	9,036	4,730	4,730	4,653	2,233
9,002	5,220	5,211	1,100	7,554	5,712	8,127

23.90	18.63	56.09	1,590.23	1,256.31	6,251.38
6.09	37.23	60.94	1,806.31	1,608.21	9,053.36

Add 16.1, 53.25, 523.161, and 5.09.   Add 23.69, 0.10, 86.081, and 92.76.

2. Word problems (5 points each)

a. If a business owner paid salaries for the month totaling $1,750.50, a $324.16 utility bill, and $631.17 for miscellaneous expenses, what were the total expenses for the month?

b. A used-car dealer sold five autos today for $1,700, $3,699.99, $495, $1,999.99, and $5,000. What were the total sales for the day?

c. Norburg, Inc. operates three delivery trucks that consumed 150.7, 210.3, and 195 gallons of gasoline, respectively, during March. What was the total amount of gasoline consumed?

d. Three offices contain 500, 496.3, and 510.25 square yards of floor space. How many square yards of carpeting will be needed to cover the entire area, including an entry area measuring 21.5 square yards?

3. Subtraction (1 point each)

400	322	850	736	390	752	905
−123	− 16	−397	− 23	−463	−243	−560

420.02	687	401.60	569	133.70	179	349.96	206	102
−395.01	− 26	−108.06	− 55	−148.68	− 15	−134.20	− 45	− 21

Find the difference between:

16.93 and 76.18   21.94 and 94.98   470.267 and 31.56   18.12 and 9.6

4. Word Problems (5 points each)

a. If an employee earned $18,500.75 last year and $19,775.15 this year, how much more was this year's income than last?

b. The Ramco Company bought a building in 1982 for $759,000 and sold it in 1986 for $855,500. What was their gain from the sale?

c. If the price of a new pickup truck is $12,259 and the amount allowed on a trade-in of a used vehicle is $1,950, what is the balance due?

d. If a business customer purchases merchandise valued at $16,132.12 but returns items costing $976.95 the following day, what amount is still owed?

e. If a student earns $158.50 per week at a part-time job, from which $5.60 is deducted for taxes and $10.62 is deducted for Social Security, how much money is left as take-home pay?

f. If a customer hands you a $20 bill in payment of items costing $3.29, $5.16, and $8.76, plus a sales tax of 86¢, how much change should you return to the customer?

1. **Multiplication (2 points each)**

442	434	246	164	328
× 45	× 23	× 78	× 12	× 45

240	49,096	500	3,258	8800
× 70	× 10	× 60	× 100	× 30

248	16.5	2.48	804	4.88
× 8.3	× 71	× 60	× 0.24	× 0.53

2. **Word Problems (5 points each)**

a. Joan Smith earns $3.75 per hour and worked 35.5 hours last week. How much money did she earn?

b. If a truck driver buys 75 gallons of diesel fuel at a price of $1.09 per gallon, how much does the fuel cost?

c. If a customer buys 3.5 pounds of apples at 69¢ per pound, what is the amount to be paid including 18¢ tax?

d. If a bookstore buys 120 copies of a book at $13.25 each less an 89¢ discount on each book, what is the publisher's total price?

3. Short division (2 points each)

$2\overline{)11.40}$ $9\overline{)439.2}$ $3\overline{)49.2}$ $0.7\overline{)112.91}$ $5.0\overline{)1260}$

$163.45 \div 10 =$ $2,1243.16 \div 100 =$ $18,164.42 \div 1,000 =$ $185 \div 10 =$ $0.323 \div 10 =$

4. Long division (2 points each)

$11\overline{)18,480}$ $15\overline{)83,475}$ $45\overline{)154,710}$ $25\overline{)135,725}$ $13\overline{)3,458}$

$11\overline{)63.25}$ $2.2\overline{)11.572}$ $0.25\overline{)12.3090}$ $0.16\overline{)62400}$ $1.01\overline{)88.678}$

5. Word problems (5 points each)

a. Having just bought a building that contains 12 separate apartments, how much rent must you charge for each apartment to realize a total monthly income (before expenses) of $4,440?

b. A trucking firm has 7 drivers who have driven a total of 6,540 miles. If each truck gets 5 miles per gallon, how many gallons of fuel did the firm use?

c. If a utility bill of $2,750 is to be divided equally among 4 divisions of a company, how much will be charged to each division?

d. Directors of the Nortex Corporation have decided to distribute evenly a $240,000 bonus among 48 managers. How much bonus money will each manager receive?

Review of Fractions

After reading Chapter 2, you will be able to

- Describe equivalent fractions, that is, why fractions such as 1/2, 2/4, 4/8, and 8/16 have the same value.
- Reduce fractions to lowest terms.
- Convert proper and improper fractions to mixed numbers and vice versa.
- Add, subtract, multiply, and divide fractions.

Key Terms

numerator	improper fraction
denominator	mixed number
proper fraction	lowest common denominator (LCD)

In business transactions we do not enjoy the convenience of dealing with only whole numbers. The average weight of a case of canned goods may weigh $27\frac{1}{2}$ pounds rather than an even 27 pounds. Similarly, an employee may have worked $47\frac{1}{2}$ hours last week, with the time in excess of 40 hours being paid at $1\frac{1}{2}$ the hourly (whole) rate.

Converting Fractions

The **numerator** is the top number in a fraction (the one above the line in the following example), and the **denominator** is the bottom number (the one below the line).

$$\frac{1}{2} \quad \begin{array}{l}\text{(numerator)}\\ \text{(denominator)}\end{array}$$

Equivalent fractions are fractions that are equal but do not look the same. We state equivalent fractions in a number of ways, as illustrated in Figure 2.1. As you can see, the shaded area remains the same (1/2), regardless of whether the square is divided into two pieces (halves), four (quarters), eight (eighths), or sixteen (sixteenths).

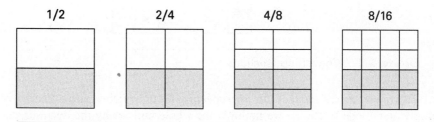

Figure 2.1 Equivalent Fractions

To *reduce fractions to their lowest terms*, we must divide both the numerator and the denominator by the largest number that will divide evenly into both of them.

$$\frac{2 \div 2}{4 \div 2} \quad \frac{1}{2}$$

$$\frac{4 \div 4}{8 \div 4} \quad \frac{1}{2}$$

$$\frac{8 \div 8}{16 \div 8} \quad \frac{1}{2}$$

Proper fractions are those in which the numerator is smaller than the denominator and include such numbers as 1/2, 3/4, and 5/8. They always represent a portion (part) of a whole — 1/2 of a whole hour, 3/4 of a whole dollar (75 cents), 5/8 of a whole truckload.

Improper fractions are fractions in which the numerator is larger than the denominator, such as 3/2, 5/2, and 5/4. **Mixed numbers** consist of a combination of whole numbers and fractions, such as $1\frac{1}{2}$, $2\frac{1}{2}$, and $1\frac{1}{4}$. As illustrated in Figure 2.2, we *convert improper fractions to mixed numbers* by dividing the numerator by the denominator. To convert 3/2 to $1\frac{1}{2}$, the 2 goes into the 3 one time with a remainder of 1, which we place over the denominator to form 1/2. In the fraction 5/2, the 2 divides into 5 two times with a remainder of 1 (or 1/2), and in the fraction 5/4, the 4 divides into the 5 one time with a remainder of 1 (or 1/4).

Improper		Mixed	

Figure 2.2   Converting Fractions

To *convert mixed numbers to improper fractions*, which is often necessary to multiply and divide fractions, we multiply the whole number by the denominator of the fraction and then add in the numerator.

Mixed	*Calculation*	*Improper*
$3\frac{1}{2}$	3 × 2 + 1	$\frac{7}{2}$
$4\frac{2}{3}$	4 × 3 + 2	$\frac{14}{3}$
$1\frac{3}{5}$	1 × 5 + 3	$\frac{8}{5}$

─────── **Self-Check 2A**   Converting Fractions ───────

Mark the following numbers as either (P) proper fraction, (I) improper fraction, or (M) mixed number:

1. $\frac{7}{8}$ _____ $\frac{365}{5}$ _____ $1\frac{7}{8}$ _____ $\frac{4}{3}$ _____ $\frac{1}{32}$ _____

Change the following fractions from:

2. Mixed to improper $2\dfrac{7}{8} =$ $\qquad$ $15\dfrac{3}{5} =$ $\qquad$ $3\dfrac{5}{9} =$ $\qquad$ $2\dfrac{5}{7} =$

3. Improper to mixed $\dfrac{16}{3} =$ $\qquad$ $\dfrac{102}{5} =$ $\qquad$ $\dfrac{23}{6} =$ $\qquad$ $\dfrac{11}{3} =$

4. Reduce the following fractions to the lowest terms:

$\dfrac{8}{16} =$ $\qquad$ $\dfrac{105}{150} =$ $\qquad$ $\dfrac{12}{15} =$ $\qquad$ $\dfrac{7}{20} =$

5. Which is greater: $\dfrac{2}{15}$ or $\dfrac{4}{30}$? $\qquad$ $\dfrac{7}{8}$ or $\dfrac{24}{32}$? $\qquad$ $\dfrac{5}{15}$ or $\dfrac{5}{10}$?

Adding Fractions

Adding fractions that have identical denominators is easy. As shown in Figure 2.3, we simply add the numerators and keep the same denominator.

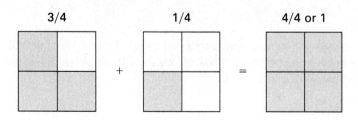

Figure 2.3 Adding Fractions

When the denominators differ, however, we must first find the **lowest common denominator (LCD)**, which is the lowest number into which each denominator divides evenly. To add 1/2 and 1/8, as in Figure 2.4, we can easily see that 8 is the LCD.

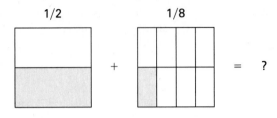

Figure 2.4 Different Denominators

To derive an answer, we must state 1/2 as 4/8, and place the sum of the two numerators over the common denominator — as shown in Figure 2.5.

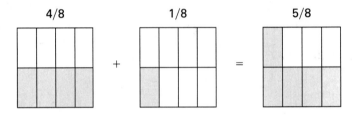

Figure 2.5 Common Denominator

To increase the denominator from 2 to 8, we multiply it by 4. To maintain the value of the fraction, we must also multiply the numerator by 4.

$$\frac{1 \times 4}{2 \times 4} = \frac{4}{8}$$

We are now ready to add:

$$\frac{1}{2} = \frac{4}{8}$$

$$\frac{4 + 1}{8} = \frac{5}{8} \quad \text{or} \quad \begin{array}{r} \frac{4}{8} \\ + \frac{1}{8} = \frac{1}{8} \\ \hline \frac{5}{8} \end{array}$$

Let's apply the same problem to a dollar bill. To add 1/2 and 1/8 of a dollar, as is often done in the purchase of stocks, we must think of the dollar bill as consisting of eight pieces. Eight is the LCD:

One dollar

$$\boxed{\frac{1}{8} \;\Big|\; \frac{1}{8} \;\Big|\; \frac{1}{8} \;\Big|\; \frac{1}{8} \;\Big|\; \frac{1}{8} \;\Big|\; \frac{1}{8} \;\Big|\; \frac{1}{8} \;\Big|\; \frac{1}{8}} = \frac{8}{8} = \$1.00$$

$$\frac{4}{8} + \frac{1}{8} = \frac{5}{8}$$

The easiest way to add mixed numbers, such as $7\frac{3}{5}$ and $8\frac{2}{10}$, is to place one above the other. Then convert the fractions to the LCD and add. In the following problem, our LCD is 10:

$$7\frac{3}{5} = 7\frac{6}{10}$$

$$+8\frac{2}{10} = +8\frac{2}{10}$$

$$15\frac{8}{10} = 15\frac{4}{5}$$

Finding the LCD for some numbers requires a special procedure. To add or subtract fractions with the denominators 4 and 8, for example, we can readily observe the LCD (the lowest number into which both numbers will divide evenly) to be 8. To determine the LCD of 3/4, 1/8, 1/15, and 2/3, on the other hand, we must continue dividing the denominator by the lowest common divisor as long as two or more of the denominators are divisible.

Example 1

$$2\overline{|4\ \ 8\ \ 15\ \ 3}$$
$$2\overline{|2\ \ 4\ \ 15\ \ 3}$$
$$3\overline{|1\ \ 2\ \ 15\ \ 3}$$
$$1\ \ 2\ \ \ 5\ \ 1$$
$$2 \times 2 \times 3 \times 1 \times 2 \times 5 \times 1 = 120$$

We may select 4 as a divisor that will divide evenly into at least two of the four numbers. The 4 divides into 4 one time and into 8 two times. Because 4 will not divide evenly into 15 or 3, we simply bring those two numbers down into our second row. Observing the newly formed second row, we see that 3 will divide evenly into 15 and 3. After bringing the 1 and 2 into the third row, we can divide no further because no two numbers in that row are evenly divisible by any one number.

We then multiply our divisors at the side by the numbers in our final row, resulting in an LCD of 120—the lowest number into which all denominators in our four fractions will divide evenly. Because multiplication by the number 1 does not change the answer, we may ignore that number when calculating the LCD.

Example 2

$$3\overline{|4\ \ 8\ \ 15\ \ 3}$$
$$4\overline{|4\ \ 8\ \ \ 5\ \ 1}$$
$$1\ \ 2\ \ \ 5\ \ 1$$
$$3 \times 4 \times 2 \times 5 = 120$$

Whether we divide the 4 and 8 by 4 first (Example 1) or 15 and 3 by 3 first (Example 2) is not important. Both approaches result in the same set of highlighted numbers, which, when multiplied, results in an LCD of 120.

We may also find the LCD of two or more numbers using a **short-cut method**. If any one denominator will divide exactly into another denominator, the number may be eliminated from the calculation. Of the numbers 4, 8, 15, and 3, we eliminate the 4 because it divides into 8 exactly 2 times. We also eliminate the 3 because it divides into 15 exactly 5 times. We then multiply the two remaining numbers:

$$8 \times 15 = 120 \text{ (the LCD of } 4, 8, 15, \text{ and } 3)$$

Knowing that the LCD is 120, we may add the four fractions.

$$\frac{3}{4} + \frac{1}{8} + \frac{1}{15} + \frac{2}{3}$$

$$= \frac{90 + 15 + 8 + 80}{120}$$

$$= \frac{193}{120}$$

$$= 1\frac{73}{120}$$

Three-fourths was converted to 90/120 by dividing 4 (the denominator) into 120 (the LCD) and then multiplying the answer (30) by 3 (the numerator). For 1/8, we divided 8 into 120, then multiplied the answer (15) by 1, and so on.

Self-Check 2B   Adding Fractions

---

1. $\dfrac{4}{8} + \dfrac{5}{16} =$

2. $1\dfrac{3}{10} + 6\dfrac{4}{5} + \dfrac{1}{15} =$

3. Of every dollar that a business receives from sales, 2/5 goes to wages and 1/3 to other costs. What fraction of every dollar goes to pay total costs?

4. What is the LCD for adding 1/12, 2/33, 7/11, and 5/6?

5. Find the LCD for 12, 30, and 9.

Subtracting Fractions

To subtract fractions with identical denominators, as shown in Figure 2.6, we subtract the numerators and place the difference over the original denominator.

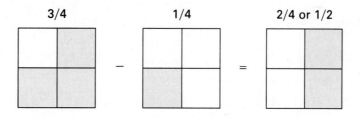

Figure 2.6   Subtracting Fractions

To subtract fractions with different denominators, such as 1/8 from 1/2, we must find the LCD of the two denominators and arrange the problem in either of the following two ways:

$$\frac{4-1}{8} = \frac{3}{8} \quad \text{or} \quad \begin{array}{r} \frac{1}{2} = \frac{4}{8} \\ -\frac{1}{8} = -\frac{1}{8} \\ \hline \frac{3}{8} \end{array}$$

Again using a dollar bill to illustrate, we think of the dollar as consisting of eight pieces, since 8 is the LCD. One-half of a dollar is 4/8, and when we subtract 1/8 from 4/8, we have a remainder of 3/8:

$$\frac{4}{8} = \boxed{\begin{array}{c|c|c|c} \frac{1}{8} & \frac{1}{8} & \frac{1}{8} & \frac{1}{8} \end{array}} = \text{One-half dollar}$$

$$\frac{4}{8} - \frac{1}{8} = \frac{3}{8}$$

You may use either of the following methods when subtracting mixed numbers, such as subtracting $7\frac{3}{5}$ from $8\frac{2}{10}$.

Step 1

Change mixed numbers to improper fractions.

$$8\frac{2}{10} = \frac{82}{10} \quad \text{and} \quad 7\frac{3}{5} = \frac{38}{5}$$

Step 2

Convert 38/5 to LCD of 10, and subtract 76 from 82.

$$\frac{82 - 76}{10} = \frac{6}{10} = \frac{3}{5}$$

In the second method,

Step 1

Convert fractions to LCD of 10.

$$
\begin{array}{r}
8\frac{2}{10} \\
-7\frac{3}{5} \\
\hline
\end{array}
=
\begin{array}{r}
8\frac{2}{10} \\
-7\frac{6}{10} \\
\hline
\end{array}
$$

Step 2

Subtract.

$$
\begin{array}{r}
7\frac{12}{10} \\
-7\frac{6}{10} \\
\hline
\frac{6}{10} = \frac{3}{5}
\end{array}
$$

In the second method, it was necessary to borrow a whole number from the 8 because we cannot subtract 6/10 from 2/10. Since the denominator is 10, the borrowed whole number is 10/10, which increases the 2/10 to 12/10. Subtracting 6/10 from 12/10 gives us an answer of 6/10, or 3/5.

Self-Check 2C   Subtracting Fractions

---

1. $\dfrac{5}{8} - \dfrac{1}{4} =$

2. $16\dfrac{1}{6} - \dfrac{3}{5} =$

3. The containers for canned apples weigh $6\frac{3}{4}$ ounces each. If each container is reduced in weight by $1\frac{5}{8}$ ounces, what is the weight of the new container?

4. $3\dfrac{2}{3} - 1\dfrac{1}{7} =$

5. A can of sweet peas weighs $20\frac{1}{4}$ ounces. If the can weighs $3\frac{1}{2}$ ounces, what is the weight of the peas inside the can?

Multiplying Fractions

Multiplying fractions is generally much easier than adding or subtracting them. We first reduce the fractions where possible by canceling (dividing) diagonally and up and down, and we then multiply across:

Example 3

$$\frac{8}{9} \times \frac{1}{7} = \frac{8}{63}$$

Example 4   ### Example 5

$$\frac{\overset{2}{\cancel{8}}}{\underset{3}{\cancel{9}}} \times \frac{\overset{1}{\cancel{3}}}{\underset{1}{\cancel{4}}} = \frac{2}{3} \qquad \frac{\overset{1}{\cancel{4}}}{\underset{\underset{1}{\cancel{2}}}{\cancel{16}}} \times \frac{\overset{1}{\cancel{2}}}{5} \times \frac{\overset{1}{\cancel{2}}}{9} = \frac{1}{45}$$

In Example 3, because no cancellation is possible, we simply multiply across: $8 \times 1 = 8$ and $9 \times 7 = 63$.

In Example 4, the 8 and 4 are reduced to 2 and 1 by dividing both by 4; the 3 and 9 are reduced to 1 and 3 by dividing both numbers by 3. Multiplication of the reduced numbers results in $2 \times 1 = 2$ and $3 \times 1 = 3$, giving us 2/3.

In Example 5, we begin by dividing the 4 and 16 by 4 or dividing the 2 and 16 by 2; either way is correct. In this instance, the 4 and 16 were divided by 4, reducing the fraction to 1/4. The 4 in that fraction and the 2 in the middle fraction are then divided by 2, reducing them to 2 and 1, respectively. Finally, the 2 in the denominator of the first fraction and the 2 in the numerator of the third fraction are divided by 2, reducing both numbers to 1. We then multiply across: $1 \times 1 \times 1 = 1$ and $1 \times 5 \times 9 = 45$, giving us 1/45.

When using a calculator to multiply fractions, we treat the line in each fraction as a division sign, so that the fraction 2/5 is the same as 2 divided by 5.

The operations of multiplication and division within the same problems may be in any order; that is, we may multiply first and then divide or divide first and then multiply.

$$240 \times 2 \div 5 = 96$$

or

$$240 \div 5 \times 2 = 96$$

As with the manual multiplication of fractions, however, we must first convert any mixed numbers to improper fractions before multiplying with calculators. For example, $3\frac{1}{3} \times 5\frac{1}{2}$ must be stated as $10/3 \times 11/2$.

Self-Check 2D   Multiplying Fractions

---

1. $320 \times \dfrac{3}{4} =$

2. $\dfrac{4}{20} \times \dfrac{5}{40} \times \dfrac{16}{32} =$

3. If a salesperson receives 1/4 of all sales dollars as commission, 1/3 of which must be given to an assistant, what fraction of total sales does the assistant receive?

4. How much money is represented by a 2/7 share of $63,000?

5. $3\dfrac{5}{8} \times 2\dfrac{4}{5} =$

Dividing Fractions

Dividing fractions is the same as multiplying them, except the divisor must be inverted (turned upside down) and the sign changed from division to multiplication. To divide 1/8 by 1/4, for example, we change the 1/4 to 4/1 and then multiply:

$$\overset{\text{change sign}}{\frac{1}{8} \div \frac{1}{4}} = \frac{1}{8} \times \underset{\text{invert}}{\frac{4}{1}} = \frac{1}{2}$$

As a second example, let's divide two mixed numbers:

$$1\frac{2}{3} \div 4\frac{3}{8} = \overset{\text{change sign}}{\frac{5}{3} \div \frac{35}{8}} = \frac{5}{3} \times \underset{\text{invert}}{\frac{8}{35}} = \frac{8}{21}$$

─────────────────── **Self-Check 2E**   Dividing Fractions ───────────────────

1. $\dfrac{3}{7} \div \dfrac{9}{21} =$

2. $5\dfrac{2}{11} \div \dfrac{1}{11} =$

3. A forest-grower owns $15\frac{3}{4}$ acres of land on which he intends to grow pine trees for pulpwood. If one pine tree requires 1/60 of an acre, how many seedlings (young trees) should he buy for planting?

4. If only 810 cubic feet of space remains in a storage area, how many containers measuring $5\frac{5}{8}$ cubic feet may be stored?

─────────────────── **Answers to Self-Checks** ───────────────────

Self-Check 2A	Self-Check 2B	Self-Check 2C	Self-Check 2D	Self-Check 2E
1. P, I, M, I, P	**1.** $\dfrac{13}{16}$	**1.** $\dfrac{3}{8}$	**1.** 240	**1.** 1
2. $\dfrac{23}{8}, \dfrac{78}{5}, \dfrac{32}{9}, \dfrac{19}{7}$	**2.** $8\dfrac{1}{6}$	**2.** $15\dfrac{17}{30}$	**2.** $\dfrac{1}{80}$	**2.** 57
3. $5\dfrac{1}{3}, 20\dfrac{2}{5}, 3\dfrac{5}{6}, 3\dfrac{2}{3}$	**3.** $\dfrac{11}{15}$	**3.** $5\dfrac{1}{8}$	**3.** $\dfrac{1}{12}$	**3.** 945
4. $\dfrac{1}{2}, \dfrac{7}{10}, \dfrac{4}{5}, \dfrac{7}{20}$	**4.** 132	**4.** $2\dfrac{11}{21}$	**4.** \$18,000	**4.** 48
5. $\dfrac{2}{15} = \dfrac{4}{30}$ $\dfrac{7}{8} > \dfrac{24}{32}$ $\dfrac{5}{15} < \dfrac{5}{10}$	**5.** 180	**5.** $16\dfrac{3}{4}$	**5.** $10\dfrac{3}{20}$	

1. **Converting mixed numbers to improper fractions (1 point each)**

$3\frac{1}{4} =$ *13/4* $6\frac{1}{2} =$ $12\frac{3}{5} =$ $5\frac{3}{7} =$ *38/7* $7\frac{2}{5} =$

$33\frac{1}{3} =$ *100/3* $4\frac{3}{8} =$ *35/8* $3\frac{5}{7} =$ $21\frac{2}{3} =$ $6\frac{7}{8} =$

2. **Converting improper fractions to mixed numbers (1 point each)**

$\frac{4}{3} =$ $\frac{22}{5} =$ $\frac{91}{8} =$ $\frac{143}{6} =$ $\frac{7}{3} =$

$\frac{11}{8} =$ *1 3/8* $\frac{61}{7} =$ *8 5/7* $\frac{5}{4} =$ $\frac{45}{15} =$ $\frac{16}{3} =$

3. **Finding the lowest common denominator (LCD) (3 points each)**

7 and 3 *- 21*   15 and 25 *- 75*   8 and 6 *24*   12 and 11

7, 3, and 8 *168*   15, 25, and 30 *150*   5, 25, and 14

9, 16, and 3   24, 12, 9, and 6   48, 15, 11, and 33

4. **Reducing fractions to lowest terms (1 point each)**

$\frac{4}{8} =$ $\frac{2}{42} =$ $\frac{15}{45} =$ $\frac{3}{9} =$ $\frac{16}{64} =$

$\frac{15}{40} =$ $\frac{6}{15} =$ $\frac{8}{45} =$ $\frac{16}{24} =$ $\frac{27}{45} =$

5. Addition (2 points each)

$$\frac{1}{2} + \frac{1}{2} =$$

$$\frac{7}{6} + \frac{19}{3} + \frac{5}{12} =$$

$$\frac{3}{8} + \frac{1}{4} + \frac{9}{16} =$$

$$\frac{5}{12} + \frac{7}{14} + \frac{1}{3} =$$

$$6\frac{1}{8} + 9\frac{3}{4} =$$

6. Subtraction (2 points each)

$$\frac{3}{4} - \frac{1}{8} = \qquad \frac{4}{5} - \frac{1}{3} = \qquad 3\frac{13}{15} - \frac{4}{5} = \qquad 6\frac{1}{3} - \frac{7}{9} = \qquad 6\frac{1}{5} - 1\frac{5}{7} =$$

7. Word problems (5 points each)

a. If you mail 5 dozen tennis balls weighing a total of $6\frac{1}{2}$ pounds, 12 tennis rackets weighing $8\frac{3}{4}$ pounds, and 6 cartons of golf balls weighing $18\frac{3}{5}$ pounds, what is the total weight involved?

b. If a case of canned dog food weighs $25\frac{1}{2}$ pounds and the manufacturer wants to reduce the weight $4\frac{1}{4}$ pounds by using aluminum cans (instead of tin), how much will the new case of dog food weigh?

c. In cubic yards, what is the total amount of top soil needed to landscape if the west side of a lawn needs $9\frac{3}{4}$ cubic yards; the east side, $7\frac{1}{8}$ cubic yards; and if two flower beds need $3\frac{2}{3}$ cubic yards each?

d. A bolt of cloth contains $5\frac{1}{4}$ yards of material. If a customer buys $3\frac{2}{3}$ yards, what amount remains?

Multiplying and Dividing Fractions

1. **Multiplication (2 points each)**

$\dfrac{3}{4} \times \dfrac{2}{3} =$ $\dfrac{4}{5} \times \dfrac{1}{2} =$ $\dfrac{9}{11} \times \dfrac{1}{3} =$ $\dfrac{1}{2} \times \dfrac{4}{7} =$ $\dfrac{7}{8} \times \dfrac{4}{9} =$

$\dfrac{16}{19} \times \dfrac{3}{8} =$ $\dfrac{39}{40} \times \dfrac{10}{39} =$ $\dfrac{25}{51} \times \dfrac{3}{5} =$ $\dfrac{15}{22} \times \dfrac{2}{9} =$ $\dfrac{6}{7} \times \dfrac{2}{3} =$

$\dfrac{3}{28} \times \dfrac{4}{9} \times \dfrac{7}{8} =$ $\dfrac{4}{7} \times 2\dfrac{5}{8} =$

2. **Word problems (5 points each)**

a. Wages are 3/4 of the cost of manufacturing television sets, and overtime pay constitutes 1/8 of all wages paid. Overtime pay is what fraction of total costs?

b. Three-fourths of a ship's cargo consists of fresh pineapple. If one-third of the pineapple becomes spoiled, what fraction of the total cargo is spoiled?

c. One-third of Lawry's take-home pay of $24,000 is budgeted for housing, including utilities. If utilities account for one-fourth of the housing budget, how much money should be allocated for utilities?

d. Garden Rock Company advertised volcanic rock at $60 per ton. If the company had $20\frac{3}{4}$ tons available and sold 2/3 of that amount, how much money did the company receive for the rock?

3. Division (3 points each)

$$\frac{1}{2} \div \frac{3}{4} = \qquad \frac{9}{12} \div \frac{3}{6} = \qquad 8 \div \frac{2}{3} = \qquad \frac{1}{2} \div \frac{1}{4} =$$

$$\frac{3}{14} \div \frac{7}{8} = \qquad \frac{4}{9} \div \frac{2}{3} = \qquad \frac{13}{4} \div \frac{12}{8} = \qquad \frac{7}{9} \div \frac{5}{6} =$$

$$\frac{5}{60} \div \frac{3}{10} = \qquad 33\frac{4}{5} \div 5\frac{1}{5} = \qquad 2\frac{3}{30} \div \frac{9}{15} = \qquad 8\frac{4}{9} \div \frac{19}{36} =$$

4. Word problems (5 points each)

a. If a jeweler has 5/8 of an ounce of gold and one pair of earrings requires 1/24 ounce of gold, how many pairs of earrings can the jeweler make from the amount of gold he has?

b. A health-food packer uses 5/6 pound of oats to make 1 pound of granola. How many 1-pound packages can he produce from 500 pounds of oats?

c. A dress manufacturer imports 10 bolts of designer fabric, each containing 60 yards of material. If it takes 3 3/4 yards to make one dress, how many dresses can be made?

d. A food wholesaler receives 50 boxes of oranges, each weighing 40 pounds, and redistributes them into $4\frac{1}{2}$ pound bags. How many bags of oranges will be produced? (Round to whole numbers.)

Review of Percents and Decimals

After reading Chapter 3, you will be able to

- Change percents to decimals and decimals to percents.
- Change fractions to decimals and decimals to fractions.
- Apply from memory commonly used decimal-fraction relationships.

Key Terms

percent	decimal equivalent
insignificant zero	repetend

The majority of business problems involve the use of percents and decimals. Many commercial transactions are calculated on a percentage basis, and because our monetary system is based on the decimal fraction, a thorough understanding of percents and decimals is essential to your success in business. This chapter provides a review of the relationships between percents and decimals and between fractions and percents. The word **percent** is used to describe anything on the basis of 100 parts. A dollar is divided into 100 parts, for example, with 5 cents being 5/100ths or 5% of one dollar.

Changing Percents to Decimals

How would you respond if someone asked you the following question: What is 13% of 250? You should multiply to solve this simple problem. But before you can multiply 250 by 13%, you must remove the percent sign and move the decimal two places to the left. But where is the decimal in 13%? Although the decimal is always to the immediate right of a whole number (in this case, 13 is the whole number), it is not shown; it is assumed to be there. For practical purposes, therefore, the number might read 13.%. We then remove the percent sign and move the decimal two places to the left, giving us 0.13.

Multiplying a number by 13% is the same as multiplying a number by 13¢. The ¢ sign is removed and the decimal is moved two places to the left, just as the percent sign is removed and the decimal is moved two places to the left. Expressed in decimal form, therefore, 13% and 13¢ both become 0.13.

For percents such as 13.5% and 0.5%, decimals must be used to show that part of the number is a whole number and that part of the number is a fraction. The number 13.5% is the same as $13\frac{1}{2}$%, and the number 0.5% is the same as 1/2%, or one-half of one percent. You would change these numbers from percents to decimals by moving the decimals two places to the left:

$$13.5\% = 0.135 \qquad 0.5\% = 0.005$$

Additional zeros are added to the left of the second number to enable us to move the decimal two places to the left. Notice also that the zeros to the left of the decimals in both answers are **insignificant zeros.** They are (unneeded) and used only for appearance.

Self-Check 3A   Changing Percents to Decimals

---

1. 33% =   22.5% = $22\frac{1}{2}\%$ = $\frac{1}{2}\%$ =

2. 120% =   50% =   5.1% =   3.25% =

3. 12¢ = $21\frac{1}{2}$¢ =   7.5¢ =   83¢ =

4. Multiply $653 by 5.5%. (Round to even cents.)

Changing Decimals to Percents

To change decimals to percents, you simply reverse the previous operation by moving the decimal two places to the right and adding the percent sign. When dealing in percentages, therefore, you would convert 0.65 to 65% and 0.755 to 75.5%.

--- **Self-Check 3B**   Changing Decimals to Percents ---

1. 0.28 =   0.5 =   0.06 =   0.333 =

2. 0.067 =   0.105 =   1.0 =   0.1625 =

3. Multiply 1.3 by 7.5 and state your answer as a percent.

Changing Fractions to Decimals

As we rely more heavily on electronic calculators for business transactions, it becomes increasingly necessary to convert fractions to decimals. Because we cannot enter mixed numbers (whole numbers combined with fractions) into calculators, we must change fractions to their **decimal equivalents.** We do this by dividing the numerators by the denominators.

$$\frac{1}{2} = 2\overline{)1.0}^{.5}$$

Because 2 will not divide into 1, we add a 0 to the dividend, and in doing so we place a decimal (which is usually assumed) to the right of the 1 to show that the number is 1, not 10. As shown, the 1/2 is the same as 0.5, and, from preceding discussion, we know that 0.5 is the same as 50% (if we were to move the decimal two places to the right and add a percent sign). Therefore, 1/2 is the same as 50%. To calculate 1/2 of another number, we may multiply the number by either 1/2 or by 0.5. Let's do so with $2.40:

$$\frac{\overset{1.20}{\cancel{2.40}}}{1} \times \frac{1}{\underset{1}{\cancel{2}}} = 1.20 \quad \text{or} \quad \begin{array}{r} 2.40 \\ \times\ 0.5 \\ \hline 1.200 \end{array}$$

Is 1.20 the same as 1.200? Yes, it is, because any zeros standing alone to the right of the decimal may be disregarded. Therefore, we may view both answers as being 1.2 or, if we are speaking of money, as $1.20.

Self-Check 3C   Changing Fractions to Decimals (round answers to thousandths)

1. $\dfrac{1}{5} =$ $\dfrac{2}{5} =$ $\dfrac{1}{8} =$ $\dfrac{5}{6} =$ $\dfrac{1}{3} =$

2. $\dfrac{3}{10} =$ $\dfrac{1}{9} =$ $\dfrac{2}{9} =$ $\dfrac{2}{3} =$ $\dfrac{1}{10} =$

3. Multiply 3/4 by 2/3 and convert the answer to a decimal.

4. Rewrite the following numbers to omit any insignificant zeros.

00.138 =	16.001 =
0.1590 =	0093.015 =
1,000 =	931.50 =
10 =	0.5 =
0.10 =	10.01 =

Changing Decimals to Fractions

To change decimals to fractions, let's check to make sure that you remember the sequential positions to the right of the decimal. Numbers to the left of decimals are always whole numbers, and numbers to the right of decimals are always fractions of whole numbers. Using the number 9.3512 to illustrate, the 9 to the left of the decimal is a whole number. The fractional numbers 3512 to the right of the decimal may be read as

> 3 tenths
> 5 hundredths
> 1 thousandth
> 2 ten-thousandths

Knowing this, we can convert the following decimal numbers to fractions:

$$0.5 = \frac{5}{10}$$

$$0.05 = \frac{5}{100}$$

$$0.005 = \frac{5}{1,000}$$

$$0.0005 = \frac{5}{10,000}$$

We may also change these decimal numbers to fractions by removing the decimal, placing the 5 as the numerator, and placing 1 below the line followed by as many zeros as there are places to the right of the decimal. Using this method, 0.5 becomes 5/10. (One zero is added to the number 1 to form the denominator, because 5 is only one place to the right of the decimal.) Because the 5 in 0.05 is two places to the right of the decimal, two zeros are added to a 1, giving us 5/100, and so on. Also consider the following examples:

$$0.003 = \frac{3}{1,000}$$

$$2.5 = 2\frac{5}{10}$$

$$10.007 = 10\frac{7}{1,000}$$

Self-Check 3D   Changing Decimals to Fractions

1. 0.2 =   **2.** 0.75 =   **3.** 1.75 =

4. 14.005 =   **5.** 21.0007 =

6. Rather than multiply another number by 3/8, what decimal equivalent may be used?

Common Relationships

You will find it useful to memorize several of the relationships between fractions and decimals because they are encountered so frequently in business transactions. The most common relationships are listed below:

$$\frac{1}{2} = 0.5 \qquad\qquad \frac{3}{5} = 0.6$$

$$\frac{1}{3} = 0.333 \text{ (repetend)} \qquad \frac{4}{5} = 0.8$$

$$\frac{2}{3} = 0.666 \text{ (repetend)} \qquad \frac{1}{6} = 0.166 \text{ (repetend)}$$

$$\frac{1}{4} = 0.25 \qquad\qquad \frac{1}{8} = 0.125$$

$$\frac{3}{4} = 0.75 \qquad\qquad \frac{3}{8} = 0.375$$

$$\frac{1}{5} = 0.2 \qquad\qquad \frac{5}{8} = 0.625$$

$$\frac{2}{5} = 0.4 \qquad\qquad \frac{7}{8} = 0.875$$

Rather than multiplying with fractions, you can use the decimal equivalents. As mentioned previously, the fractional part of mixed numbers *must* be converted to decimals when using most calculators. To find $3\frac{2}{5}$ of 240, for example, you must multiply 240 by 3.4.

$$240 \times 3\frac{2}{5} =$$

$$240 \times 3.4 = 816$$

Rather than multiplying fractions such as 3/4 times 1/2, you may find it easier to multiply by the decimal equivalents of these fractions:

$$0.75 \times 0.5 = 0.375$$

To multiply or divide by a repetend, such as 2/3 (.666666), we must round the number. If you are figuring a price for a consumer item, you might round to the cents (100ths) position, with 0.666666 becoming 0.67 (67¢). When bankers compute interest charges, however, they often round to as many as eight or ten places to the right of the decimal, because rounding to two places would result in a difference of several dollars over the course of many years.

―――――――――――――――――― **Answers to Self-Checks** ――――――――――――――――――

Self-Check 3A	Self-Check 3B	Self-Check 3C	Self-Check 3D

Self-Check 3A

1. 0.33
   0.225
   0.225
   0.005

2. 1.2
   0.5
   0.051
   0.0325

3. $0.12
   $0.215
   $0.075
   $0.83

4. $35.92

Self-Check 3B

1. 28%
   50%
   6%
   $33\frac{1}{3}\%$

2. 6.7%
   10.5%
   100%
   16.25%

3. 975%

Self-Check 3C

1. 0.20
   0.40
   0.125
   0.833
   0.333

2. 0.3
   0.111
   0.222
   0.667
   0.1

3. 0.5

4. .138   16.001
   .159   93.015
   1,000   931.5
   10   .5
   .1   10.01

Self-Check 3D

1. $\dfrac{1}{5}$

2. $\dfrac{3}{4}$

3. $1\dfrac{3}{4}$

4. $14\dfrac{1}{200}$

5. $21\dfrac{7}{10,000}$

6. 0.375

1. **Changing percents to decimals (1 point each)**

    40% =   33% =   2.5% =   0.5% =

    150% =   0.05% =   0.026% =   26.0% =

    25% =   100% =   0.16% =   16% =

    3.67% = $\frac{1}{4}$% =   200% =   16.01% =

    0.20% =   19% =   50% =   120% =

2. **Changing decimals to percents (1 point each)**

    0.5 =   0.67 =   0.75 =   0.13 =

    0.99 =   0.05 =   0.005 =   0.145 =

    0.333 =   0.036 =   0.0025 =   0.19 =

    0.165 =   1.5 =   9.75 =   2.0 =

    1.0 =   2.25 =   1.1 =   1.11 =

3. **Word problems (5 points each)**

    a. Rather than multiplying another number by
    1/7, what decimal equivalent may be used?
    (Round answer to 1,000ths.)

    b. Rewrite the following numbers, omitting any   1.0 =
    insignificant zeros.   3.05 =
    99.10 =
    1.50 =
    0.1 =

4. Changing fractions to decimals (round to thousandths) (1 point each)

$\dfrac{2}{5} =$ $\dfrac{3}{5} =$ $\dfrac{5}{5} =$ $\dfrac{2}{3} =$

$\dfrac{3}{4} =$ $\dfrac{1}{8} =$ $\dfrac{3}{8} =$ $\dfrac{7}{8} =$

$\dfrac{1}{6} =$ $\dfrac{1}{15} =$ $\dfrac{5}{6} =$ $\dfrac{1}{3} =$

$\dfrac{1}{4} =$ $\dfrac{2}{4} =$ $\dfrac{3}{4} =$ $\dfrac{44}{11} =$

$\dfrac{5.5}{5} =$ $3\dfrac{3}{5} =$ $7\dfrac{1}{25} =$ $\dfrac{12}{11} =$

5. Changing decimals to fractions (reduce to lowest terms) (1 point each)

$0.4 =$ $0.25 =$ $0.5 =$ $0.05 =$

$0.62 =$ $0.005 =$ $0.22 =$ $0.333 =$

$0.875 =$ $0.2 =$ $2.2 =$ $0.75 =$

$0.30 =$ $0.300 =$ $0.125 =$ $0.375 =$

$0.8 =$ $0.008 =$ $0.6 =$ $0.0033 =$

6. Word problems (5 points each)

a. Multiply 3/4 by 1/2 and state your answer as a percent.

b. Multiply $720 by the decimal equivalent of 3 1/2%.

1. Changing percents to decimals (1 point each)

4% =	25% =	1.25% =	19.3% =
233% =	8.7% =	$\frac{3}{4}$% =	$1\frac{1}{2}$% =
200% =	1.5% =	$\frac{1}{8}$% =	0.3% =
17.2% =	12% =	10% =	120% =
2,600% =	0.1% =	0.12% =	$33\frac{1}{4}$% =

2. Changing decimals to percents (1 point each)

1.8 =	0.026 =	2.1 =	0.88 =
3 =	2.11 =	0.125 =	0.088 =
$1\frac{1}{2}$ =	1 =	12.5 =	0.008 =
25 =	1.7 =	1.25 =	0.25 =
2 =	0.9 =	0.001 =	3.25 =

3. Word problems (5 points each)

a. Multiply $112.15 by the decimal equivalent of $5\frac{1}{4}$%.

b. Multiply 1/8 by 4/5 and state your answer as a percent.

4. Changing fractions to decimals (round to thousandths) (1 point each)

$\dfrac{1}{4} =$ $\dfrac{3}{75} =$ $\dfrac{8}{25} =$ $\dfrac{9}{50} =$

$2\dfrac{1}{8} =$ $\dfrac{1}{2} =$ $\dfrac{4}{5} =$ $\dfrac{9}{10} =$

$\dfrac{11}{20} =$ $26\dfrac{3}{4} =$ $\dfrac{2}{5} =$ $\dfrac{7}{20} =$

$\dfrac{9}{20} =$ $\dfrac{11}{50} =$ $8\dfrac{3}{5} =$ $\dfrac{2}{25} =$

$\dfrac{7}{25} =$ $\dfrac{9}{25} =$ $\dfrac{12}{25} =$ $1\dfrac{7}{8} =$

5. Changing decimals to fractions (reduce to lowest terms) (1 point each)

$0.8 =$ $0.333 =$ $1.25 =$ $0.5 =$

$0.2 =$ $0.80 =$ $0.81 =$ $0.05 =$

$0.625 =$ $0.007 =$ $0.005 =$ $0.875 =$

$1.6 =$ $5.5 =$ $0.7 =$ $0.16 =$

$0.176 =$ $0.111 =$ $5.75 =$ $0.375 =$

6. Word problems (5 points each)

a. Rather than multiplying another number by
7/8, what decimal equivalent may be used?
(Round answer to 1,000ths.)

b. Rewrite the following numbers, omitting any
insignificant zeros.

$2.50 =$
$018.301 =$
$100.00 =$
$0.63 =$
$120.30 =$

CHAPTER

4

Review of Equations

After reading Chapter 4, you will be able to

- Explain precisely the meaning of signed numbers.
- Add, subtract, multiply, and divide signed numbers.
- Gather terms by separating signed and unsigned numbers.
- Solve simple equations.
- Work proportional problems through the use of a short-cut method.

Key Terms

signed number   directly proportional

coefficients   indirectly proportional

Solving equations involves not only the basic operations of addition, subtraction, multiplication, and division, which we review in the first three chapters, but also an ability to work with signed numbers. This chapter discusses only the simplest types of mathematical equations, but a working knowledge of the materials is useful in solving many of the problems presented in later chapters, especially those problems relating to retailing and banking transactions.

Working with Signed Numbers

Before attempting to solve equations, let's review the use of **signed numbers.** A signed number is a number that is either positive or negative, which includes all numbers except zero. We may identify positive numbers by either preceding them with the plus sign (+) or with no sign at all, and we may identify negative numbers with either a minus sign (−) or by placing them within parentheses. As Figure 4.1 illustrates, the **addition of two positive numbers** results in a positive answer.

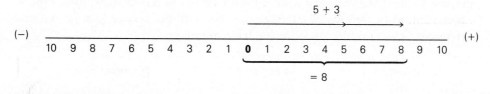

Figure 4.1   Adding Positive Numbers

If a gambler wins $5 to begin with and later wins an additional $3, for example, a total of $8 is won. No plus signs (+) are required with positive numbers because a number that is not preceded by a negative sign (−) is considered to be positive.

As shown in Figure 4.2, the **addition of two negative numbers** results in a negative answer.

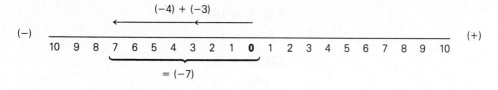

Figure 4.2   Adding Negative Numbers

If a gambler loses $3 to begin with and later loses an additional $4, a total of $7 is lost. Notice in Figure 4.2 that minus signs are used to identify negative numbers. Parentheses are used here to make it clear that the "−4" and the "−3" are set apart from the plus sign that separates them.

As illustrated in Figure 4.3, the **addition of numbers with mixed signs** may result in either positive or negative answers.

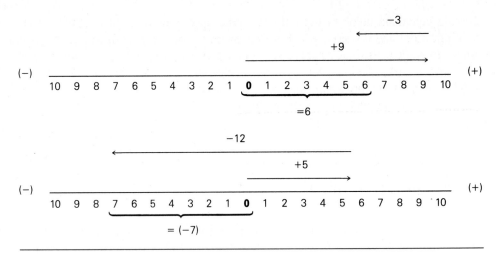

Figure 4.3   Adding Numbers with Mixed Signs

In the first instance, our imaginary gambler won $9 and later lost $3, resulting in a net gain of just $6. In the second instance, an initial win of $5 (positive) is followed by a loss of $12 (negative), resulting in an overall loss of $7. In losing $12, the gambler lost $7 more than was first won. To add numbers of mixed signs, therefore, we subtract and place the sign of the larger number with the answer (that is, with the difference). Also consider the following three examples:

Example 1	*Example 2*	*Example 3*
$-7 + 6 = -1$	$1 + 7 - 6 = 2$	$7 - 6 + 1 - 3 = -1$

In Example 1 the answer is negative (-1) because the negative number (-7) exceeds the positive number ($+6$) by one. The positive 8 ($1 + 7$) in Example 2 exceeds the negative value (-6) by 2, making the answer positive ($+2$). In Example 3 the negative numbers ($6 + 3 = 9$) exceed the positive numbers ($7 + 1 = 8$) by one, resulting in a negative answer (-1).

In the **multiplication of signed numbers,** we may use the times sign, a dot, or parentheses; thus the following problems are all 2 times 5:

$$2 \times 5 = 10$$
$$2 \cdot 5 = 10$$
$$(2)(5) = 10$$
$$2(5) = 10$$

Because all of these numbers are positive, the answers also are positive. Positive answers also result when we multiply two negative numbers, such as -2 times $-5 = 10$. Negative answers, on the other hand, result when we multiply numbers with mixed signs:

Example 4	*Example 5*	*Example 6*
$(-6)(-5) = 30$	$7 \cdot 6 = 42$	$(7)(-6) = -42$

In Example 4, two negative numbers equal a positive answer. In Example 5, two positive numbers equal a positive answer. In Example 6, the multiplication of one positive number and one negative number equals a negative answer.

In the **division of signed numbers** the signs work the same as with multiplication. When dividing two positive numbers or two negative numbers, the answer is positive. A negative answer results only when the numbers being divided are of different signs. Consider the following examples:

Example 7	*Example 8*	*Example 9*
$15 \div 3 = 5$	$15 \div (-3) = -5$	$(-15) \div (-3) = 5$

In Example 7, dividing two positive numbers gives a positive answer. A negative number results in Example 8 when numbers with mixed signs are divided, and in Example 9 a positive number results when two negative numbers are divided.

Remember that numbers placed as fractions are actually division problems, so that $48/12$ is the same as $48 \div 12 = 4$ and $-33/11$ is the same as $-33 \div 11 = -3$.

Self-Check 4A   Working wth Signed Numbers

1. $4 - 6 - 2 =$

2. $(-8)(2) =$

3. $45 \div (-9) =$

4. $-18 + 9 - 1 =$

5. $15 \cdot 3 =$

6. $\dfrac{21}{-7} =$

7. $6 + 3 - 2 =$

8. $(-3) + (-2) =$

9. $(-7) + (4) =$

10. $\dfrac{-24}{-3} =$

11. $\dfrac{18}{-6} =$

12. $\dfrac{-3.5}{7} =$

Gathering Terms

The first step in solving an equation is to gather the terms, or place the numbers with letters on one side of the equal sign and the numbers without letters on the opposite side of the equal sign. In the problem "$2x + 5 = 10 - 3x$," for example, we must gather the numbers associated with the letter x (the unknown number) on one side of the equal sign and gather those numbers not associated with x on the opposite side. The numbers associated with a letter are called **coefficients**. Example 10 shows the mathematical process that is used to gather the terms, and Example 11 shows an easier thought process that accomplishes the same result.

Example 10

Original equation	$2x + 5 = 10 - 3x$	
Add $+3x$	$3x$	$3x$
Add -5	-5	-5
Which leaves	$5x$	$= 5$

Example 11

Move $-3x$ to left of the equal sign and change to $+3x$

Move $+5$ to right of equal sign and change to -5

Which gives us

$$2x + 5 = 10 - 3x$$
$$+3x \quad \longrightarrow -5$$
$$5x \quad = 5$$

To understand the concept of equations, we should think of them as balancing scales. When a quantity is added, subtracted, multiplied, or divided on one side of an equation, we must maintain equality by doing the same to the other side. To eliminate the $-3x$ on the right side of the equation in Example 10, we add a positive $3x$ ($+3x$ plus $-3x$ = zero). Then, to maintain equality, we also add a positive $3x$ to the left side of the equation, resulting in $5x$ ($2x + 3x = 5x$). We use the same procedure to remove the $+5$ from the left side; that is, we add a -5 to both sides of the equation, resulting in a positive 5 ($10 - 5 = 5$) at the right side. We then have the numbers associated with x positioned to the left of the equal sign and those numbers not associated with x to the right of the equal sign.

The result in Example 10 is the same as if we had moved numbers from one side of the equal sign to the other and changed their signs, which is exactly the procedure illustrated in Example 11. Using either of these two methods, consider the following examples:

Example 12	*Example 13*	*Example 14*
$5x - 13 = 7$	$x + 8 = 16 - 3x$	$3x = 25 + 5x$
$5x = 7 + 13$	$x + 3x = 16 - 8$	$3x - 5x = 25$
$5x = 20$	$4x = 8$	$-2x = 25$

In Example 12, we changed the sign of -13 to $+13$ and moved it to the right of the equals sign. In Example 13, we moved the $+8$ to the right and changed it to a -8, and we moved the $-3x$ to the left and changed it to a $+3x$. In Example 14, we changed the $+5x$ to a $-5x$ in moving it to the left of the equal sign. Notice also that if there is no coefficient associated with a letter, the assumed coefficient has a value of one, so that "$x + 3x$" (Example 13) is actually "$1x + 3x = 4x$."

Self-Check 4B   Gathering Terms

---

1. $6x + 3 = 3x + 18$ **2.** $x + \dfrac{1}{4}x = 10$ **3.** $8 + x = 32 - 3x$

4. $5x = 16 - 1$ **5.** $7x - 3 = 18$ **6.** $4x + 9 = x - 3$

Finding an Unknown Number

In the final step of equation solving, we use division to find the value of the unknown x. After gathering terms in Example 12, for instance, we had "$5x = 20$." We must now eliminate the number alongside the unknown x by dividing it by itself; and, to maintain equality, we must also divide the opposite side by the same number, as shown in Example 15.

Example 15

Equation	$5x = 20$
Divide both sides by 5	$\dfrac{\overset{1}{\cancel{5}}x}{\underset{1}{\cancel{5}}} = \dfrac{\overset{4}{\cancel{20}}}{\underset{1}{\cancel{5}}}$
Which gives us	$1x = 4$
Which is actually	$x = 4$

In dividing $5x$ by 5, we derive a quotient of 1 ($5 \div 5 = 1$). One what? $1x$ or simply x. In also dividing the right side of the equation by 5 we derive 4 ($20 \div 5 = 4$), so that our answer reads "$x = 4$"; the value of x is 4.

We may prove our answer by plugging the newly found value into the original equation; that is, by changing x to 4.

$$\text{Originally:}\quad 5x - 13 = 7$$
$$\text{Proof:}\ 5(4) - 13 = 7$$
$$20 - 13 = 7$$
$$7 = 7$$

Also consider Examples 16 and 17:

Example 16

Original equation	$1 + 4x = 9$
Gather Terms	$4x = 9 - 1$
Add	$4x = 8$
Divide by 4	$x = 2$

Example 17

Original equation	$3x + 3 = 5x + 12$
Gather terms	$3x - 5x = 12 - 3$
Add	$-2x = 9$
Divide by -2	$x = -4.5$

Self-Check 4C   Finding an Unknown Number

1. $25 = 5x$

2. $(-8) + (x) = (3x) + (16)$

3. $4x + 5 = x + 20$

4. $8 + x = 32 - 3x$

5. $29 - 5x + x = 10 + 16 - x$

Using Simple Equations

Now let's see how such equations can help us solve the following problems.

Situation 1

If a number is added to 3 times the number and the sum is 88, what is the number?

Instead of x, let's refer to the unknown number as N, which gives us

A number:	N
Added to:	$+$
Three times the number:	$3N$
Is:	$=$
The sum:	88
Giving us:	$N + 3N = 88$
	$4N = 88$
	$N = 22$

$$
\begin{aligned}
\text{Proof:} \quad N + 3N &= 88 \\
22 + (3 \cdot 22) &= 88 \\
22 + 66 &= 88
\end{aligned}
$$

The word problem flows easily into an equation, making problem solving almost routine.

Situation 2

A storeowner can sell a certain model of a small radio at $156. If a profit of 20 percent of cost is to be realized, how much can the storeowner afford to pay the manufacturer for each radio?

Cost: C

Add: $+$

20% of cost: $0.2C$

Is: $=$

Selling price: **156**

Giving us: $C + 0.2C = 156$
$$1.2C = 156$$
$$C = \$130$$

Proof: $C + 0.2C = 156$
$$130 + 0.2(130) = 156$$
$$130 + 26 = 156$$

The storeowner may pay $130 for each radio, add 20 percent of the cost as profit, and still sell the item for $156.

Now use the following self-check section to gauge your understanding of these concepts, to make certain that you will be able to solve many business problems the easy way — with simple equations.

Self-Check 4D   Using Simple Equations

---

1. If 5 is subtracted from 3 times a number, the remainder is 40. Find the number.

2. Housing represents about one-fourth (25%) of a family's annual budget. If housing costs total $9,000 a year, what is the family's annual income?

3. The assembly department was charged $1,904 for electricity during March. If that department was charged 34% of the total electric bill, what was the total?

4. If Ray and Gloria had combined sales of $116,340 during the month, and Gloria sold 1 1/2 times the volume that Ray sold, what was the total dollar amount of Ray's sales?

Proportional Problems

If we know that a truck will run 50 miles on 5 gallons of fuel, we can determine the distance that the truck will run on 12 gallons (or any other amount) of fuel. Such problems are said to be proportional, and they can be solved with the simplest type of equation. We arrange the problems as follows:

5 gallons : 50 miles
12 gallons : x miles

We now have three numbers and one unknown (x) to work with, which enables us to cross multiply:

$$5x = 50 \times 12$$
$$= 5x = 600$$
$$x = 600 \div 5$$
$$x = 120 \text{ miles}$$

Let's try another proportional problem. If a certain number of workers can produce 3,120 parts in 5 days, how many days will be required for them to produce 7,800 parts?

$$\frac{3{,}120 \text{ parts} : 5 \text{ days}}{7{,}800 : x \text{ days}} =$$

$$3{,}120x = 7{,}800 \times 5$$
$$3{,}120x = 39{,}000$$
$$x = 39{,}000 \div 3{,}120$$
$$x = 12\frac{1}{2} \text{ days}$$

In solving proportion problems, you should be especially certain to check the logic of your answer. The two previous illustrations were **directly proportional**— we would expect a truck to run farther on 12 gallons of fuel than on 5 gallons, and we would expect the same number of workers to take more days to produce a greater number of parts.

The following problems are **indirectly proportional,** which means that an inverse (opposite) relationship applies.

**If 12 employees can perform a task in 16 days,
how many employees will be required to
perform the same task in 6 days?**

If we tried to work this problem using cross multiplication, as with the two previous examples, our answer would suggest that the task could be accomplished in fewer days using fewer employees, which is nonsense. When we see that the problem is indirectly proportional (that fewer days will require additional employees), we use horizontal multiplication:

$$
\begin{array}{ll}
\text{12 employees : 16 days} & 6x = 12 \times 16 \\
& 6x = 192 \\
\text{x employees : } \text{6 days} & x = 192 \div 6 \\
& x = 32 \text{ employees}
\end{array}
$$

We multiply 12 and 16 on one side of the equal sign and the 6 and x on the other side—across, rather than diagonally. Problems that are indirectly proportional (requiring horizontal rather than cross multiplication) are generally problems that relate the use of workers or machines to the time required to accomplish a task.

Self-Check 4E   Proportional Problems

1. If a bank deposit of $700 earns $48 interest, how much will a deposit of $950 earn during the same period?

2. If a company can process a government order in 12 days with the use of 8 drill presses, how many drill presses will be required to complete the order in only 7 days?

3. If 25 employees can produce 1,200 machined parts in 1 day, how many employees will it take to produce 1,550 parts in 1 day?

Answers to Self-Checks

Self-Check 4A	Self-Check 4B	Self-Check 4C	Self-Check 4D	Self-Check 4E
1. -4	1. $3x = 15$	1. $5 = x$	1. 15	1. $\$65.14$
2. -16	2. $\frac{5}{4}x = 10$	2. $x = -12$	2. $\$36,000$	2. 14
3. -5	3. $4x = 24$	3. $x = 5$	3. $\$5,600$	3. 33
4. -10	4. $5x = 15$	4. $x = 6$	4. $\$46,536$	
5. 45	5. $7x = 21$	5. $x = 1$		
6. -3	6. $3x = -12$			
7. 7				
8. -5				
9. -3				
10. 8				
11. -3				
12. -0.5				

1. Adding signed numbers (1 point each)

$-5 + 4 =$	$17 - 3 + 6 =$	$21 + 7 + 7 =$	$-8 - 9 + 3 - 2 =$
$6 - 4 =$	$4 + 16 - 5 =$	$15 + 5 - 6 + 3 =$	$16 + 18 - 3 - 7 =$
$-10 - 4 =$	$-4 - 8 - 6 =$	$39 + 30 + 7 - 2 =$	$23 + 7 + 7 - 6 =$
$-4 + 5 =$	$18 - 4 + 8 =$	$-6 - 14 - 12 - 2 =$	$42 + 16 - 4 - 2 =$
$5 - 4 =$	$12 - 6 + 9 =$	$16 - 7 - 2 - 5 =$	$24 + 15 - 7 - 3 =$

2. Multiplying signed numbers (1 point each)

$7 \times 4 =$	$(-3) \times (-6) =$	$3(16) =$	$8 \cdot 7 =$
$8(-2) =$	$(+2)(-6) =$	$(4)(10) =$	$6 \cdot 5 =$
$(+7)(+4) =$	$3 \cdot 7 =$	$(2)(9) =$	$(-8)(-4) =$
$(9)(3) =$	$12(-2) =$	$(-6)(20) =$	$5(-11) =$
$2(15) =$	$2(-10) =$	$4(-12) =$	$(-3)(+9) =$

3. Dividing signed numbers (1 point each)

$15 \div 5 =$	$16 \div (-4) =$	$-80 \div (20) =$	$36 \div (06) =$
$(-54) \div (-6) =$	$\dfrac{44}{4} =$	$\dfrac{0.33}{1.1} =$	$\dfrac{-48}{4} =$
$\dfrac{27}{-9} =$	$\dfrac{-5}{10} =$	$\dfrac{105}{3} =$	$90 \div (-15) =$
$48 \div 8 =$	$(-48) \div (-12) =$	$\dfrac{-28}{7} =$	$\dfrac{24}{(4)(3)} = \dfrac{24}{12} =$
$\dfrac{-20}{(2)(10)} =$	$\dfrac{-30}{(-2)(15)}$	$\dfrac{80}{(-40)(-2)} =$	$\dfrac{(-12)(+5)}{(-5)(+3)} =$

4. Finding an unknown number (2 points each)

$3x + 5 = 20$ $\qquad$ $4x - 5 = 15$ $\qquad$ $-6 + 3x = 24$ $\qquad$ $8 - 3x = 23$

$4x + 3 = 6x - 15$ $\qquad$ $5x - 18 = 3x$ $\qquad$ $-50 + 20x = 10x + 50$ $\qquad$ $3 + 6x = -3x + 30$

$7 + 12x = 5x - 14$ $\qquad$ $4x - 13 = 7 + 2x$ $\qquad$ $5x - 4 = 2x + 32$ $\qquad$ $25 - 5 = 5x$

$21 = 8x + 5$ $\qquad$ $6x + 3 = 3x + 12$ $\qquad$ $4x - 18 = 10x$ $\qquad$ $x - 12 = 20 - 3x$

$5x - 13 = 3x - 3$ $\qquad$ $-3x - 9 = 6x + 27$ $\qquad$ $9x + 2 = 2x + 30$ $\qquad$ $2x + 4 = 6x + 20$

1. Word problems (10 points each)

a. A company paid two-thirds as much money to advertise Product A as it did to advertise Product B. If total advertising expenses were $4,000, how much was spent on each product?

b. Sarah earns $225 weekly, which is three times the amount received by Bob. How much money does Bob earn?

c. Margaret and Albert are business partners. Because Margaret invested 2½ times as much as Albert, she receives 2½ as much of the profits as Albert does. Determine Albert's share of the $5,689.25 profits for this month.

d. The sum of two numbers is 310, with one of the numbers being four times the amount of the other number. Find the two numbers.

e. During a telephone survey, Dan made 125 calls, which was five more than two times as many as Sylvia made. How many telephone calls did Sylvia make?

2. Word problems (10 points each)

a. If a grocer charges $4.80 for 6 dozen apples,
how much will he charge for 11 dozen
apples?

b. After all taxes, fees, and claims were paid,
an estate was valued at $510,000. If the
surviving spouse received twice as much as
the daughter, how much did each receive?

c. If 16 workers can erect 1,500 feet of wall in
5 days, how many workers will be required
to erect 1,500 feet of wall in just 2 days?

d. Partner A and Partner B realized $10,400 net
profit from their business during August. If
Partner B's share is 3/5 that of Partner A,
how much money will Partner A receive?

e. If a gas station owner added 14,950 gallons
of gasoline to an underground tank, with the
new gas including 2 1/4 times as much
premium as regular, how much of each type
was added?

You may use this practice test to measure your preparation for the actual part test. Answers begin on page 413.

Review of Math Basics

1. Addition and subtraction (2 points each)

1,899	$2.48 + 3.19 + 0.52 + 51 =$	6,521.14	8,901.16	48
5,332		$-3,115.01$	-117.93	-56
2,919				

2. Multiplication and division (2 points each)

491	260.2	$0.8\overline{)32.8}$	$11\overline{)4631}$	$2.6\overline{)107.12}$
$\times212$	$\times1.05$			

3. Fractions (1 point each)

Change to improper fractions	$3\dfrac{3}{8} =$	$9\dfrac{3}{4} =$	$7\dfrac{1}{8} =$	$33\dfrac{1}{3} =$
Change to mixed numbers	$\dfrac{15}{4} =$	$\dfrac{17}{3} =$	$\dfrac{19}{3} =$	$\dfrac{17}{5} =$
Reduce to lowest terms	$\dfrac{30}{65} =$	$\dfrac{21}{105} =$	$\dfrac{9}{48} =$	$\dfrac{24}{54} =$

4. Fractions (reduce to lowest terms) (2 points each)

$$\frac{1}{5} + \frac{2}{6} =$$

$$2\frac{3}{14} + 1\frac{7}{10} =$$

$$1\frac{1}{8} - \frac{1}{4} =$$

$$5\frac{1}{4} - 1\frac{3}{8} =$$

$$\frac{5}{6} \times \frac{3}{10} =$$

$$\frac{9}{12} \times \frac{6}{15} \times 2\frac{5}{3} \times \frac{1}{22} =$$

$$\frac{5}{6} \div \frac{20}{35} =$$

$$4\frac{4}{5} \div \frac{12}{25} =$$

5. Decimals and percents (1 point each)

Change to decimals: 65% =   1.5% = $\frac{1}{2}$% =

Change to percents: 0.005 =   3.5 =   0.26 =

6. Fractions (1 point each)

Change to decimals: $\frac{7}{8}$ = $\frac{3}{5}$ = $\frac{3}{4}$ =

Change to fractions: 0.3 =   0.003 = $0.1\dot{7}$ =

7. Equations (5 points each)

$6x - 4 = 20 - 2x$ $x = 2x + 13$ $12 - 3 = 3x$ $16x - 10 = 40 - 4x$

8. Word problems (10 points each)

a. Of a total U.S. work force of 90 million people, there are approximately 3 1/2 times more nonunion employees as there are employees who belong to unions. How many unionized employees are there?

b. If 16 employees can produce 1,240 units during an 8-hour day, how many units will 20 workers produce during a similar time period?

PART

2

Foundational Math
of Business

5. Weights and Measures

Quantities
Weights
Capacity
Lengths and Areas
Volume
Summary of Common Weights and Measures
Time

6. Percentage Applications

Finding the Portion
Finding the Base
Finding the Rate
Finding the Base, Rate, or Portion
Rate of Change

7. Important Averages

Arithmetic Mean
Mean, Median, and Mode
Modified and Weighted Means
Price Indexes

8. Graphic Illustrations

Tables
Line Graphs
Bar Graphs
Circle Graphs
Component Graphs

Weights and Measures

After reading Chapter 5, you will be able to

- Determine cost on the basis of both quantity (units, dozens, gross) and weight (ounces, pounds, tons).

- Calculate price on the basis of capacity (pints, quarts, gallons), length (inch, foot, yard, mile), area (square feet and square yards), and volume (cubic feet and cubic yards).

- Compare local time with the variations represented by the several time zones within the United States and Canada.

Key Terms

gross	square yard
unit price	volume
cwt	cube
per M	cubic foot
ton	cubic yard
capacity	time zone
square foot	daylight saving time (DLS)

A working knowledge of our most widely used weights and measures is essential in areas of business such as production, warehousing, purchasing, traffic, and distribution. This knowledge also is important to each of us in our everyday lives as consumers.

Quantities

When we buy, sell, ship, or receive products, we deal either in single units or in various quantities. A *unit* of anything is one, so when ordering 25 cases of canned goods at $23.15 per case, we multiply units times price to determine total cost.

$$\textbf{Units} \times \textbf{price} = \textbf{total cost}$$
$$25 \quad \times \quad 23.15 = \quad \$578.75$$

A dozen is, of course, 12 units. When we order 4 dozen pencils, for example, we are referring to 48 pencils, which, if priced at $3.48 per dozen, would cost $13.92.

$$\begin{matrix} \textbf{Number} \\ \textbf{of dozen} \end{matrix} \times \begin{matrix} \textbf{price} \\ \textbf{per dozen} \end{matrix} = \textbf{total cost}$$
$$4 \quad \times \quad 3.48 \quad = \quad \$13.92$$

When dealing with many small items, such as pencils, we often use the term **gross**. One gross is 144, or 1 dozen dozen.

$$\textbf{One dozen} \times \textbf{one dozen} = \textbf{one gross}$$
$$12 \quad \times \quad 12 \quad = \quad 144$$

At $36 per gross, therefore, the total cost of five gross is $180.

$$\begin{matrix} \textbf{Number} \\ \textbf{of gross} \end{matrix} \times \begin{matrix} \textbf{price} \\ \textbf{per gross} \end{matrix} = \textbf{total cost}$$
$$5 \quad \times \quad 36 \quad = \quad \$180$$

In business, we must often determine the total cost per order. Occasionally, however, we may need to verify the amount ordered or the cost per unit. To determine the **unit price,** we divide the total cost by the number ordered. For example, if 4 dozen pencils cost $13.92, what is the cost per dozen?

$$\textbf{Total cost} \div \textbf{number ordered} = \textbf{unit price}$$
$$13.92 \quad \div \quad 4 \quad = \quad \$3.48$$

Self-Check 5A   Quantities

1. At 8¢ each, what is the cost of 1 gross of pencils? *11.52*

2. What is the cost of 42 shirts at a price of $98 per dozen?

    3 50 × 98   343

3. At a price of $180 per dozen shirts, what is the cost per unit?

         12/180   15⁰⁰

4. If a store orders 36 shirts at $180 per dozen and 15 men's jackets at $43 each, what is the total cost to the store?

5. If a merchant purchased one gross of ballpoint pens for a total cost of $36.72, how much profit will be made on each pen at a selling price of 36¢ per unit?

144

Weights

Ounces, pounds, and tons are the most common weights used in the United States. An ounce is 1/16 of a pound, or, stated another way, a pound consists of 16 ounces. To determine the number of ounces in a package that weighs 2.5 pounds, therefore, we multiply by 16.

$$\text{Ounces per lb} \times \text{number of pounds} = \text{total ounces}$$
$$16 \times 2.5 = 40$$

To find the per-ounce price of a product, we divide the price by the number of ounces. If we wish to determine the price per ounce of a 2 1/2-pound (40 ounce) item that is priced at $7.80 to compare it to the per-ounce price of another item, we divide.

$$\text{Price} \div \frac{\text{total}}{\text{ounces}} = \frac{\text{price}}{\text{per ounce}}$$
$$7.80 \div 40 = 0.195 = 19\frac{1}{2}¢$$

In the *unit pricing* system, per-ounce prices of products are posted on the edge of grocery shelves, enabling customers to compare the unit (per ounce) savings, if any, to be realized by purchasing large-sized containers.

Transportation companies generally charge rates (prices) on the basis of **cwt** (100 weight); that is, per each 100 pounds. To determine shipping costs, we must first find the number of 100s in the weight. For a shipment weighing 52,225 pounds that is rated at $2.25 per cwt, for instance, we divide the weight by 100 (move the decimal two places to the left) to find the number of 100s in the shipment.

$$\text{Weight} \div 100 = \text{cwt}$$
$$52{,}225 \div 100 = 522.25$$

Finding that the shipment contains $522\frac{1}{4}$ 100s, we multiply the figure by the rate.

$$\text{100s} \times \text{rate} = \text{cost}$$
$$522.25 \times 2.25 = \$1{,}175.06$$

If a shipment rate is quoted **per M** (per 1,000 pounds), we divide the weight by 1,000 before multiplying. The shipping charges on a 110,250-pound shipment at $26.70 per M, for instance, total almost three thousand dollars.

$$\text{Weight} \div 1{,}000 = \text{Ms}$$
$$110{,}250 \div 1{,}000 = 110.250$$

$$\text{Number of 1,000s} \times \text{rate} = \text{cost}$$
$$110.25 \times 26.70 = \$2{,}943.68$$

A **ton** consists of 2,000 pounds, so we must divide the weight by 2,000 before multiplying by the price (rate). If a mining company is selling coal at $125 per ton, for example, an order for 31,000 pounds would cost almost two thousand dollars.

$$\text{Weight} \div 2{,}000 = \text{tons}$$
$$31{,}000 \div 2{,}000 = 15.5$$

$$\text{Tons} \times \text{price} = \text{cost}$$
$$15.5 \times 125 = \$1{,}937.50$$

Self-Check 5B Weights

---

1. What is the price per ounce of a can of tomatoes weighing 28 ounces and selling two for $1? (Round answer to 10ths of a cent.)

2. One and one-fourth pounds equals how many ounces?

3. What is the charge for 250 pounds at a rate of $1.10 per cwt?

4. What is the charge for 22,250 pounds at a rate of $10 per ton?

5. Which is the better buy, an 8-ounce can of sweet peas that sells for 34¢ or a 17-ounce can priced at 45¢? (Round all calculations to 10ths of a cent.)

6. If a shipment weighing 32,018 pounds is rated at $16.25 per M, what are the shipping costs?

Capacity

Capacity is the measure of liquid volume, and the units of capacity that you should remember are the pint, quart, and gallon. One pint consists of two 8-ounce cups. A quart consists of two pints, and one gallon equals four quarts.

Self-Check 5C   Capacity

1. How many pints are there in one gallon?

2. If a cleaning service has only pint-sized cans of cleaning fluid and $6\frac{1}{2}$ quarts of the fluid are needed, how many cans must be used?

3. If gasoline is selling for 1.15\frac{9}{10}$ per gallon, how much will 3 pints for your lawnmower cost? (Round answer to cents.)

4. If a pint of varnish sells for $1.50 and a quart sells for $2.75, how much would you save if you bought a quart?

5. How many gallons of cleaning fluid will be required to fill 1,000 6-ounce cans? (Round answer to even gallons.)

Lengths and Areas

The inch is our shortest linear measure, which we may divide into fractional lengths such as 1/8 and 3/4. A foot consists of 12 inches, and a yard is either 36 inches or 3 feet. A mile, our longest measure, consists of 5,280 feet.

These measures are used not only to determine lengths, but also to calculate surface areas. A **square foot** is a square that is one foot long on all four sides, as shown in Figure 5.1.

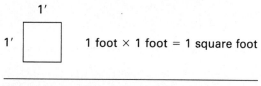

Figure 5.1 One Square Foot

To determine the number of square feet of any surface, we multiply its length by its width. To find the number of square feet of the floor illustrated in Figure 5.2, for instance, we multiply its width of 10 feet by its length of 15 feet.

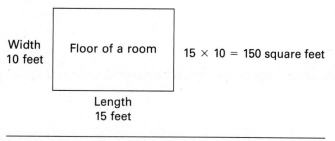

Figure 5.2 Area of a Floor (in square feet)

A **square yard** consists of 9 square feet, as shown in Figure 5.3.

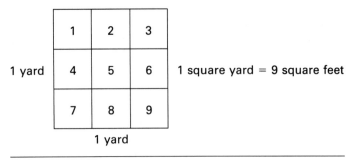

Figure 5.3   One Square Yard

To determine the number of square yards in the room pictured in Figure 5.2, therefore, we divide the number of square feet by 9.

$$\text{Square feet} \div 9 = \quad \text{square yards}$$

$$150 \quad \div 9 = 16\frac{2}{3} \text{ square yards}$$

Self-Check 5D   Lengths and Areas

1. One square foot contains how many square inches?

2. How many square feet are there in an area measuring 20 feet by $15\frac{1}{2}$ feet?

3. How many square yards of carpeting are required for a room measuring 15 feet by 15 feet?

4. How many square feet are there in a counter that measures $6\frac{1}{2}$ feet long and $2\frac{1}{2}$ feet wide? (Round answer to 100ths.)

5. How many tiles measuring 1 square foot would be required to cover a square room measuring 30 feet on each side?

Volume

The **volume** of a space consists of its cubic measure — not only its length and width as in square footage, but also its height. A **cube** is an even-sided object (such as a toy block) or an even-sided space (such as an empty square box), as diagramed in Figure 5.4.

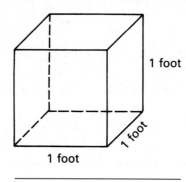

1 foot

1 foot

1 foot

Figure 5.4   A Cube

To find the cubic measure of a space, we multiply length times width times height, as illustrated in Figure 5.5.

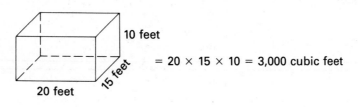

10 feet

15 feet

20 feet

$= 20 \times 15 \times 10 = 3{,}000$ cubic feet

Figure 5.5   Volume of a Space (in cubic feet)

A **cubic foot** contains 1,728 cubic inches ($12 \times 12 \times 12 = 1{,}728$), so that a container with a volume of one cubic foot would hold 1,728 square blocks that measure one inch on each side. A **cubic yard** contains 27 cubic feet, which means that a container with a volume of one cubic yard would hold 27 square containers that measure one cubic foot each. To convert cubic feet in the volume depicted in Figure 5.5 to cubic yards, therefore, we divide cubic feet by 27.

$$\frac{\text{Cubic}}{\text{feet}} \div 27 = \frac{\text{cubic}}{\text{yards}}$$

$$3{,}000 \div 27 = 111.11$$

The container in Figure 5.5 contains 3,000 cubic feet or a little more than 111 cubic yards.

Self-Check 5E   Area and Volume
---

1.   If the length of a room is 32 feet and its width is $25\frac{1}{2}$ feet, what is the square footage?

2.   How many square yards of carpeting would be needed to cover the entire floor of the room described in Question 1? (Round answer to even yards.)

3.   What is the volume of a railcar that has a length of 50 feet, a width of $10\frac{1}{2}$ feet, and a height of 12 feet?

4.   What is the volume of the railcar in Question 3 as expressed in cubic yards? (Round answer to even yards.)

5.   How many boxes could be placed in a square room that contains 3,000 cubic feet, if the boxes measure 1 foot at each edge?

Summary of Common Weights and Measures

The following summary of weights and measures is intended as a handy reference source for your continued convenience:

Quantities

12 units = 1 dozen
144 units = 1 gross
12 dozen = 1 gross

Weights

16 ounces = 1 pound
2,000 pounds = 1 ton

Capacities

1 cup = 8 ounces
2 cups = 1 pint
2 pints = 1 quart
8 pints = 1 gallon
4 quarts = 1 gallon

Lengths

12 inches = 1 foot
36 inches = 1 yard
3 feet = 1 yard
5,280 feet = 1 mile

Areas

Length × width = square area
9 square feet = 1 square yard
Square feet ÷ 9 = square yards

Volume

Length × width × height = cubic volume
27 cubic feet = 1 cubic yard
Cubic feet ÷ 27 = cubic yards

Time

When transacting business within the continental United States and Canada, we have four **time zones** to consider. When the time is 10:00 A.M. on the West Coast, as illustrated in Figure 5.6, it is 1:00 P.M. on the East Coast. Although there are four time zones, there is only a three-hour difference in time between the eastern and western United States. Notice at the base of the map the one hour time difference between the West Coast (Pacific time) and Alaska and the two hour difference with Hawaii. For instance, when it is 10:00 A.M. on the West Coast, it is 9:00 A.M. in Alaska and 8:00 A.M. in Hawaii.

If you were working in California and someone in New York asked you to phone at 3:00 P.M. their time, you would call at 12 noon Pacific time (3:00 − 3 hours = noon). Conversely, if you asked someone in New York to call you at 3:00 P.M. your time, the call would have to be placed at 6:00 P.M. Eastern time (3:00 + 3 hours = 6:00 P.M.).

An airplane departing New York at 8:00 A.M. and taking 4 hours to fly to the West Coast will arrive in California at 9:00 A.M. The 8:00 A.M. departure time from New York is only 5:00 A.M. in California, and the airplane gains 1 hour as it enters each of the different time zones for a total of 3 clock hours during the 4 actual hours

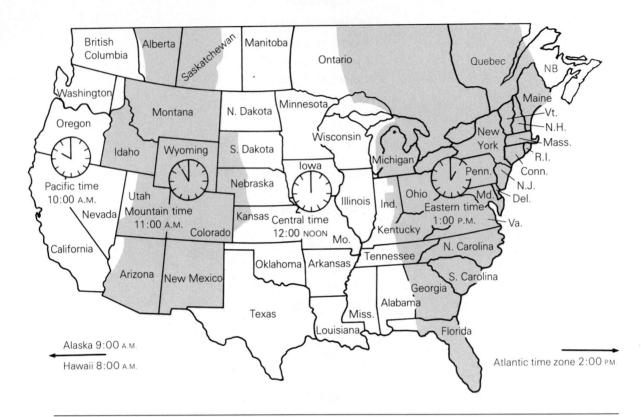

Figure 5.6   Standard Time Zones within the United States and Canada

of flying time. When flying from the west to the east, on the other hand, travelers lose 1 hour as they enter each time zone, so that a 4-hour flight leaving California at 8 A.M. will arrive in New York at 3 P.M. — 7 clock-hours later.

Long-distance transactions are further complicated by **daylight saving time (DLS).** When daylight saving time is in effect, from the first Sunday of April to the last Sunday of October, people observing the time change advance their watches and clocks 1 hour. Although you might still be arising at 6:30 A.M. according to the alarm clock, you are actually arising an hour earlier each morning according to the position of the earth relative to the sun.

Daylight saving time would not be very complicated if everyone observed it, but two states (Arizona and Hawaii) have exempted themselves from the program. When people in California set their timepieces ahead by 1 hour and the people in Arizona do not, the usual 1-hour difference between the two time zones is eliminated. When it is 11:00 A.M. in San Francisco, for instance, it is also 11:00 A.M. in Phoenix, Arizona. The usual time differences between Arizona and points east, on the other hand, are increased by 1 hour. When people in New York City set their clocks ahead 1 hour and the people in Arizona do not, the usual 2-hour difference is increased to 3 hours. Additionally, some sections of Indiana observe daylight saving time throughout the entire year.

—————————————— **Self-Check 5F**   Time ——————————————

1. When it is 9:30 A.M. in Colorado, what time is it in St. Louis?

2. Assuming 3 hours actual flying time, what time would you have to leave New York City to arrive in San Francisco at 9:00 A.M.?

3. If it is 8:00 A.M. in Arizona on June 10, what time is it in New York?

4. A business person in Detroit, Michigan, decides at 9 A.M. to call a company in Anchorage, Alaska. What time would it be in Anchorage?

5. If a group of business people in Chicago must be in New York City at 3:00 P.M. what time must they leave Chicago—assuming travel time of $2\frac{1}{2}$ hours?

—————————————— **Answers to Self-Checks** ——————————————

Self-Check 5A	**Self-Check 5B**	**Self-Check 5C**	**Self-Check 5D**	**Self-Check 5E**
1. $11.52	1. 1.8¢ per oz	1. 8 pints	1. 144 sq in	1. 816 sq ft
2. $343	2. 20 oz	2. 13 cans	2. 310 sq ft	2. 91 sq yd
3. $15	3. $2.75	3. 44¢	3. 25 sq yd	3. 6,300 cu ft
4. $1,185	4. $111.25	4. 25¢	4. 16.25 sq ft	4. 233 cu yd
5. $10\frac{1}{2}$¢	5. 17-ounce can	5. 47	5. 900 tiles	5. 3,000 boxes
	6. $520.29			

Self-Check 5F

1. 10:30 A.M.   4. 5:00 A.M.

2. 9:00 A.M.   5. 11:30 A.M.

3. 11:00 A.M.

Measurements: Quantities and Weights (5 points each)   Score _____

1. At a price of 24¢ per unit, what is the cost of 1 gross of pencils?

2. At a price of $6\frac{1}{2}$¢ each, what is the price of a 5-gross carton of grommets?

3. What is the total cost of a gross of windshield wipers if the price is $2.25 per wiper?

4. If you can buy short-sleeve men's shirts in plain colors for $15.50 each, how much would you pay for 8 boxes containing 4 shirts each?

5. If packages of yellow paper can be purchased for $108.60 per dozen, what is the cost per package?

6. One supplier sells ballpoint pens for $21.60 per gross, and another supplier sells similar pens for $1.98 a dozen. What is the difference in the cost of each pen?

7. What is the total cost for the following items:
   150 paperback books @ $1.50 per unit
   15 dictionaries at $8.50 each
   12 pencil sharpeners @ $4.25 each

8. What is the cost of 150 gift-wrapped handkerchiefs that are listed at $93.60 per gross?

9. How much more expensive are apples that are selling at 69¢ per pound than bananas that are priced at 4 pounds for a dollar?

10. What is the difference in price of hand calculators if one costs $16.55, including an adapter for recharging the batteries, and the other calculator costs $12.60 plus $2.05 for the adapter?

11. What is the price per ounce of a can of tuna weighing 6 ounces and costing $1.29?

12. If a 1-pound box of powder is priced at $2.08 and an 8-ounce package of the same powder costs $1.16, how much would you save per ounce by purchasing the larger package?

13. What is the price per ounce of a can of tomatoes weighing 1 pound and 9 ounces and priced at 0.75¢ each?

14. Find the per-unit difference between regular aspirin selling 500 for $2.59 and 30 extra-strength aspirin selling for $1.19. (Round answer to 10ths of a cent.)

15. If auto stores have been selling a certain brand of motor oil for $1.10 per quart, how much more money will they make on each carton of 24 cans sold if they raise the price by 12 cents per quart?

16. What is the cost for shipping 150 pounds if the rate per cwt is $5.20?

17. If a manufacturer offers to sell you 2,000 cartons of merchandise at $15 per carton plus freight charges of 25¢ per carton, how much must you pay?

18. What is the cost of shipping 5,500 pounds if the shipping charges are figured at $25.50 per M?

19. What is the cost of a 55,000-pound shipment at a rate of $50 per ton?

20. If canned tomatoes weigh $16\frac{1}{2}$ ounces each, how much does it cost to ship 100 24-can cartons of tomatoes at a rate of $2.25 per cwt? Add 4 ounces for each cardboard carton used.

Measurements: Capacities, Lengths, Volume, and Time (5 points each)

1. What is the cost of 15 gallons of unleaded gasoline if the price is $1.15\frac{9}{10}$ per gallon?

2. If you buy 10 gallons of gasoline that is priced at $1.70\frac{9}{10}$ per gallon, how much does the extra $\frac{9}{10}$¢ cost you?

3. If olive oil is selling for $6.50 per quart, how much could a person save per quart by buying a half-gallon selling for $13.00?

4. How many gallons of vinegar must be processed to produce 25,000 pints and 2,000 quarts?

5. What is the square footage of a floor that is 22.5 feet long and 18 feet wide?

6. If an office floor measures $25\frac{1}{4}$ feet by $30\frac{1}{2}$ feet, how many square yards of carpeting will be required to cover it from wall to wall? (Round answer to 100ths.)

7. If a section of a steamship measures 40 feet long, 50 feet across, and 20 feet high, how large is the area in terms of cubic yards? (Round answer to whole numbers.)

8. If the inside of a railcar measures 40 feet long, 10 feet wide and $10\frac{1}{2}$ feet high, what is its volume in terms of cubic feet?

9. If $67\frac{1}{2}$ cubic feet were subtracted from an area measuring 30 cubic yards, how many cubic yards of space would remain?

10. What is the difference in square footage between a storage room that measures $8\frac{1}{2}$ by 11 feet and one that measures 9 by $11\frac{1}{2}$ feet?

11. Name the four time zones within the continental United States.

12. You have promised to meet some business people at the Los Angeles airport at 2:00 P.M. today. At what time must you depart the New York City airport in your private jet, which cruises at a speed of 500 miles per hour? (The distance from New York City to Los Angeles is approximately 3,000 miles.)

13. On Wednesday at 9:00 A.M. you are to arrange a conference call from company headquarters in San Francisco that will connect you simultaneously with company representatives in Denver, Colorado, Dallas, Texas, and Philadelphia, Pennsylvania. At what time will you ask the representatives to be standing by for the call?

14. Your Arizona branch office closes at 5:00 P.M. If it is 4:30 P.M. on July 3 in your California office, will you be able to reach the Arizona branch office by phone? Explain.

15. If daylight saving time is in effect, what is the difference in time between New York City and San Francisco?

16. If it is 3:00 P.M. in New York City (DST), what time is it in Hawaii?

17. How much would carpeting cost at $25 per square yard for a room that measures 25 feet by 25 feet? (Round to whole yards.)

18. If the floor of a 12-foot high storage room contains 625 square feet, how many cubic feet does the room contain?

19. What is the total square footage of the floor diagramed below?

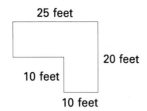

20. What is the measurement of the following space in cubic yards? (Round to 100ths.)

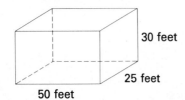

CHAPTER

6

Percentage Applications

After reading Chapter 6, you will be able to

- Find the portion, base, and rate (percent) in a wide variety of problems.
- Determine the rate of increase or decrease between two numbers from one time period to another.

Key Terms

base

portion

rate

Many educators consider a study of percents to be the most important segment of business mathematics, because these types of problems are so prevalant in business. Business people calculate the percent of increase or decrease in transactions such as sales, costs, expenses, and profits. Government employees compute the percent of economic growth and unemployment. Most of us are concerned with the percent of change in the cost of living, as well as the percent of our salaries that is paid in taxes.

The most efficient way of learning to calculate percentages is to define the different parts of percentage problems as being the base, rate, or portion. The **base** is the total or whole amount of whatever we are dealing with—total salary, total population, total price, total work force. The **portion** is a part (a fractional amount) of the base, and the **rate** determines the size of the portion in relation to the whole. Consider the diagram of a pie in Figure 6.1.

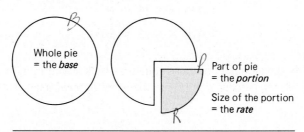

Figure 6.1   The Relationship of Base, Rate, and Portion

Placing the segments in the following equation will help us solve a wide variety of business problems.

$$\text{Base} \times \text{Rate} = \text{Portion}$$

or, more simply

$$BR = P$$

When we know the value of any two of these segments, we may use the equation to find the unknown third value.

Finding the Portion

We find the portion by multiplying the base (B) times the rate (R):

$$BR = P$$
$$\uparrow$$
the unknown

If the base is $1 and the rate is 10 percent, we find the portion by multiplying the base times the rate:

$$BR = P$$
$$\$1 \times 10\% = P$$
$$\$1 \times 0.10 = 0.10, \text{ or } 10\cancel{c}$$

Similarly, if our company employs 6,420 persons and 15 percent of them are women, we can multiply the total number of employees (the base) by the percent of women employees (the rate) to find the fraction (portion) of the total that are women:

$$BR = P$$
$$6,420 \times 0.15 = P$$
$$6,420 \times 0.15 = 963$$

You may simplify development of these equations by keeping in mind that any number associated with the percent sign (%) or the word *percent* itself is always the rate.

Self-Check 6A   Finding the Portion

1.   What is 21% of 600?

126

2.   If the population of a community is 96,000 and 12% of them are 65 years or older, what portion of the population is younger than 65 years of age?

11520   *84480*

3.   In the preceding problem, how many persons in the community are 65 years or older?

1382.4

4.   If a sales tax of 7.5% is assessed, what amount of tax must be paid on the purchase of an automobile priced at $12,250?

9187.5

5. How much commission will a real estate agent receive if the commission rate is 6% of the sales price of $125,500? *753*

Finding the Base

In the preceding discussion, the base and rate were provided, and we had to find the portion; that is, P was the unknown. In other types of business problems, the rate and portion may be given so that we have to find the base:

$$BR = P$$
$$\uparrow$$
the unknown

If we don't know the total number of employees working for a company (the base), for example, we can find the base if we know that 963 women work there (the portion) and that they represent 15 percent (the rate) of the total number of employees:

$$B \times R = P$$
$$B \times 0.15 = 963$$

Recalling that we may reverse the order of the numbers (multiplicand and multiplier) when we multiply, we may change $BR = P$ to $RB = P$ (reversing the order of B and R) so that $0.15B = 963$.

Now let's apply some of the knowledge of equations that you acquired in Chapter 4, having substituted the letter B for x as the unknown.

$$0.15B = 963$$
$$B = 963 \div 0.15$$
$$B = 6{,}420 \text{ employees}$$

If it is easier for you to memorize a formula, on the other hand, the formula for finding the base is the portion divided by the rate:

$$B = \frac{P}{R} = \frac{963}{0.15} = 6{,}420 \text{ employees}$$

Self-Check 6B Finding the Base

1. If 5% of a number is 125, what is the number? *2500*

2. 490 is 20% of what number?

    2450

3. If you pay the bank $780 as a down payment on a new car, which amounts to 15% of the selling price, what is the selling price?   *5200*

4. If a sales merchant who earns a 12% commission receives commissions of $1,536 for March, what was the value of this person's sales for that month? *12800* ✓

5. If 3,835 of the employees at Armar Corporation are minority members, which amounts to 32½% of total employees, how many people are employed at the company? *108,028 – 11,800*

Finding the Rate

When the base and the portion are provided, the rate becomes the unknown, and we use the same procedure to find an unknown rate as we did to find an unknown base — we divide. If we know that a company employs 6,420 workers, for example, of which 963 are women, we can proceed by either of the following steps to find the rate (the percent):

Equation

$$BR = P$$
$$6{,}420R = 963$$
$$R = 963 \div 6{,}420$$
$$R = 0.15 = 15\%$$

Formula

$$R = \frac{P}{B} = \frac{963}{6,420} = 15\%$$

One very important point to remember is that when you want to know the rate (percent) that one number is of another number, you divide it by the other number. In the example just given, we are actually asking what percent 963 is of 6,420, so we divide 963 by 6,420.

Self-Check 6C   Finding the Rate

1. 1,728 is what percent of 7,200?   24%

2. What percent is 3,825 of 8,500?

3. If your gross pay is $550 and your take-home pay is $357.50, what percent of your pay was withheld for taxes, insurance, etc.?

4. If an airline ticket costing $278.20 includes a federal transportation tax of $18.20, what is the tax rate?

5. If Partner A receives profits of $162,500 and Partner B receives $87,500, what is Partner B's percent of total profits?

Finding the Base, Rate, or Portion

Many people use the pyramid scheme presented in Figure 6.2 to identify the correct formula to apply.

We can easily remember that *P* (portion) is placed at the point of the pyramid and that *B* (base) is placed at the base, which leaves only one slot (bottom right) for the *R* (rate).

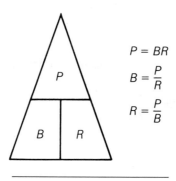

$$P = BR$$
$$B = \frac{P}{R}$$
$$R = \frac{P}{B}$$

Figure 6.2   The $BR = P$
Pyramid

Keeping these guidelines in mind, let's consider a mixture of percentage problems.

If a city government employs 523,201 persons, 120,336 of whom are on monthly salaries (rather than hourly rates), what is the percent of employees earning monthly salaries?

$$BR = P$$
$$523{,}201R = 120{,}336$$
$$R = 120{,}336 \div 523{,}201$$
$$R = 23\%$$

The base is 523,201 (the total number of employees), and 120,336 is a portion of the base; rate (the percent) is the unknown.

Of a total of 222,416 television sets manufactured, 12.5% had defects. How many sets were defective?

$$BR = P$$
$$222{,}416 \times 0.125 = P$$
$$222{,}416 \times 0.125 = 27{,}802$$

The total number (222,416) is the base, the percent (12.5% = 0.125) is the rate, and the portion is the unknown.

If Joyce Palmer received an end-of-year bonus of $3,534, which represents 1 1/2% of her total sales for the year, what was the dollar amount of her sales?

$$BR = P$$
$$B \times 0.015 = 3,534 \text{ (or } 0.015B = 3,534)$$
$$B = 3,534 \div 0.015$$
$$B = \$235,600$$

The rate is 1.5 (1.5% = 0.015), and the bonus of \$3,534 is a portion of her total sales, leaving total sales as the unknown base.

Self-Check 6D   Finding the Base, Rate, or Portion

1. What percent is \$257.92 of \$1,612.00?

2. What number is 13% of \$250,000?

3. \$3,960 is 12% of what amount?

4. If an employee earns a bonus of \$225, which amounts to 8% of her monthly income, what amount does she earn per month?

5. If a customer is to make a down payment of 15% of the sales price for a clothes dryer priced at \$559, in what amount must a check be written?

6. If an investor received $750 last year from a company in which he invested $6,250, what percent is the payment of the investment?

Rate of Change

Percentages are used extensively in business to measure the rate of change in such things as prices, costs, expenses, and profits. To calculate the percent of change, you find the difference between the current value and original value, and then divide the difference by the original value. If a can of tomatoes that has been selling for 35¢ is increased to 42¢, for example, you calculate the **percent increase** by dividing the difference between the new price and the earlier price by the earlier price.

Step 1

New price − Earlier price = Difference

$$0.42 - 0.35 = 0.07¢$$

Step 2

Difference ÷ Earlier price = % change

$$0.07 \div .35 = 0.20 = 20\% \text{ increase}$$

A **percent decrease** is calculated the same way as an increase. Assume, for example, that company sales declined from $85,320 in 1989 to $81,054 in 1990. As before, we compute the percent change by finding the difference between the two amounts and dividing the difference by the earlier (1989) figure:

Step 1

$$81,054 - 85,320 = -4,266 \text{ difference}$$

Step 2

$$-4,266 \div 85,320 = 5\% \text{ decrease}$$

In addition to the minus sign and the word *decrease,* as used here, we may place numbers within parentheses to note a decline in value.

——————— **Self-Check 6E** Rate of Change (round answers to tenths of a percent) ———————

1. If you earned $11,000 in 1988, and your income for 1989 was $12,000, what was the percent change in your income?

2. If the price of your favorite whole wheat bread increases from 80¢ a loaf to 95¢, what is the rate of increase?   *18.8%*

3. If the salaries paid employees totaled $60,000 last year and $55,000 this year, what is the percent change?

    6.3

4. If an automobile manufacturer charges $11,726.04 for a sedan that was priced at $11,248.00 the preceding year, what is the percent of increase?   *4.3%*

——————— **Answers to Self-Checks** ———————

Self-Check 6A	Self-Check 6B	Self-Check 6C	Self-Check 6D	Self-Check 6E
1. 126	1. 2,500	1. 24%	1. 16%	1. 9.1%
2. 84,480	2. 2,450	2. 45%	2. $32,500	2. 18.8%
3. 11,520	3. $5,200	3. 35%	3. $33,000	3. (8.3%)
4. $918.75	4. $12,800	4. 7%	4. $2,812.50	4. 4.3%
5. $7,530	5. 11,800	5. 35%	5. $83.85	
			6. 12%	

1. What is 18% of 920?

2. $45.90 is what percent of $180.00?   ⊃ 5. 5

3. What is 120% of 9,600?   − 25.5 11,520

4. If company sales in 1989 were $750,000, compared with $700,000 in 1990, what was the percent change? (Round to tenths of a percent.)

   5% − 750 ⎯⎯ 50⟌50 6.7%
         700

5. 645 is 15% of what number?   ⊂ 43

6. What is 33% of $9,900?   3 267

7. If an airline had 1,500 flights last month, compared with 1,100 flights for the same month last year, what is the percent change? (Round to tenths of a percent.)

   400   36.4   1,500
              − 1,100
              ⎯⎯⎯⎯
                400

8. If an investor receives $270 interest at the end of 1 year on a deposit that earns 6% interest, how much money did the investor deposit in the bank?

9. If an investor receives $4,250 income on an investment of $50,000, what rate of return does he realize?   8.5

10. If you sell a $350 electric clothes dryer to a customer on terms of 15% down, how much money must you collect from the customer prior to delivery of the dryer?   52.50

11. $92.75 is what percent of $700? (Round answer to tenths of a percent.)

12. 150% of what number is $1,462.50?

13. A purchaser must make a down payment of 15% on an automobile priced at $10,275. How much money is this?

14. If the price of a package of mints is increased from 5¢ to 15¢, what is the percent increase?

15. If your gross pay each month is $620 and $198.40 is withheld for taxes, social security, insurance, and union dues, what percent of your pay is left over for other uses?

16. If the bank requires you to pay $2,325 as a 15% down payment on a new car, what is the total cost of the new car, including the down payment?

17. If 22% of our employees are 40 years of age or older, of a total of 32,000 employees, how many employees are younger than 40 years of age?

18. If the average employee at Hurley Electronics earns a gross income of $1,260 per month, from which the company deducts $504, what percent of total income is the average employee's take-home pay?

19. In 1973 many of the oil-producing countries increased the average price of a barrel of crude oil from $2.60 to $11.00. What was the percent of increase?

20. If there are 80 students in the class and 5% of them fail the course, how many students passed?

Name _____

Percentage Applications (5 points each)

Score _____

1. What is $18\frac{1}{4}\%$ of 8,400?

2. What percent is 363 of 1,100?

3. 75% of what number is 270?

4. What percent is 105 of 700?

5. If profits for 1990 are $84,000 compared with $80,000 for 1989, what is the percent change?

6. If you made $15 profit on an item that you sold for $45, what percent of the selling price is profit? (Round answer to tenths of a percent.)

7. If a retailer loses $184 on the sale of a new refrigerator, which amounts to 46% of the price he paid the manufacturer for the item, how much did the retailer pay the manufacturer?

8. If the price of 60¢ for an item includes 3¢ for transportation charges, what percent of the price is the transportation charge?

9. If a real estate agent receives $2,550 in commissions, which is 6% of the selling price of the property, what was the selling price?

10. If the number of employee absences was 1,550 last year and only 1,240 this year, what was the percent decrease?

11. What is $3\frac{1}{4}$ percent of $1,500?

12. What percent is $15,990 of $24,600?

13. If your salary this year is $11,880, compared with $11,000 last year, what is your percent increase in salary?

14. If a can of peaches is now selling for 48¢ and we increase the price by 2%, what is the new price?

15. If a purchaser of a personal computer made a down payment of $440, which was 16% of the purchase price, what was the purchase price?

16. If a business charged a customer $33.50 in late charges in the payment of an invoice totaling $1,675.00, what percent of the amount was the penalty charge?

17. Production workers agreed to wage cuts of 50 cents per hour on an average wage of $18.20 per hour. What was the rate of change? (Round answer to tenths of a percent.)

18. What were the total sales this year, if we realized a 12% increase over the $33,000 sales last year?

19. Exactly 12% of all sales by Nortex Corporation were written off as bad debts, totaling $33,038.88. What were the total sales for the year?

20. What amount did a salesperson receive on the sale of merchandise priced at $199.95 if the commission rate is 15 percent of the selling price? (Round answer to cents position.)

CHAPTER

7

Important Averages

After reading Chapter 7, you will be able to

- Compute the arithmetic mean, median, and mode.
- Describe the applications to which each of these three averages is best suited.
- Calculate and explain the usefulness of the modified mean.
- Apply the weighted mean as a short-cut method of computation.
- Prepare and interpret price indexes.

Key Terms

average   modified mean
arithmetic mean   weighted mean
median   price indexing
mode   Consumer Price Index (CPI)

Business people rely heavily on averages when making important comparisons — average salaries within a company or an industry, average prices that competitors are charging, average amounts of inventories on hand, average earnings during the month or year, and many others. In setting their own prices and when adjusting wage levels for their employees, business managers also depend on average prices that are reflected in price indexes published by the federal government.

Arithmetic Mean

When most people think of an **average**, they think of the mean, or more properly, the arithmetic mean. The **arithmetic mean** is an average that is derived by dividing the total of all observed values by the number of observations involved. Consider the seven observations of daily high temperatures in Table 7.1.

Day	Temperature	Sequential Order	
		down 4	
Sunday	70	74	*middle*
Monday	65	71	
Tuesday	69	70	*most*
Wednesday	71	median → 70	mode - *common repeated #*
Thursday	70	70	
Friday	74	69	
Saturday	70	65	
	7/489		
	69.9 = mean	up 4	

Table 7.1   Daily High Temperatures

We calculate the mean to be 69.9 by adding the seven temperatures and dividing the total by 7, the number of observations.

Mean, Median, and Mode

The **median** is the value that divides a set of numbers into two equal parts, so that half of the numbers are higher than the average and half are lower. The median is often more helpful than the mean. For example, the mean annual income of Americans includes salaries of more than $1 million per year, resulting in an average suggesting that Americans are better off than they actually are. The median income of Americans, on the other hand, indicates that one-half of the population is receiving incomes higher than the average and one half are receiving lower incomes.

The median is the middle value in the odd number of temperatures listed in Table 7.1. After placing the data in sequential order, from the largest to the smallest or from the smallest to the largest, we can readily identify the middle value as 70. A slightly different approach is necessary when working with an even number of values, as explained later in this section.

The **mode**, when one exists, is the value that is repeated more often than any other value. In Table 7.1, 70 degrees is the mode (as well as the median), because 70 appears more frequently (three times) than any other reading. In business, the mode is mainly used to determine the most popular or preferred colors, styles, or sizes.

To further illustrate these three averages, let's consider the ages of ten employees in the distribution department of a manufacturing company. These ages are listed in Table 7.2.

			down $5\frac{1}{2}$	
Bill Brown	19		64	
Rae Charles	17		35	
Bob Downing	19		21	
Kate Fowler	64		21	
Jack Harris	21		20	← 19.5 = median
Mary Jones	19		19	
Nancy Love	35	mode	19	
Jim Moore	17		19	
Barry Nelson	20		17	
Diane Smith	21		17	
	10 $\overline{)252}$		up $5\frac{1}{2}$	
	25.2 = mean			

Table 7.2   Ages of Employees

To calculate a mean of 25.2, we add the ages and divide the sum by the total number of employees ($252 \div 10 = 25.2$). Because we have an even number of observations (employees in this instance), the median (counting $5\frac{1}{2}$ from either the top or bottom of the array) is between ages 19 and 20 (see arrows). Therefore, we take an average of these two numbers to find the median age to be 19.5.

$$\text{Median: } \frac{19 + 20}{2} = \frac{39}{2} = 19\frac{1}{2}$$

The mode is 19 because that age appears more frequently than any other age.

─────────────── **Self-Check 7A**   Arithmetic Mean and Median and Mode ───────────────

1.   What is the mean of 263, 483, 622, and 918?

2. What is the median of 16, 18, 22, 20, 19, and 21?

3. What is the mode of 70, 65, 80, 65, 75, 83, and 77?

4. If a store had weekly sales during March of $1,112.65, $1,444.10, $1,398.16, and $1,500.02, what were the average (mean) weekly sales for the month?

Modified and Weighted Means

A **modified mean** is derived by removing any extreme values before calculating the mean. The one extreme age in Table 7.2 is 64. With 8 of the 10 employees being 21 years of age or younger, a mean average of 25.2 is not truly representative of the group. By averaging all ages except 64, we find that the modified mean is 20.9 (or almost 21 years of age), which is much more representative of this group of employees.

Sometimes it is more convenient to compute a **weighted mean,** in which individual values are multiplied by a factor indicating their relative importance before averaging. The weighted mean is a shortcut in calculating the arithmetic mean, as it enables us to group identical values. To illustrate, let's consider the scores on a final examination shown in Table 7.3.

Number of Students		Score Earned		Weighted Score
1	×	99	=	99
2	×	92	=	184
3	×	88	=	264
1	×	78	=	78
5	×	75	=	375
3	×	70	=	210
1	×	65	=	65
16				1275 ÷ 16 = 79.7 = mean

Table 7.3   Final Examination Scores

We multiply each score by the number of students earning the score. To find the mean, we then add the weighted scores and divide the sum by the total number of students. We could have derived the same answer without using the weighted scores by adding 99, 92, 92, 88, 88, 88, 78, 75, 75, 75, 75, 75, 70, 70, 70, 65, and dividing the total by 16. It is much easier to compute the weighted mean, however, especially when the quantity of data is great. Imagine the difference involved with each method, for example, if 100 or more students were involved.

Self-Check 7B   Modified and Weighted Means

---

1. Using the weighted mean, determine the average price of the following sales of sandwiches:

Number of Sandwiches	Unit Price
1,212 hamburgers	$2.25
918 cheeseburgers	2.50
525 chicken	2.60

2. Which average or averages would you use to determine the representative salary for the following incomes received by the personnel in a small firm: $19,500, $19,000, $21,000, $45,000, $25,000, and $23,500?

Price Indexes

Price indexes, which are based on average prices, are important in today's business world because they enable us to measure the effects of inflation on the purchasing power of the dollar. In addition, many of our incomes are adjusted periodically in response to changes in price indexes. Without such measurements, we would be unable to determine with certainty whether our purchasing power is improving or deteriorating each year.

Price indexing is easy; we simply identify a number as the base and compare it with all other numbers. For example, you may decide to identify your weight for January as the base and compare all subsequent weights as a percent of your January weight, as shown in Table 7.4.

In comparing the January and February weights, we are actually asking: What percent is 123 of 119? So we divide 123 by 119, resulting in an answer of 1.0336. We then multiply 1.0336 by 100 (or simply move the decimal two places to the right) to state the figure in terms of a percent.

Months	Index
January	119 lb ÷ 119 × 100 = 100.0
February	123 lb ÷ 119 × 100 = 103.3
March	124 lb ÷ 119 × 100 = 104.2
April	130 lb ÷ 119 × 100 = 109.2
May	120 lb ÷ 119 × 100 = 100.8
June	118 lb ÷ 119 × 100 = 99.2
July	126 lb ÷ 119 × 100 = 105.9
August	128 lb ÷ 119 × 100 = 107.6
September	130 lb ÷ 119 × 100 = 109.2
October	125 lb ÷ 119 × 100 = 105.0
November	120 lb ÷ 119 × 100 = 100.8
December	120 lb ÷ 119 × 100 = 100.8

Table 7.4 Monthly Weight

Although indexes are actually percents, it is customary to omit the percent sign.

So what does this information tell us? The resulting 103.3 for February indicates that your weight increased 3.3 percent during the one-month period (103.3 − 100.0 = 3.3). Looking next at the March index of 104.2, we find that your weight increased 4.2 percent from January.

The **Consumer Price Index (CPI),** our most widely used index, is calculated in a similar fashion each month. The government priced thousands of consumer items in 1967, the base year, that were representative of products normally purchased by most households in the United States. The total cost of those 1967 goods became the base (and the divisor) in the comparison of total prices for similar products in future years. Each month the Bureau of Labor Statistics strives to price goods that are similar to the 1967 selection, the total cost of which is divided by the cost of the original selection in 1967. The results are shown in Table 7.5.

Although the Bureau of Labor Statistics is also compiling averages with 1980 as the base year, we will continue to use 1967 as the base for the next several years.

The CPI tells us that in 1988 we had to pay $3.63 to purchase the same quantity and value of items that would have cost $1.00 in 1967. The inflation rate during that 21-year period, therefore, was 262.7 percent (362.7 − 100 = 262.7).

In comparing the price levels for any two of the above years, we figure the *rate of change* just as we did in Chapter 6. That is, we find the difference between the two averages and divide that difference by the average of the earlier year. Let's use the years 1979 and 1980 as an illustration.

Year	Index	% of Inflation
1967	100.0	2.9
1968	104.2	4.2
1969	109.8	5.4
1970	116.3	5.9
1971	121.3	4.3
1972	125.3	3.3
1973	133.1	6.2
1974	147.7	11.0
1975	161.2	9.1
1976	170.5	5.8
1977	181.5	6.5
1978	195.3	7.6
1979	217.7	11.5
1980	245.5	12.8
1981	272.3	10.9
1982	288.6	10.6
1983	298.4	3.4
1984	311.1	4.3
1985	322.2	3.6
1986	331.1	2.8
1987	346.1	4.5
1988	362.7	4.8

Table 7.5   Consumer Price Index (1967 = 100)

Step 1

Find the difference.

245.5 − 217.7 = 27.8

Step 2

Divide the difference by the earlier average.

27.8 ÷ 217.7 = 0.127698

Step 3

Move the decimal two places to the right and round to the 10ths position.

0.127698 = 12.8% increase in the cost of living from one year to the next

How would a 12.8 percent increase in the CPI have affected a person's income and savings in 1980? If a person had an income of $20,000 in 1979, he or she would have had to earn $22,560 in 1980 (a $2,560 increase) just to stay even in purchasing power. Similarly, if that same person had $1,000 in a savings account in 1979 that paid 5 percent interest, the $1,000 would have lost 7.8 percent of its purchasing power during the year (12.8% − 5.0% = 7.8%).

Self-Check 7C   Price Indexes
---

1. Compute index numbers for a 1-pound can of coffee, using 1983 as the base year.

Year	$/lb.
1980	3.10
1981	3.20
1982	3.33
1983	3.45
1984	3.75
1985	3.80
1986	3.85
1987	3.90
1988	3.95

2. The CPI for 1980 was 245.5, compared with a CPI for 1988 of 362.7. What was the rate of inflation during this period?

3. If an item cost $10 in 1980, how much did that item cost in 1988?

Answers to Self-Checks

Self-Check 7A

1. 571.5

2. $19\frac{1}{2}$

3. 65

4. $1,363.73

Self-Check 7B

1. $2.41

2. Modified mean or the median

Self-Check 7C

1. 89.9; 92.8; 96.5; 100.0; 108.7; 110.1; 111.6; 113.0; 114.5

2. 47.7%

3. $14.77

1. **Mean, median, mode (10 points each)**

handwritten:
16.232
17,141
———
2)33,373 = 16.

a. If sales in March and April were $16,232 and $17,141, respectively, what were the average sales for the 2-month period?

b. If the ages of five vice-presidents are 48, 50, 52, 55, and 60, what is their average (mean) age? Their median age?

c. Using monthly incomes of $425, $432, $550, $660, $675, and $950, compute the mean and median incomes.

d. In Problem 1.c, which average is the most representative of the incomes, the mean or the median? Why?

e. Compute a modified mean using the incomes in Problem 1.c.

f. What is the mode of 33, 26, 33, 27, 32, 26, 37, 28?

2. **Price indexes (10 points each)**

a. Calculate the rate of inflation on a $48 pair of shoes that sold for $22 five years ago. (Round to one place.)

b. Compute a price index for a 7-ounce can of salmon at the following prices, using 1984 as the base year:

Year	Price
1984	$1.10
1985	1.13
1986	1.15
1987	1.28
1988	1.45

3.   Weighted mean (a = 10 points, b = 5 points, c = 5 points)

Tickets for a concert were priced according to the distance of the seats from the stage. The following sales figures summarize the number of tickets sold at different prices:

Price	Number Sold
$15.00	300
10.00	1,500
7.50	2,500
5.00	5,000
2.50	7,500

a. What is the mean price that was paid for a ticket?

b. What is the median price that was paid for a ticket?

c. What is the mode?

ASSIGNMENT 7B

Name _____

Important Averages

Score _____

1. Mean, Median, and Mode (10 points each)

During the first day of their semiannual sale, Gerard's Furniture Store sold 12 items for $200, $500, $2,000, $2,500, $500, $1,800, $700, $1,000, $1,200, $500, $300, and $1,000.

a. What is the average (mean) sales price?

b. What is the median price?

c. What is the mode?

d. If the annual salaries for five employees in a small consulting firm are $20,000, $22,000, $23,000, $25,000, and $65,000, which average is the most representative of the incomes and why?

e. Using the salaries in Problem 1.d, compute a modified mean.

f. Gentry Apparel sold 12 men's suits on the first day of their spring sale. Prices varied considerably: $75, $95, $105, $210, $95, $175, $105, $190, $95, $105, $95, $75. What was the mean price of the 12 suits?

2. **Determine the weighted mean of all of the following audio systems that were sold during one year (20 points).**

Name	Units Sold	Price	Sales Revenues
Toshiba	24	$ 600	
JVC	6	1,200	
Fisher	7	1,100	
Sanyo	20	700	
Panasonic	10	900	

3. **Price Indexes (10 points each)**

a. Using the following prices for office visits to a medical doctor, what was the rate of inflation between 1975 and 1985? (Round answer to one place.)

1967	$ 6 = 100.0
1970	12
1975	15
1980	20
1985	23

b. With a CPI of 114.9 in 1980 for food items, compared with a CPI of 228.7 in 1988, how much would it cost in 1988 for food items that would have cost $25 in 1980?

Graphic Illustrations

After reading Chapter 8, you will be able to

- Prepare tables.
- Describe the reasons that business people generally rely on just two of the four available quadrants in the preparation of graphic illustrations.
- Plot multiple line graphs and bar graphs.
- Draw, segment, and label circle graphs.
- Describe the strengths and limitations of line, bar, and circle graphs.
- Prepare and interpret component graphs.

Key Terms

table	protractor
line graph	compass
quadrant	legend
bar graph	component graph
circle graph	

The old saying, one picture is worth a thousand words, is certainly true regarding business data. When business people begin writing or talking in numbers, they soon lose the interest of their audience — unless they accompany their remarks with graphic illustrations. Business and government publications typically include tables and graphs to illustrate data relating to elements such as costs, prices, and profitability. It is important, therefore, that you learn to construct and interpret tables and graphs.

Tables

People in business commonly use **tables** to place numerical data in columns and rows, where the reader can more easily see the relationships and meaning of the numbers. Rather than trying to convey product sales information in paragraph form, for example, we may construct a table similar to Table 8.1.

Tables must be properly labeled, so that they tell the reader exactly what the data represent.

Year	Product A	Product B	Product C
1982	$40,000	$25,000	$ 5,000
1983	45,000	27,500	7,500
1984	37,500	25,000	10,000
1985	40,000	28,000	15,000
1986	32,000	22,500	15,000
1987	35,000	29,000	17,000
1988	30,000	23,000	18,000
1989	28,500	24,750	21,750

Table 8.1 Annual Sales of Products A, B, and C for Years 1982 through 1989

Table 8.1 tells the reader that the data are for sales of three separate products for an 8-year period and that (1) sales of Product A have declined to a notable degree, (2) sales of Product B have fluctuated from year to year, but with no marked increase or decrease for the 8-year period, and (3) sales of Product C have increased continuously.

Self-Check 8A Tables

During 1986 Smith Bros. Construction, Inc. employed 74 people who earned wages totaling $1,320,000; in 1987, 89 employees earned $1,505,000; in 1988, 93 employees earned $1,613,000; and in 1989, 105 employees earned $1,715,000. Construct and label a table, on page 124, containing this information.

Line Graphs

We may present a clearer picture of the sales data given in Table 8.1 with a line graph. Although **line graphs** may consist of as many as four **quadrants** (sections), as shown in Figure 8.1, most line graphs in business contain only one quadrant, also as shown in Figure 8.1, with the bottom line being the horizontal axis and the side line the vertical axis.

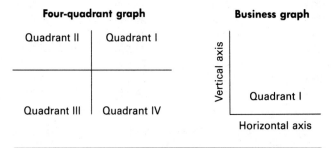

Figure 8.1 Four Quadrants and One Quadrant

We may prepare line graphs by following the three-step process of (1) plotting the data, (2) connecting the marks, and (3) labeling the data.

Step 1

Let's begin a line graph by plotting the sales data from Table 8.1 for Product A. Time is generally placed on the horizontal axis and dollar amounts on the vertical axis, as shown in Figure 8.2. We place a dot directly above the year 1982 at 40 ($40,000) level. We place dots above each of the years in the same manner, plotting our entries in thousands of dollars rather than listing lengthy numbers.

Step 2

We then connect the dots with continuous lines, as shown in Figure 8.3. The dots should be entered lightly (lighter than shown here), so that they are not apparent after they have been connected with a line.

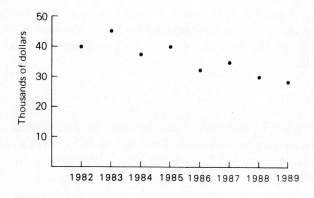

Figure 8.2   Data Entries for Product A

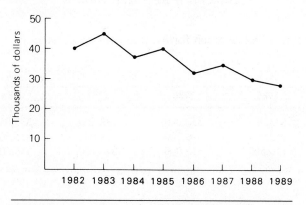

Figure 8.3   Connecting Line for Product A

The same procedure is followed for Products B and C, as shown in Figure 8.4.

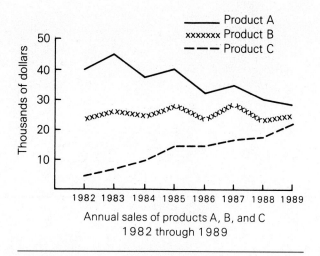

Figure 8.4   Completed Line Graph

Notice that Product A is represented by a continuous line, Product B by a series of small crosses, and Product C by dashes, so that readers can distinguish one product from another. Such distinctions are especially important when the lines cross each other, as these three product lines seem destined to do. We may also distinguish one line from the other by using a different colored pen or pencil for each line.

Step 3

Label the graph so that readers may interpret the data without having to read any accompanying explanations. The labeling in Figure 8.4 informs readers that the plotted data are for annual sales of Products A, B, and C for an eight-year period.

Self-Check 8B   Line Graphs

Construct and label as "Figure 1" a line graph for the following sales data:

	1985	**1986**	**1987**	**1988**	**1989**
Department A	$33,990	$30,000	$32,500	$35,000	$38,110
Department B	$19,900	$20,500	$18,003	$11,000	$11,200
Department C	$10,500	$15,000	$16,100	$16,500	$17,500

Bar Graphs

We sometimes use **bar graphs** to present business data. Although a single-bar graph cannot be used to illustrate the sales data shown in Table 8.1 (page 123) for the three products and for each of the eight years, we can plot the sales on a bar graph for a single time period (one year). Figure 8.5 shows a vertical-bar graph for 1989 sales, and Figure 8.6 presents the same data in a horizontal-bar graph. Notice in the vertical-bar graph that the dollar amount of sales is shown on the vertical axis and that the individual products are placed on the horizontal axis. In the horizontal-bar graph, these relationships are reversed. In Figure 8.6, product identification is placed directly on the horizontal bars rather than on the vertical axis.

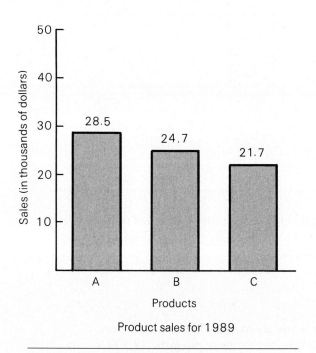

Figure 8.5 Vertical-Bar Graph

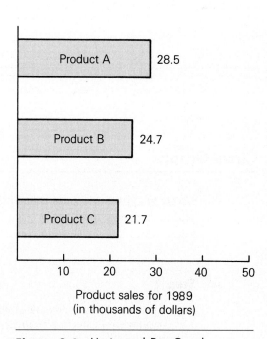

Figure 8.6 Horizontal-Bar Graph

Self-Check 8C Bar Graphs

Construct and label a vertical-bar graph, on page 128, showing earnings by Smith Bros. Construction, Inc., of $1,500,021 in 1985; $1,950,332 in 1986; $2,130,450 in 1987; $3,212,616 in 1988; and $4,100,225 in 1989. (Show in millions of dollars, rounding to the tenths position, so that $1,500,021 becomes $1.5 million.)

Circle Graphs

Circle graphs, sometimes called pie graphs, provide us with another method of presenting business data. Again using the data given in Table 8.1 on page 123 for 1989 sales, we follow six steps to construct a circle graph.

Step 1

Compute the total amount of whatever it is you are plotting. Because we are concerned with sales for 1989, we total the sales for the three products: 28,500 + 24,750 + 21,750 = $75,000.

Step 2

Calculate the percentage that each segment is of the total by dividing each segment by the total. (Sum of percentages should always be 1.00.)

28,500 ÷ 75,000 = 0.38
24,750 ÷ 75,000 = 0.33
21,750 ÷ 75,000 = 0.29
                   1.00

Step 3

Multiply the percentages by 360, the number of degrees in a circle. (Sum of degrees should always be 360.)

$$0.38 \times 360 = 136.8$$
$$0.33 \times 360 = 118.8$$
$$0.29 \times 360 = \underline{104.4}$$
$$360.0$$

Step 4

Draw a circle with a **compass,** marking the place where the steel point is placed on the paper. The size of the circle depends on your needs, and the same steps are taken for a very small circle as for a very large one.

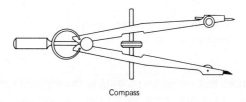

Compass

Step 5

Use a **protractor** to mark the degrees.

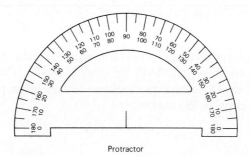

Protractor

After drawing a line from the center to the top of the circle, place the flat part of the protractor on that line, with the line on the protractor at the center of the circle and the rounded part to the right. Then, reading from the left (zero side) of the scale, place a mark at 136.8 (137 is close enough), remove the protractor, and draw a line from the mark to the center of the circle. Label that section "Product A, 38%." Proceed by placing the flat part of the protractor on the newly drawn line and plotting 118.8 (119 is close enough). Draw a line and label this second section "Product B, 33%" and the remaining section "Product C, 29%."

Step 6

Label the graph as illustrated in the completed version in Figure 8.7.

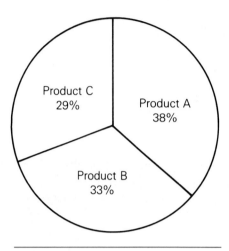

Figure 8.7 Product Sales for 1989
(Percent of Total Sales)

Good form dictates that we begin plotting at the top of a circle and move to the right (clockwise), beginning with the largest segment first, the next largest segment second, and so on. Any category labeled "other" or "miscellaneous" should be placed last, regardless of size, just to the left of the top center of the graph.

─────── **Self-Check 8D** Circle Graphs ───────

At Nelson Electronics, per-employee earnings in 1989 averaged $18,300, from which $2,745 was withheld for taxes, $1,464 for medical coverage, and $915 for other purposes. Construct a circle graph showing the percent of wages that went to (1) the average employee as take-home pay, (2) taxes, (3) medical, and (4) other. (Hint: One-half of a circle is 180 degrees.)

Step 1

Step 3

Step 2

Steps 4, 5, and 6

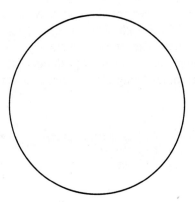

Component Graphs

In the preceding section we used a circle graph to picture different parts of a whole — not just salary but also the deductions and take-home pay that equaled the total salary of employees at Smith Bros. As illustrated in the **component graph** shown in Figure 8.8, we can also use line graphs and bar graphs to show the various components that, together, comprise a whole.

Figure 8.8 provides us with information not just of total company income (as specified by the top line), but also a clear picture of the relationships between costs, expenses, and net income (profit). Costs for 1984 were $240,000, the three zeros at the top left indicating that the dollar amounts are being stated in thousands. Costs were $280,000 in 1985, $300,000 in 1986, and so on.

Before plotting dollar amounts, we must calculate a range of numbers for the vertical axis that will be great enough to accommodate the three layers (costs, expenses, income) for each of the years. The total for 1984 is $340,000 (240,000 + 60,000 + 40,000), compared with approximately $410,000 for 1989. We make the range of dollar amounts on the vertical axis great enough to include $410,000, the highest total for the six-year period. Figure 8.8 also includes a **legend,** the three small boxes at the top that identify each segment of the graph.

Expenses for 1984 were $60,000. Rather than plotting (placing a dot for) that amount above 1984, however, we add the $60,000 to the $240,000 in costs, totaling $300,000. Similarly, we plot our $40,000 in profits for 1984 at $340,000 (an accumulation of the $240,000 in costs; $60,000 in expenses; and $40,000 net income).

After plotting company data in this manner for the remaining years, we can easily see that costs have increased steadily each year, that a leveling off of expenses in 1986 resulted in a widening (increasing) of net income (profits), and that a subsequent acceleration in costs and expenses resulted in a narrowing (decreasing) of net income. This graphic illustration has enabled us to identify relationships that would be difficult to interpret from lists of figures.

Figure 8.9 is a graphic illustration of the relationship between the earnings of a company and the dividends paid to stockholders. Notice that the amounts of money on the left are shown in units ($1, $2, etc.), not in thousands of dollars as in Figure 8.8, and that the amounts shown are "per share." From the $4.80 earnings per share in 1989, for instance, owners of the company received dividends (shares of company earnings) of $1.75 for each share owned. The main information that we obtain from this graph is that, except for a relatively small dividend in 1984, the payout (portion of earnings paid to owners as dividends) has remained fairly constant, with increases in earnings being closely matched with increases in dividends.

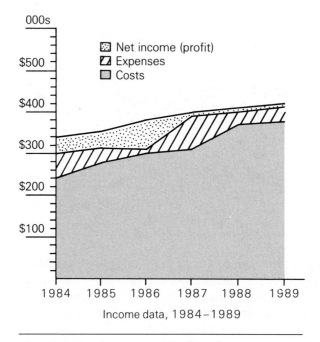

Figure 8.8 Component Line Graph

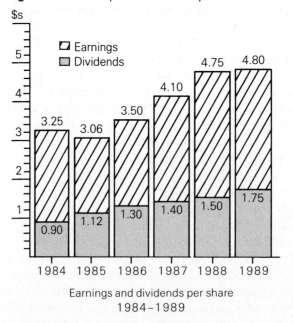

Figure 8.9 Component Bar Graph

—————————— **Self-Check 8E**   Component Graphs ——————————

1. In Figure 8.8, what was the net income for 1984?

2. In Figure 8.8, what was the amount of costs for 1986?

3. In Figure 8.9, what percent of earnings per share was paid to stockholders as dividends in 1989? (Round to tenths.)

4. Was the dividend in 1988 (shown in Figure 8.9), as a percent of earnings per share, higher or lower than in 1989?

—————————— **Answers to Self-Checks** ——————————

Self-Check 8A

Year	Number of Employees	Total Wages Earned
1986	74	$1,320,000
1987	89	$1,505,000
1988	93	$1,613,000
1989	105	$1,715,000

Table 1 Number of Employees and Total Wages Earned 1986 through 1989

Self-Check 8B

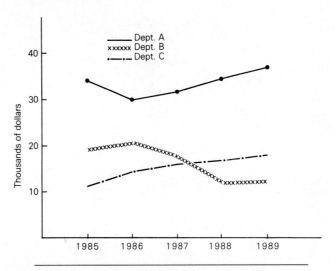

Figure 1   Departmental Sales, 1985–89

Self-Check 8C

Self-Check 8D

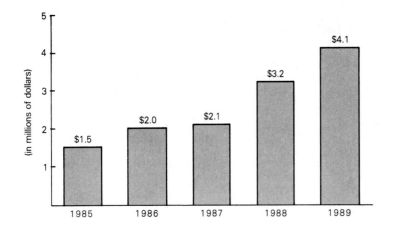

Yearly earnings 1985 through 1989

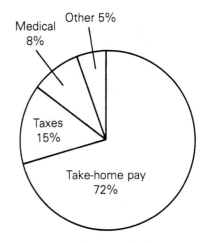

Average distribution
of wages, 1989

Self-Check 8E

1. $40,000 2. almost $300,000 3. 36.5% 4. 1989; 31.6% < 36.5%

Using the data given in the following table, construct and label the graphs described in Problems a, b, and c.

Year	Western Division	Eastern Division	Southern Division
1982	$ 60,000	$165,000	$25,000
1983	70,000	167,000	33,000
1984	72,000	179,000	47,000
1985	77,000	171,000	58,000
1986	88,000	164,000	63,000
1987	99,000	154,000	68,000
1988	120,000	144,000	78,000
1989	122,500	140,000	87,500

Company Sales by Division (1982 through 1989)

a. Line graph for each of the three divisions, in thousands of dollars (35 points)

b.   Vertical-bar chart showing sales (in thousands of dollars, rounded to the 10ths position) for each of the three divisions in 1989 (25 points)

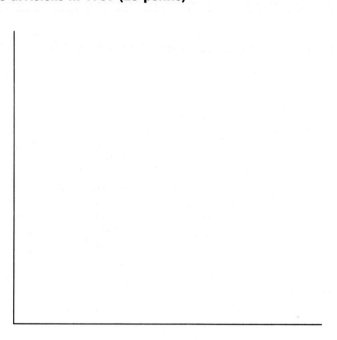

c.   Circle graph showing the percentage of sales for each division in 1989 (40 points)

Step 1

Step 2

Step 3

Steps 4, 5, and 6

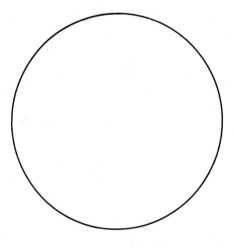

Graphic Illustrations

1. **Complete a component line graph for the following sales data (30 points).**

   (Place the data for Department A at the
   bottom, Department B in the middle, and
   Department C at the top.)

	Dept. A	Dept. B	Dept. C
1975	$30,000	$15,000	$ 5,000
1980	25,000	15,000	10,000
1985	22,000	10,000	15,000
1990	20,000	13,000	17,000

2. **Using the same data in Problem 1, complete a component bar graph (30 points).**

   (Place the data for Department A at the
   bottom, Department B in the middle, and
   Department C at the top.)

3. The following three questions pertain to Problems 1 and 2 (5 points each):

a. Which department has had declining sales in each of the four periods?

b. Which department has had the greatest expansion of sales between 1970 and 1985?

c. Which department suffered the greatest decline of sales in 1980?

4. The following five questions pertain to the accompanying graph (5 points each):

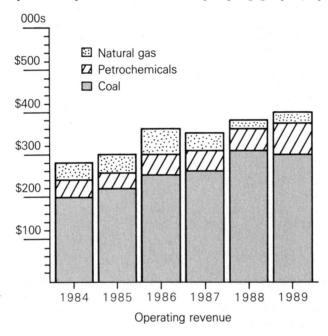

a. Most of this company's operating revenue is realized from the sale of which energy products?

b. What amount of revenues was realized from the sale of natural gas in 1984?

c. What amount of revenues was realized from the sale of coal in 1986?

d. What amount of revenues was realized from the sale of petrochemicals in 1987?

e. Natural gas accounted for what percent of total sales in 1984? (Show your computations and round to 10ths of a percent.)

You may use this practice test to measure your preparation for the actual part test. Answers begin on page 414.

Foundational Math of Business

1. Weights and measures (5 points each)

a. At a price of $6.60 for 1 dozen men's handkerchiefs, what is the cost per unit?

b. What is the price per ounce of a can of beans weighing 15 ounces and selling three for $1?

c. Rather than buying 2 pints of paint for $3.65 each, how much would you save by purchasing 1 quart for $7.10?

d. How many square yards of carpet are required for a room measuring 15 by 20 feet?

e. If an airplane requires 4 hours to fly from San Francisco to New York City, what time must the plane leave (California time) to arrive in New York City at 12 noon (New York time)?

2. Percentage applications (5 points each)

a. 8% of what number equals 550?

b. What is $12\frac{1}{2}$% of $76.24?

c. 1,216 is what percent of 7,600?

d. If Armstrong Floors had total sales of $220,000 last year, of which $92,400 was for carpeting installations, what percent of total sales was in carpeting?

e. If Aero Electronics sold supplies to the government last year totaling $92,400, which represented 42% of total sales, what was the amount of total sales?

f. The owners of an apartment complex rented 92% of a total of 2,000 apartments. How many apartments remained unrented?

g. If your income increases from $9,500 last year to $10,500 this year, what is the percent increase? (Round answers to tenths of a percent.)

h. If the terms of sale on a new refrigerator costing $1,195 is 15% down, how much must a buyer pay at the time of purchase?

3. Averages (5 points each)

a. If Joyce Randolph had sales of $61,852 in January, $73,904 in February, and $93,612 in March, what were her average monthly sales for the quarter?

b. If 150 theater seats are priced at $40.00 each, 350 at $30.00 each, and 800 at $15.50 each, what is the mean price of the tickets? (Round answer to even cents.)

4. Graphic illustrations (25 points)

Complete a **line graph** for the following sales (in thousands of dollars) for City Center Appliances.

Year	Household Appliances	Entertainment Systems
1986	$18,000	$14,000
1987	22,000	19,500
1988	21,000	28,000
1989	24,000	35,500
1990	25,000	43,000

PART
3

Mathematics of Banking

9. Simple Interest

Calculating Simple Interest
Calculating Amount
Calculating Principal
Calculating Rate
Calculating Time

10. Credit Transactions

Installment Loans
Partial Payment
Rule of 78
Charge Accounts

11. Banking Records

Writing Checks
Recording Checks and Deposits
Interest-Earning Checking Accounts
Statement-Register Reconciliation

12. Bank Discounting

Discounting Loans
Finding the Principal of a Discounted Loan
Discounting Negotiable Instruments

13. Compound Interest

Calculating Compound Amount
Using Compound-Interest Tables
Finding Present Value
Sinking Funds
Amortization

CHAPTER

9

Simple Interest

After reading Chapter 9, you will be able to

- Calculate approximate and exact interest.
- Compute the amount (principal plus interest) of a deposit or loan.
- Find the principal, rate, or time when two of these elements are known.

Key Terms

interest

principal

rate

time

simple interest

compound interest

approximate interest

exact interest

amount

Interest is a rental fee for the use of money. When we loan money to others we charge them interest, and when we borrow money from lending institutions or from individuals, we repay the quantity borrowed plus interest. The **principal** is the quantity of money being borrowed or loaned. The **rate** is a percent of the principal, and **time** is the number of years (or fraction thereof) that the money is to be rented (borrowed or loaned).

Calculating Simple Interest

The two types of interest are simple and compound. **Simple interest** is figured on the principal, whereas **compound interest** (discussed in Chapter 13) is figured on the sum of principal and accumulated interest. We compute the simple interest (I) that a borrower pays or that a lender collects by multiplying principal (P) times rate (R) times time (T).

$$\text{Interest} = \text{Principal} \times \text{Rate} \times \text{Time}$$

or, in symbols

$$I = PRT$$

If we borrow $1,000 for 2 years at 12 percent simple interest, for example, the principal is $1,000, the rate is 12 percent, and the time is 2 years, resulting in an interest charge of $240:

$$I = PRT$$
$$I = 1{,}000 \times 0.12 \times 2$$
$$I = \$240$$

When the term of a loan involves a fraction of a year, we must decide whether to calculate interest on the basis of **approximate interest,** which assumes a 360-day year, or **exact interest,** which is based on a 365-day year. Large institutions, such as banks and insurance companies, use both, depending on whether they are paying or collecting interest.

Using approximate interest of 12 percent to figure interest on $1,000 for 6 months, we may state time in either months (6/12), days (180/360), or fraction of a year (1/2).

$$I = PRT$$
$$I = \$1{,}000 \times 0.12 \times \frac{6}{12}$$
$$I = 1{,}000 \times 0.12 \times 0.5$$
$$I = \$60$$

In determining time (T) for approximate interest, we can easily find the number of applicable days by placing the year, month, and day of the ending date above the year, month, and day of the beginning date and then subtracting. For a loan on January 12, 1989, which is repaid on November 3 of the same year, we have the following:

	Year	Month	Day
Ending date	1989	11	3
Beginning date	1989	1	12

The loan ends on the third day of November (the 11th month of the year), after beginning on the twelfth day of January (the first month of the year). We then subtract, beginning at the right (as shown below), but because we cannot subtract 12 from 3 we borrow one month (30 days in approximate interest), giving us 33 days from which to subtract 12 days. We then determine the number of months by subtracting 1 from 10, and the number of years (zero) by subtracting 1989 from 1989.

	Year	Month	Day
Ending date	1989	$\overset{10}{\cancel{11}}$	$\overset{33}{\cancel{3}}$
Beginning date	1989	1	12
	0	9	21

$$\textbf{9 mos} \times \textbf{30 days} = \textbf{270 days}$$

$$\textbf{270 days} + \textbf{21 days} = \textbf{291 days}$$

After changing the 9 months to 270 days (9 × 30 = 270), we add the 21 days so that our fraction for time (T) would be 291/360.

To illustrate further this method of computing time (T), let's consider a loan that begins on June 1, 1989, and is repaid on February 28, 1993:

	Years	Months	Days
Ending date	$\overset{1992}{\cancel{1993}}$	$\overset{14}{\cancel{2}}$	28
Beginning date	1989	6	1
	3	8	27

$$\textbf{3 years} \times \textbf{360 days} = \textbf{1,080 days}$$

$$\textbf{8 months} \times \textbf{30 days} = \textbf{240 days}$$

$$\textbf{1,080} + \textbf{240} + \textbf{27} = \textbf{1,347 days}$$

Because we couldn't subtract 6 months from 2 months without deriving a negative number, we borrowed one year (12 months), decreasing the 1993 to 1992 and increasing 2 months to 14 months. In computing $I = PRT$, therefore, our figure for time (T) becomes 1,347/360. Keep in mind that this method of determining time works only when calculating approximate interest.

To determine time (T) for exact interest, we must figure the exact number of days from the start of the loan to the repayment date. Correspondingly, a 6-month loan on July 1, on which payment comes due on December 31, has 183 days:

Month	Days
July 1	30 (31 − 1 = 30)
August	31
September	30
October	31
November	30
December	31
	183 days

For exact interest, therefore, time (T) is 183/365, and interest on a $1,000 loan is computed as follows:

$$I = PRT$$
$$I = 1,000 \times 0.12 \times 183/365$$
$$I = \$60.16$$

If you do not already know the number of days in each month, the following jingle provides a useful memory aid:

> **Thirty days has September,**
> **April, June, and November.**
> **All the rest have 31,**
> **Except February which has 28 (29 in leap years).**

When figuring exact interest, you must also remember that the numerator is the exact number of days in the term of the loan, over a denominator of 365.

An easier way to compute the exact number of days between two dates is to use Table 9.1.

With the same set of dates (July 1 to December 31), we read down the day column (at the far left or the far right) and find that July 1 is the 182nd day of the year. And, of course, December 31 is the 365th day of the year (bottom right, where December and the 31st day of the month intersect at the corner of the table). We then find the difference between the two numbers to be 183 days:

$$365 - 182 = 183 \text{ days}$$

Day of Month	Jan.	Feb.	Mar.	Apr.	May	June	July	Aug.	Sept.	Oct.	Nov.	Dec.	Day of Month
1	1	32	60	91	121	152	182	213	244	274	305	335	1
2	2	33	61	92	122	153	183	214	245	275	306	336	2
3	3	34	62	93	123	154	184	215	246	276	307	337	3
4	4	35	63	94	124	155	185	216	247	277	308	338	4
5	5	36	64	95	125	156	186	217	248	278	309	339	5
6	6	37	65	96	126	157	187	218	249	279	310	340	6
7	7	38	66	97	127	158	188	219	250	280	311	341	7
8	8	39	67	98	128	159	189	220	251	281	312	342	8
9	9	40	68	99	129	160	190	221	252	282	313	343	9
10	10	41	69	100	130	161	191	222	253	283	314	344	10
11	11	42	70	101	131	162	192	223	254	284	315	345	11
12	12	43	71	102	132	163	193	224	255	285	316	346	12
13	13	44	72	103	133	164	194	225	256	286	317	347	13
14	14	45	73	104	134	165	195	226	257	287	318	348	14
15	15	46	74	105	135	166	196	227	258	288	319	349	15
16	16	47	75	106	136	167	197	228	259	289	320	350	16
17	17	48	76	107	137	168	198	229	260	290	321	351	17
18	18	49	77	108	138	169	199	230	261	291	322	352	18
19	19	50	78	109	139	170	200	231	262	292	323	353	19
20	20	51	79	110	140	171	201	232	263	293	324	354	20
21	21	52	80	111	141	172	202	233	264	294	325	355	21
22	22	53	81	112	142	173	203	234	265	295	326	356	22
23	23	54	82	113	143	174	204	235	266	296	327	357	23
24	24	55	83	114	144	175	205	236	267	297	328	358	24
25	25	56	84	115	145	176	206	237	268	298	329	359	25
26	26	57	85	116	146	177	207	238	269	299	330	360	26
27	27	58	86	117	147	178	208	239	270	300	331	361	27
28	28	59	87	118	148	179	209	240	271	301	332	362	28
29	29	*	88	119	149	180	210	241	272	302	333	363	29
30	30	—	89	120	150	181	211	242	273	303	334	364	30
31	31	—	90	—	151	—	212	243	—	304	—	365	31

*In leap (election) years, add one day if February 29 falls between the two dates.

Table 9.1   The Number of Each Day of the Year

When we do not have access to such a table, we must proceed through the time period month by month as in the first example. Notice also that when computing time, with or without the table, we do not include in the loan period the day on which the loan was made.

―――――――   **Self-Check 9A**   Calculating Simple Interest   ―――――――

1.   What is the due date on a 90-day loan that is dated February 12, applying exact interest?

2. To compute approximate interest, what fraction do we use for time (T) in connection with a loan dated March 28, 1989, that is due on June 12, 1991?

3. Using Table 9.1, determine time (T) for a loan dated February 15 that matures on October 4.

4. How much interest should be charged for a $900 loan for 3 years at $15\frac{1}{2}\%$ simple interest?

5. Figure the approximate interest that will be charged for a 5-month loan of $150 at 14%.

6. What is the exact interest for a $600 loan from June 15 to December 10, at a $17\frac{1}{2}\%$ rate of simple interest?

Calculating Amount

The **amount** of a loan is the maturity value — that is, the sum of the principal and the interest charge that must be repaid. For a 2-year loan of $150 at 8 percent simple interest, the amount is $174:

$$\text{Amount} = \text{Principal} + PRT$$
$$\text{Amount} = 150 + (150 \times 0.08 \times 2)$$
$$\text{Amount} = 150 + 24$$
$$\text{Amount} = \$174$$

At the end of 2 years the borrower must repay $174.

Note that figuring simple interest is similar to computing percentages (see Chapter 6), except that with interest we have four elements ($I = PRT$) and with percentages we have three ($BR = P$).

Self-Check 9B   Calculating Amount

---

1. If the principal is $665 and the interest is $17, what is the amount of the loan?

2. At simple interest of 9%, what is the amount of a 6-month loan for $450?

3. What is the amount of a $1,200 loan dated May 10, 1990, that is due November 10, 1990, with an exact interest rate of 8%?

Calculating Principal

Up to this point we have been finding interest; I has been the unknown. When principal is the unknown, we must find P. If the interest on a 2-year loan at 8% is $56, we can use either an equation or a formula to find the principal (P):

Equation	*Formula*
$I = PRT$	$P = \dfrac{I}{RT}$
$56 = P(0.08)(2)$	
$56 = 0.16P$ or	$P = \dfrac{56}{(0.08)(2)}$
$P = 56 \div 0.16$	
$P = \$350$	$P = 56 \div 0.16$
	$P = \$350$

Using the now familiar equation $I = PRT$, we simply plug in the information that is provided in the problem. Knowing that interest is $56, rate is 8%, and time is 2 years, we solve for P, the unknown, just as we would solve for x or any other unknown number. We are doing the same thing when using the formula, except that we must memorize the fact that principal may be found by multiplying the rate by time and dividing the answer into interest.

Self-Check 9C   Calculating Principal
---

1. Find the principal of a 6-month, 15% loan that earns interest of $112.50.

2. If the interest received is $1,662.50 and the rate is 9.5% for a 5-year term, what is the principal of the loan using approximate interest?

3. If a borrower must pay interest of $98.04 on March 12 on a loan that was made on October 11 of the preceding year at a rate of 14% (using exact interest) how much money was borrowed?

Calculating Rate

If we know the interest, principal, and time, we can calculate the rate (R) in much the same way that we find principal. For a $1,500 loan that earns $360 in interest during a 2-year period, we find the rate to be 12 percent:

Equation	*Formula*

$$I = PRT$$
$$360 = (1,500)(R)(2)$$

$$R = \frac{I}{PT}$$

$$\frac{360}{1,500(2)} = R \qquad \text{or} \qquad R = \frac{360}{1,500 \times 2}$$

$$R = 360 \div 3,000 \qquad\qquad R = 360 \div 3,000$$
$$R = 0.12 = 12\% \qquad\qquad R = 0.12 = 12\%$$

Self-Check 9D   Calculating Rate

1. What is the rate for a $600 loan that earns $189 interest over a 3-year period?

2. If the interest is $1,890 on a 9-month loan for $18,000, what is the rate?

3. A lender collected interest of $63 at maturity on a 6-month, $1,200 loan. What is the interest rate?

Calculating Time

Similarly, we may solve for time (T) when it is the unknown. If, for example, we know that the principal of a loan is $3,200, that the interest charge is $116, and that the simple interest rate is $14\frac{1}{2}\%$, we can use either an equation or a formula to find that time is 1/4 year or 3 months.

<table>
<tr><td align="center">*Equation*</td><td></td><td align="center">*Formula*</td></tr>
</table>

$$I = PRT$$
$$116 = 3,200(0.145)T$$

$$\frac{116}{3,200(0.145)} = T$$

or

$$T = \frac{I}{PR}$$

$$T = \frac{116}{3,200 \times 0.145}$$

$$T = 116 \div 464$$

$$T = 0.25 = \frac{1}{4} \text{ year}$$

$$T = 116 \div 464$$

$$T = 0.25 = \frac{1}{4} \text{ year}$$

Be certain to check the logic of your answer. Because simple interest is based on whole years, any fraction in the answer is a fraction of a year, so that the answer 0.25 is 1/4 year, or 3 months. Correspondingly, an answer of 0.50 would be 1/2 year, or 6 months.

Self-Check 9E   Calculating Time

1. If you paid $229.50 interest for borrowing $1,200 at $12\frac{3}{4}\%$ simple interest, what is the time period of the loan?

2. If the interest rate is $8\frac{1}{2}\%$ and the interest expense is $127.50, for how long did the bank lend $500.00 to the borrower?

3. How long did it take an investor to earn interest of $341.40 on a bank deposit of $2,600.00 if the annual rate of interest was $7\frac{1}{2}\%$?

Answers to Self-Checks

Self-Check 9A

1. May 13

2. $\dfrac{794}{360}$

3. $\dfrac{231}{365}$

4. $418.50

5. $8.75

6. $51.21

Self-Check 9B

1. $682

2. $470.25

3. $1,248.39

Self-Check 9C

1. $1,500

2. $3,500

3. $1,681.61

Self-Check 9D

1. 10.5%

2. 14%

3. 10.5%

Self-Check 9E

1. $1\frac{1}{2}$ years

2. 3 years

3. $1\frac{3}{4}$ years

1. **A mixture of simple interest problems (5 points each)**

   a. What is the exact interest for a loan of
   $2,000 from March 15 to August 15 of the
   same year, if the rate of interest is 9%?

   b. What is the rate of simple interest on a
   $1,200 loan for 18 months that calls for
   interest of $189?

   c. How much was borrowed at 8% for 2 years
   if the simple interest paid is $40?

   d. If simple interest of $21.60 is paid for
   borrowing $120.00 for 2 years, what interest
   rate was charged?

   e. If the interest received is $55.13 and the
   simple interest rate is 10.5% for a 6-year
   term, what is the principal of the loan?

   f. If the interest rate is 12% and the interest
   expense is $105, for how long did the bank
   lend $700 to the borrower?

   g. What is the approximate interest on $250 at
   $8\frac{1}{4}$% for 75 days?

   h. If a loan for $1\frac{1}{2}$ years carries simple interest
   of $13\frac{1}{2}$% and yields $607.50 to the lender,
   what is the principal of the loan?

i. What is the rate for a $750 loan that earns
$78.75 simple interest over a 1-year period?

j. If you paid $148.75 interest for borrowing
$1,750 at $8\frac{1}{2}\%$ simple interest, what is the
time period of the loan?

2. A mixture of simple interest problems (10 points each)

a. If approximate interest is used for a loan of
$15,000 from January 15, 1987, to July 12,
1989, what amount must be repaid at 10%?

b. If you wish to collect $65 interest on $500
that you have loaned to a friend at $6\frac{1}{2}\%$
simple interest, how long must you let
the friend use the money before
demanding repayment?

c. A banker loaned $25,000 to a small business
owner, who repaid $29,375, including
principal and interest at 14%. What was the
term of the loan?

d. If the borrower had to pay the bank
$1,394.25 in repayment of a 6-month loan
of $1,300.00, what was the interest
rate charged?

e. If the lender receives interest of $45 in
6 months from a loan that pays 9% simple
interest, what is the amount that must be
repaid by the borrower?

1. **A mixture of simple interest problems (5 points each)**

a. If a 6-month loan has a simple interest rate of 15% and yields $150 to the lender, how much money was loaned?

b. If the simple interest rate on a $1,300 loan is 12.5% and the interest expense is $40.63, what is the term of the loan?

c. What amount must the borrower repay in connection with a $1,200 loan for $1\frac{1}{2}$ years at $8\frac{1}{4}\%$ simple interest?

d. What amount of interest will a retailer add to a balance of $1,195 if an interest rate of $9\frac{1}{2}\%$ is assessed over a 12-month period?

e. What percent was charged for a 2-year loan of $1,650 that yielded $280.50 simple interest?

f. If a borrower repays a loan at the end of 2 years, which includes $2,430 interest at a rate of 13 1/2%, what was the principal of the loan?

g. For a loan of $5,000 to a friend on June 15, what amount should be repaid on September 21 at 8% simple interest? Use exact time.

h. An individual repaid $728 to a finance
        company for a 6-month loan of $650. What
        rate of interest was charged?

i. Compute approximate interest on a loan of
        $12,500 beginning January 15 and maturing
        September 7 at a rate of 12%.

j. How long will it take for $840 to earn
        $109.20 interest at $6\frac{1}{2}$% simple interest?

2. A mixture of simple interest problems (10 points each)

a. The owner of a small business borrowed
        $50,000 and repaid a total of $59,500
        2 years later. What was the rate of interest?

b. A payment of $4,200 was made in repayment
        of a 2-year loan of $3,500. What was the
        simple interest rate?

c. If you received $176 interest in 4 months
        from an investment that pays $16\frac{1}{2}$%, how
        much did you invest?

d. Ted James borrowed $950 on August 10 and
        agreed to repay the loan 90 days later with
        exact interest of 8%. What amount did
        he repay and on what date did he repay
        the loan?

e. At an approximate rate of 8% simple interest,
        what is the amount that must be repaid for a
        loan of $10,000 that runs from August 5,
        1989, to July 8, 1991?

Credit Transactions

After reading Chapter 10, you will be able to

- Compute the interest and payment amounts on installment loans.
- Determine the balance due when a partial payment is made on a loan.
- Explain the Rule of 78, and identify the amount of interest to be saved when a loan is paid off early.
- Calculate the amount of interest to be paid on a charge account.
- Determine the annual percentage rate.

Key Terms

installment loan   charge account

partial payment   average daily balance (ADB)

Rule of 78   annual percentage rate

Many business transactions involve an extension of credit, including transactions between businesses and those involving consumers. We receive or extend personal loans to one another. We make installment payments on such large-ticket products as refrigerators and automobiles, and we open charge accounts to purchase relatively low-priced items. This chapter shows you how to figure the interest charges for these types of credit transactions.

Installment Loans

Stores, banks, and finance companies routinely finance durable goods such as furniture, appliances, and automobiles — products that normally last longer than one year — through **installment loans.** Consumers, after having made down payments in the form of either cash or trade-ins, repay the balance in monthly installments.

If, for example, Westside Motors allows Marcor Electric $3,770 as trade-in on the replacement of a used panel truck for a new one priced at $14,550, a balance of $10,780 must be financed. Assuming an interest rate of 12 percent and a loan term of three years, the monthly payments are $407.24.

$$\text{Interest:} \quad 10,780 \times 0.12 \times 3 = \$3,880.80$$

$$\text{Total due:} \quad 10,780 + 3,880.80 = \$14,660.80$$

$$\text{Monthly payment:} \quad 14,660.80 \div 36 \text{ months} = \$407.24$$

We figure the interest on the balance due, add the interest to find the total due, and divide the total by the number of months involved to find the monthly payment.

Self-Check 10A   Installment Loans

Joe Daladas bought a 1/3-carat diamond engagement ring priced at $1,250. The jeweler required a down payment of $500 and accepted the balance in 18 monthly installments with carrying charges of 11% simple interest.

1. What amount must be financed?

2. What amount of interest is to be charged?

3. What is the monthly payment?

Partial Payment

A **partial payment** is a payment on a loan that is less than the total amount due. When borrowers make partial payments on loans, lenders usually stop charging interest on the amounts paid. A ruling by the United States Supreme Court has made if official that interest on loans to and including the date of partial payments be deducted from the partial payments, with the balance of the partial payments being applied against the principal.

If you sell a used automobile to a friend on January 1, for example, you may agree to accept $1,000 cash and give the friend 1 year to pay an additional $500, plus simple interest of 6 percent. If the friend makes a partial payment of $250 on June 30, you would collect interest and reduce the loan as follows:

Step 1

Compute interest from January 1 to June 30.

$$\$500 \times 0.06 \times \frac{6}{12} = \$15$$

Step 2

Subtract interest from payment.

Payment − Interest = Credit
$$\$250 - 15 = \$235$$

Step 3

Subtract credit from principal.

Principal − Credit = Balance
$$\$500 - 235 = \$265$$

You have charged the friend interest on the $500 for the time that he or she used it, from January 1 to June 30 (6 months or 6/12). Then, having subtracted the $15 interest from the $250 payment, you reduce the $500 loan by the remaining $235. As of June 30, therefore, the friend owes you $265.

You continue earning interest on the balance of $265 until another partial payment is received or until the loan is paid in full. If you receive a partial payment of $100 on September 30 (3 months later), you reduce the principal (amount still owed) by $96.02 (the $100 partial payment less interest):

Step 1

Compute interest from July 1 to September 30.

$$\$265 \times 0.06 \times \frac{3}{12} = \$3.98$$

Step 2

Subtract interest from payment.

Payment − Interest = Credit
$$\$100.00 - 3.98 = \$96.02$$

Step 3

Subtract credit from principal.

Principal − Credit = Balance
$$\$265.00 - 96.02 = \$168.98$$

As before, you have charged interest only on the borrowed money for the time that the borrower used it—that is, on the balance of $265 from July 1 to September 30. After subtracting the interest on $265 for 3 months, you reduce the balance of the loan by the remaining $96.02.

If the borrower pays off the loan on December 31, as agreed, the payment will be $171.51—the $168.98 balance, plus interest on that amount for the 3 months that the money was used:

Step 1

Compute interest from October 1 to December 31.

$$\$168.98 \times 0.06 \times \frac{1}{4} = \$2.53$$

Step 2

Add interest to balance.

Balance + Interest = Pay-off amount
$$\$168.98 + 2.53 = \$171.51$$

Rather than deduct the interest as before, we add it to the balance to find the pay-off amount. On making the final payment of $171.51, the borrower will have repaid the original $500 plus interest of $21.51.

Interest Payments	Date
$15.00	June 30
3.98	September 30
2.53	December 31
$21.51	

Self-Check 10B Partial Payment

---

1. If you borrowed $1,000 for 1 year at 10% simple interest, how much would you still owe if you made a $500 partial payment at the end of the first 3 months of the loan?

2. Continuing with Problem 1, what would the balance be after a $250 payment 3 months later, that is, at the end of 6 months from the original loan date?

3. How much money would you have to pay at the end of the 1-year period, after having been credited with the two partial payments?

4. How much interest would you have paid?

Rule of 78

The **Rule of 78,** which allows lenders to claim most of the interest expense during the early months of a loan, heavily penalizes borrowers who manage to pay off loans a few months early. Many states prohibit lenders from applying the Rule of 78 for this reason, but the practice remains legal in several areas of the country.

Under the Rule of 78, lenders list and add the number of months that money is being loaned, so that a 12-month loan totals 78:

Total of Months (12-month loan)

$$1 + 2 + 3 + 4 + 5 + 6 + 7 + 8 + 9 + 10 + 11 + 12 = 78$$

They then multiply the interest on a loan by a fraction, with the number of the individual months as the numerator (reversing the order) and a total of the months as the denominator. Using a 1-year loan that carries a $300 interest charge as an example, the Rule of 78 is computed as shown in Table 10.1.

Month	Fraction		Total Interest		Monthly Interest
1	12/78	×	300	=	46.15
2	11/78	×	300	=	42.31
3	10/78	×	300	=	38.46
4	9/78	×	300	=	34.62
5	8/78	×	300	=	30.77
6	7/78	×	300	=	26.92
7	6/78	×	300	=	23.08
8	5/78	×	300	=	19.23
9	4/78	×	300	=	15.38
10	3/78	×	300	=	11.54
11	2/78	×	300	=	7.69
12	1/78	×	300	=	3.85
78					$300.00

Table 10.1   Rule of 78

The numbers 1 through 12 for the months are reversed for the fractions, so that the numerators become 12 through 1. Bankers then charge 12/78 of the $300 interest for the first month of the loan, 11/78 of $300 for the second month of the loan, and so on. Notice in Table 10.1 that the total column at the right equals the total interest charge of $300. If the borrower paid off this loan one month early, the interest savings would only be 1/78 of $300 ($3.85), rather than the 1/12 ($25) that would apply if the Rule of 78 were not in effect.

Note also that the denominator 78 applies only to 1-year loans. Rather than adding the months of a loan to determine the denominator of our fractions, we may use the following formula, with n being the number of months in the loan:

$$\frac{n(n + 1)}{2} = \text{denominator of fraction}$$

Thus, for a 12-month loan, we substitute 12 for n in the formula to find the denominator of the fraction:

$$\frac{12(12 + 1)}{2} = \frac{12 \times 13}{2} = 78$$

Self-Check 10C   Rule of 78

1.   By what fraction do we multiply the interest charge for the first month of an 18-month plan?

2. By what fraction do we multiply the interest charge for the last month of an 18-month loan?

3. How much of a $200 interest charge would you save on a 5-month loan by paying the loan off at the end of the fourth month?

Charge Accounts

Stores open **charge accounts** for credit worthy customers who wish to buy products on credit and pay on monthly terms. Because Americans use credit cards or **charge accounts** for more purchases each year, it is important that we understand the costs involved. One cost that may not be obvious to consumers is the service cost that banks charge stores using credit-card service. The stores must recover these service charges by charging higher prices on all products — even those they sell to consumers paying cash. Another cost, but one consumers may avoid, is the interest charge that banks assess when consumers do not pay for their charge-account purchases in full by the due dates.

Assume that you purchased $100 worth of merchandise from a department store on January 3, charging that amount with your Visa card. If the bank bills you on the first day of the following month, which is the usual practice, you will have had use of the $100 worth of goods for almost a month before receiving the bill, with no direct charge to you. Additionally, a statement issued by the bank on February 1 will have a due date of March 1, enabling you to use the $100 worth of merchandise another 30 days with no direct charge to you. In paying the $100 by the due date, therefore, you will have postponed payment by almost 2 months without having to pay interest charges. (See calendars in Figure 10.1.)

If, instead, you pay only $10 (the minimum payment allowed) by the due date, the bank will charge you interest of $1\frac{1}{3}$ percent on the $90 balance, with interest being charged from the statement date (February 1) to the next statement date (March 1):

$$\begin{array}{ccc} \text{Account} \\ \text{balance} \end{array} \times \begin{array}{c} \text{Monthly} \\ \text{rate } 1\frac{1}{3} \end{array} = \begin{array}{c} \text{Interest} \\ \text{charge} \end{array}$$

$$\$90.00 \times 0.0133 = \$1.20$$

Charge date							Billing date							Due date						
JANUARY							FEBRUARY							MARCH						
SUN	MON	TUE	WED	THU	FRI	SAT	SUN	MON	TUE	WED	THU	FRI	SAT	SUN	MON	TUE	WED	THU	FRI	SAT
1	2	③	4	5	6	7				①	2	3	4				①	2	3	4
8	9	10	11	12	13	14	5	6	7	8	9	10	11	5	6	7	8	9	10	11
15	16	17	18	19	20	21	12	13	14	15	16	17	18	12	13	14	15	16	17	18
22	23	24	25	26	27	28	19	20	21	22	23	24	25	19	20	21	22	23	24	25
29	30	31					26	27	28					26	27	28	29	30	31	

Figure 10.1 Relationship of Charge, Billing, and Due Dates

Although an interest rate of $1\frac{1}{3}\%$, or an interest charge of \$1.20, may not seem very high, on an annual basis it is a very high 16 percent:

$$\frac{\text{Monthly}}{\text{rate}} \times \frac{\text{Months}}{\text{in year}} = \frac{\text{Annual}}{\text{rate}}$$
$$0.0133 \quad \times \quad 12 \quad = \quad 0.16 \quad = 16\%$$

Most stores that issue credit cards to their customers charge rates of interest that are even higher than those charged by banks. Instead of charging 1.2 percent each month on the unpaid balance, as MasterCard and Visa do, most stores charge 1.5 percent resulting in an annual rate of 18 percent ($1\frac{1}{2} \times 12$ months $= 18\%$). And rather than charging interest on the unpaid balance, as the major banks do, most stores begin charging interest on each new purchase from the date of the purchase.

As in the previous example, assume that you owe the store \$100 and that the due date is March 1, but you make the minimum payment of just \$10, electing to postpone payment and to pay interest on the \$90 balance. Assume further that you purchase an additional \$50 worth of goods on March 11. Because you have a balance due from the previous month (the \$90), on which you are paying interest, the store begins charging you interest immediately on the new purchase. Instead of being allowed to use the \$50 worth of merchandise from the purchase date to the billing date and from the billing date to the due date without paying any interest, you must now begin paying interest from the date of purchase. In other words, customers who do not pay their statements in full by the due dates no longer receive the 30- to 60-day grace period that is available to those who do pay in full by the due dates.

If you make only the minimum payment, a store begins charging interest on the first day of the new billing period. As shown in the department store statement in Figure 10.2, the customer made only the minimum payment for the preceding month, and the store began on January 1 charging interest on the \$90 balance. Notice also that the customer made two additional purchases during January.

Most stores charge interest on the **average daily balance (ADB),** which is computed exactly the same as a weighted average (see Chapter 7). Using Figure 10.2 to illustrate, we can see that the customer had a balance of \$90.00 from January 1 through 10, \$96.38 from January 11 through 14, and \$119.83 from January 15 through 31,

PLEASE MAKE CHECK OUT TO:

REUTER'S FASHIONS
1212 West Highland Street
Phoenix, Arizona 85015

STATEMENT
TO AVOID ADDITIONAL PERIODIC FINANCE CHARGES
ON THE NEW BALANCE, PAYMENT MUST BE RECEIVED
BY THE PAYMENT DUE DATE SPECIFIED BELOW.

MINIMUM PAYMENT	PAST DUE AMOUNT	PAYMENT DUE DATE	NEW BALANCE	ACCOUNT NUMBER	AMOUNT YOU ARE PAYING
10.00	90.00	03/01/89	121.44	3244 2500 0273 9012	

JOHN F PRINCE
ELIZABETH J. PRINCE
6000 OLIVE AVENUE
GLENDALE AZ 85301-5206

CREDIT LINE	UNUSED CREDIT	ANNUAL PERCENTAGE RATE
1000.00	878.56	1.5% X 12 = 18%

PLEASE DETACH THE ABOVE PORTION AND RETURN IT WITH YOUR PAYMENT.

- -

TRANSACTION DATE	REFERENCE NUMBER	DESCRIPTION	PURCHASES	PAYMENTS AND CREDITS
JAN 2		PAYMENT--THANK YOU		10.00
JAN 11	228102	INFANT BASICS	6.38	
JAN 15	221101	CUT N SEWN SHIRTS	23.45	

CLOSING DATE	PREVIOUS BALANCE	MINUS PAYMENTS AND CREDITS	FINANCE CHARGE	PLUS PURCHASES	NEW BALANCE
01/31/89	100.00	10.00	1.61	29.83	121.44

NOTICE: SEE REVERSE SIDE FOR IMPORTANT INFORMATION

Figure 10.2 Monthly Statement for a Charge Account

with the amount of each item being added to the balance on the date of purchase. With this information, we can compute interest in a two-step process:

Step 1

Compute the average daily balance.

$ 90.00	10 days × 90.00 =	900.00
Jan. 11 6.38	4 days × 96.38 =	385.52
Jan. 15 23.45	17 days × 119.83 =	2,037.11
119.83	31	3,322.63

3,322.63 ÷ 31 = 107.18

Step 2

Compute the interest.

Average daily balance	Interest of of 1 1/2%	January interest charge
107.18 ×	0.015	= $1.61

The store not only began charging interest on the $90 balance beginning the first day of the new accounting period (January 1), but also began charging interest on the two additional items on the very day that each was purchased. In other words, there was no interest-free grace period because of the customer's failure to pay off the entire amount for the previous month. Although an interest charge of $1\frac{1}{2}$ percent per month may not seem meaningful, the **annual percentage rate** is a very high 18 percent.

Monthly rate	Months in a year	Annual rate
0.015 ×	12	= 18%

As illustrated at the top of the statement in Figure 10.2, federal law requires all lenders to publish annual percentage rates on installment contracts and monthly statements.

Self-Check 10D Charge Accounts

---

1. If you charged a purchase of $75 to your MasterCard credit card on June 15, with a billing date of July 1 and a due date of July 31, how much interest will be charged on the purchase if you pay your account in full on or before the due date?

2. Continuing with Problem 1, if you paid only $10 on July 31, leaving a balance of $65, on what date would interest charges begin, and how much interest at $1\frac{1}{3}\%$ would you be charged on the next statement?

3. If a customer used a store credit card to charge the following amounts, what is the average daily balance for August, assuming that no additional charges or credits (payments) are involved?

   August 3 $50
   August 5 $15
   August 20 $23
   August 30 $125

4. If a store charges interest at a rate of 1.25% on the unpaid balance of a charge account, what is the annual rate?

Answers to Self-Checks

Self-Check 10A	**Self-Check 10B**	**Self-Check 10C**	**Self-Check 10D**
1. $750	1. $525	1. 18/171	1. None
2. $123.75	2. $288.13	2. 1/171	2. 86¢
3. $48.54	3. $302.54	3. $13.33	3. $76.81
	4. $52.54		4. 15%

Credit Transactions

1. **Installment loans (10 points)**

   A complete Sony audio system featuring eight speakers was offered for $1,125 with a minimum 20% down and 24 monthly payments. With interest of $12\frac{1}{2}$ percent, what is the amount of each monthly payment?

2. **Partial payments (10 points each)**

   a. If you loaned $2,000 to someone for 2 years at 8% simple interest, how much money would that person still owe you after making a partial payment of $1,000 at the end of the first year?

   b. In Problem 2.a, what would be the balance owed following a $500 payment 6 months later, that is, at the end of the 18th month?

3. **Rule of 78 (10 points each)**

   a. If, under the Rule of 78, a consumer pays off a 12-month loan at the end of 3 months, how much of the annual interest of $144 will be saved?

   b. With interest charges of $240 on a 6-month loan, how much of the interest will the lender avoid paying under the Rule of 78 if the loan is paid off at the end of the fourth month?

4. Charge accounts (50 points)

A credit card customer has a balance of $540 in a department store account after having made a payment the preceding month.

a. What is the average daily balance if the closing period for the earlier month was August 27 and the closing date for the most recent month was September 28, with the customer having made the following purchases:

$150.00 on August 31

$132.50 on September 5

$78.21 on September 20

b. At a rate of 1.75 percent per month, what amount of interest will be added to the current bill?

1. **Installment loans (10 points)**

   The Harringtons purchased an air-conditioning unit for $3,500 including installation. Their down payment consisted of a trade-in of $125 on the old unit plus a check for $675. If the balance is paid in 20 monthly installments of $185 each, how much money are the Harringtons paying in finance charges?

2. **Partial payments (20 points)**

   A friend borrows $5,000 on July 10 under terms of exact interest at 9 percent annually. He makes a $1,500 payment on August 18 and a second payment of $1,000 on December 12.

   a. What is the balance due following the first payment?

   b. What is the balance due following the second payment?

   c. What is the pay-off amount on March 3 of the following year?

3. **Rule of 78 (10 points each)**

   a. If interest charges of $175 are to be paid over the life of a 12-month contract, how much interest under the Rule of 78 will the borrower save by paying 3 months early?

   b. Compare the interest charge during the first month and twelfth month of a 1-year contract for the purchase of a $1,500 home-entertainment system, assuming that the purchaser made a down payment of $350 and financed the balance at 14% interest under the Rule of 78.

4. Charge accounts (10 points each)

a. If the interest rate is 1.4% per month, what is the annual rate?

b. If the bank bills you for $150 worth of merchandise that you have charged to your bank credit card, and if you pay only $10 of that amount this month, how much interest will the bank add to next month's statement (monthly rate is 1.33%)?

c. If you have a balance due of $90 on your department-store credit card, on which you are paying interest, how many days will the store give you to pay for a $50 purchase that you just made before they begin charging interest on the $50?

d. If you had a balance due of $80 at the beginning of March and you used your store credit card to charge $40 of purchases on the 11th and another $60 on the 31st, what is your average daily balance for the month?

e. If you have an average daily balance of $79 for credit-card purchases, how much interest will the department store add to the statement this month (monthly rate is $1\frac{1}{2}$%)?

CHAPTER
11

Banking Records

After reading Chapter 11, you will be able to

- Write checks in proper form.
- Record checks and deposits.
- Compute interest on interest-earning bank accounts.
- Reconcile bank statements with check registers.

Key Terms

check register

interest-earning checking account

bank credit

bank statement

statement-register reconciliation

ending balance

revised balance

service charge

Rather than paying bills in person or sending money through the mails, most businesses and individuals use checks. They must record every check in a check register, and they must balance their records each month with statements issued by the bank. When the word "bank" is used in this chapter, it refers equally to savings-and-loan associations, credit unions, and other institutions that offer check-writing services.

Writing Checks

Money is all that is needed to open a checking account at a bank; the people at the bank handle all of the necessary details and provide customers with checkbooks. After placing money in a bank, we may write checks to others, authorizing the bank to pay specified amounts of our money to businesses or individuals who present our checks for payment.

Most checks issued by businesses are written on typewriters or by computer printers; most checks written by individuals are handwritten. The example in Figure 11.1 is a check that was written by an individual, Jody Campbell, to make a monthly payment to MasterCard. In addition to writing the check number (161) and date in full and showing MasterCard as the payee (receiver of the money), Jody was careful to place the figures "75.10" close to the dollar sign, making it impossible for anyone to change the figure to a higher amount, such as $175.10 or $275.10.

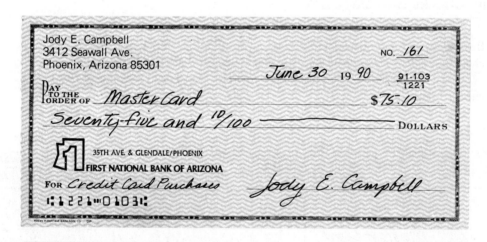

Figure 11.1 A Personal Check

Jody was also wise to place the spelling of the amount "Seventy-five" to the far left, making it impossible for anyone to increase the amount by inserting an additional word to the left of the intended amount. Finally, Jody identified the purpose of the payment as being for items that were purchased with a MasterCard credit card. Although the symbols at the lower left corner of the check are for the bank's use, the user should double-check these symbols on each batch of new checks received from the bank to make certain that they correspond with the account number. The symbols on this check represent account number 1221-0103.

Self-Check 11A   Writing Checks

Using the current date and check no. 71, assume you are Jody Campbell and make the following check out to First Federal Savings for a mortgage payment of $571.85.

Recording Checks and Deposits

Businesses and individuals must record each check that they write, at the time each check is written, using **check registers** like the one illustrated in Figure 11.2.

The $250.16 figure was brought forward from the preceding page in the check register.

CHECK NO.	DATE	CHECKS ISSUED TO OR DESCRIPTION OF DEPOSIT	AMOUNT OF CHECK		CHECK FEE (if any)	✓	AMOUNT OF DEPOSIT	BALANCE FORWARD	
								250	16
	6/30/90	To Cash Deposit					200 00	Check or Dep. 200	00
		For						Bal. 450	16
161	6/30	To Master Card	75	10	.25			Check or Dep. 75	35
		For Credit purchases						Bal. 374	81
162	7/2	To Mountain States	38	10	.25			Check or Dep. 38	35
		For Gas bill						Bal. 336	46
163	7/3	To Gazette	7	50	.25			Check or Dep. 7	75
		For Newspaper - July						Bal. 328	71
		To						Check or Dep.	
		For						Bal.	
		To						Check or Dep.	
		For						Bal.	

Figure 11.2   Check Register

After depositing $200.00 on June 30, Jody had an account balance of $450.16 (250.16 + 200.00 = 450.16). On writing a check to MasterCard for $75.10, she adds the bank's 25¢ check fee to the amount to be deducted, resulting in a deduction of $75.35 and a new balance of $374.81. After writing two additional checks, Jody has a balance of $328.71. Some banks charge higher or lower fees for writing checks, some assess monthly charges, and some make no such charges. Also, as illustrated in Figure 11.2, the complete date is shown on the first line of each page of a register, so that when dealing with old records the year of the transactions may be easily determined.

Self-Check 11B   Recording Checks and Deposits

Assume that you had a $152.25 balance in your checking account before writing check No. 121 on July 1 for $16.50 to Bell Telephone Company for telephone service, writing a check on July 10 for $64.22 to City Power Company for electric service, and making a deposit of $100.00 on July 15. Record these three transactions on the following check register to reflect a bank service charge of 15¢ for each check written.

CHECK NO.	DATE	CHECKS ISSUED TO OR DESCRIPTION OF DEPOSIT	AMOUNT OF CHECK	CHECK FEE (if any)	✓	AMOUNT OF DEPOSIT	BALANCE FORWARD	
		To					Check or Dep.	
		For					Bal.	
		To					Check or Dep.	
		For					Bal.	
		To					Check or Dep.	
		For					Bal.	

Interest-Earning Checking Accounts

Some banks offer **interest-earning checking accounts** that not only provide free checking when minimum balances are maintained, but also pay interest on the average daily balance or on the lowest balance during the month. A bank might offer 5 1/4 percent interest on the lowest balance, for example, based on a minimum balance of $250. Assuming that the balance in an account ranges from $300 to $600 during a one-month period, interest will be computed on $300 — the lowest figure.

$$I = PRT$$

$$I = 300(0.0525)\left(\frac{1}{12}\right)$$

$$I = \$1.31$$

Rather than paying a per-check charge and a monthly maintenance fee, the customer collects $1.31 at the end of the month in the form of a **bank credit** to the checking account.

Self-Check 11C   Interest-Earning Checking Accounts
---

1. If a bank imposes a minimum deposit requirement of $200 on checking accounts and a depositor's balance during the month ranged from a low of $150 to a high of $500, how much interest will be credited to the account for the month at a rate of 5%?

2. What would the interest have been if the balance had ranged from a low of $310 to a high of $500?

3. What is the average daily balance of an account during June if the balance was $200 from June 1 to 15, $220 from June 16 to 20, and $260 from June 21 to 30. (Hint: The average daily balance is actually a weighted mean.)

Statement-Register Reconciliation

Banks mail monthly statements to their customers who have checking accounts, so that they (businesses and individuals) may compare bank records (**bank statement**) with their own records (checkbook register). The bank statement in Figure 11.3 summarizes the transactions at the beginning of the statement, showing the beginning balance, three deposits (including an interest credit), ten withdrawals, and an ending balance.

The EFT notations in the bank statement stand for "electronic funds transfer," by which the depositor has his employer transfer his semimonthly earnings directly to the bank, with the depositor having instructed the bank to place $800 of that amount in a checking account and the balance in a savings account. EFT is also used by the bank on behalf of the depositor to make monthly payments to the newspaper for home delivery and to Cities Service for electricity consumed. ATM is an abbreviation for "automatic teller machine," which this depositor used in the city of Glendale on March 26 to withdraw $300 cash. The corresponding check register is shown in Figure 11.4.

DESERT VIEW FEDERAL CREDIT UNION
P.O. BOX 11350
PHOENIX, AZ 85061
(602) 242-3200

See reverse side for important
information regarding your rights
to dispute electronic fund transfer
errors.

Statement
of Account:

PAGE	SOCIAL SECURITY	STATEMENT PERIOD	ACCOUNT NUMBER
1	310 26 3044	030590 040490	27392-04

SAVINGS RATES: TO $1000=5.0%, TO $3000=5.25%, TO $10,000=6%, $10,000 AND UP=6.25%
CHECKING RATES: TO $500=0%, TO $3000=5.0%, $3000 AND UP=5.25%

DATE	NO.	TRANSACTION DESCRIPTION	BALANCE
		PREVIOUS BALANCE	$1,322.45
		THREE DEPOSITS	1,608.50
		TEN WITHDRAWALS	-838.42
		ENDING STATEMENT BALANCE	$2,092.53
		DEPOSITS AND OTHER CREDITS	
03/10	EFT	PAYROLL	$800.00
03/25	EFT	PAYROLL	800.00
04/05		INTEREST	8.50
		TOTAL	$1,608.50
		CHECK TRANSACTIONS	
03/05	EFT	NEWSPAPER	$7.50
03/08	227	CHECK	100.00
03/14	228	CHECK	45.12
03/16	EFT	CITIES SERVICE	125.00
03/20	229	CHECK	72.45
03/22	230	CHECK	75.25
03/22	*232	CHECK	7.15
03/21	233	CHECK	23.85
03/25	*235	CHECK	82.10
03/26	EFT	ATM 126 GLENDALE	300.00
		TOTAL	$838.42

Figure 11.3   Bank Statement

Check No.	Date	Checks issued to or description of deposit	Amount of check	Fee	Amount of deposit	Balance forward	
						1,912	95
225	2/28/90	To Mortgage / For	525.50			ck/dep 525	50
						bal 1,387	45
226	3/1	To Dentist / For	65.00			ck/dep 65	00
						bal (1,322	45)
227	3/3	To Payless / For	100.00			ck/dep 100	00
						bal 1,222	45
228	3/8	To Sears / For	45.12			ck/dep 45	12
						bal 1,177	33
EFT	3/10	To Payroll / For			800.00	ck/dep 800	00
						bal 1,977	33
229	3/15	To Hall's Shoes / For	72.45			ck/dep 72	45
						bal 1,904	88

Check No.	Date	Checks issued to or description of deposit	Amount of check	Fee	Amount of deposit	Balance forward	
						1,904	88
230	3/16/90	To Payless / For	75.25			ck/dep 75	25
						bal 1,829	63
231	3/16	To B. Dalton / For	25.12			ck/dep 25	12
						bal 1,804	51
232	3/17	To Revco / For	7.15			ck/dep 7	15
						bal 1,797	36
233	3/17	To Broadway / For	23.85			ck/dep 23	85
						bal 1,773	51
EFT	3/15	To Cities Service / For	125.00			ck/dep 125	00
						bal 1,648	51
234	3/20	To Ace Hardware / For	17.12			ck/dep 17	12
						bal 1,631	39

Check No.	Date	Checks issued to or description of deposit	Amount of check	Fee	Amount of deposit	Balance forward	
						1,631	39
235	3/20/90	To Safeway / For	82.10			ck/dep 82	10
						bal 1,549	29
EFT	3/25	To Payroll / For			800.00	ck/dep 800	00
						bal 2,349	29
ETM	3/26	To Cash / For	300.00			ck/dep 300	00
						bal 2,049	29
236	3/28	To Mortgage / For	525.50			ck/dep 525	50
						bal 1,523	79
		To / For				ck/dep	
						bal	
		To / For				ck/dep	
						bal	

Figure 11.4 Check Register

The depositor recorded each check as written and recorded the EFT payroll deposits on each payday (the 10th and 25th) and the ATM cash withdrawal on the 26th—even though no deposit slips or checks were written (see Figure 11.4). These transactions represent deposits to and withdrawals from the account just as though the depositor had gone to the bank to deposit the paychecks and just as though he had actually written and mailed monthly checks to the newspaper and electric companies.

In **statement-register reconciliation,** the depositor, on receipt of the bank statement (which is for the period March 5 to April 4) must reconcile (balance) the two records in a two-step process.

Step 1

Change the statement.

Ending balance	2,092.53
+ Deposits not shown (if any)	
− Checks outstanding (if any)	
231 25.12	
234 17.12	
236 525.50	−567.74
= Revised balance	1,524.79

Step 2

Change the register.

Current balance	1,523.79
+ Bank credits (if any)	8.50
− Service charges (if any)	
= Revised balance	1,532.29
Adjustment: EFT 3/5	−7.50
	1,524.79

In Step 1 the customer first enters the statement's **ending balance** for the preceding month. If any deposits were made since the bank issued the statement on April 4, the customer would add them to the beginning balance. Because all deposits are shown on the statement, no additional deposits are entered. The depositor then subtracts any checks outstanding, that is, checks that have been written that had not reached the bank by the date of the statement. As flagged (*) on the statement, Checks 231 and 234 are missing from the list of checks that had cleared, and, because Check 236 is shown in the check register but not on the statement, all three checks are outstanding. Deducting the amounts of these checks from the beginning balance results in the statement's **revised balance** of $1,524.79.

In Step 2, the depositor enters the current balance from the checkbook register. Because this is an interest-earning checking account, the bank credits the customer for interest of $8.50, which is added to the account in Step 2 and added to the individual's checkbook just as though it were a deposit.

A **service charge** may include fees for new supplies of checks, bank fees for checks that have been returned to the bank because of insufficient funds to cover them, and fees for stop-payment orders placed by depositors. Because no such fees are shown on the bank statement, the revised register balance is $1,532.29.

In comparing the two revised balances, we find that the check register is $7.50 higher than the statement.

Revised register balance	$1,532.29
Revised statement balance	−1,524.79
Difference	$ 7.50

On scanning the statement, we find the difference—an EFT transfer of $7.50 on March 5. Because the automatic transfer of funds by the bank (from this account to the newspaper company) was not recorded in the checkbook register, the depositor must make such an entry as illustrated by the third entry in Figure 11.5.

Before the checkbook register update is complete, it must reflect every entry on the bank statement. We must therefore enter the quarterly (January through March) interest payment as a deposit. The circled balance of $1,524.79 then agrees with the revised statement balance of $1,524.79. The depositor circles the ending balance in the register as a notation for next month that the record was last balanced to that point.

If we had not found the $7.50 omission so readily, we would next check the accuracy of our entries and our addition and subtraction in the check register. Although bank records are sometimes inaccurate, most mistakes are eventually located in the check registers of depositors. If we still could not balance the register with the statement, we would seek the assistance of bank employees.

Check No.	Date	Checks issued to or description of deposit	Amount of check	Fee	Amount of deposit	Balance forward 1,631 39	
235	3/20/90	To Safeway / For	82.10			ck/dep	82 10
						bal 1,549 29	
EFT	3/25	To Payroll / For			800.00	ck/dep	800 00
						bal 2,349 29	
ETM	3/26	To Cash / For	300.00			ck/dep	300 00
						bal 2,049 29	
236	3/28	To Mortgage / For	525.50			ck/dep	525 50
						bal 1,523 79	
EFT	3/5	To Gazette / For	7.50			ck/dep	7 50
						bal 1,516 29	
Cr.	4/5	To Quarterly Interest / For			8.50	ck/dep	8 50
						bal (1,524 79)	

Figure 11.5   Adjustment to Check Register

─────────── **Self-Check 11D**   Statement-Register Reconciliation ───────────

1. Reconcile the following bank statement and check register:

Bank Statement		
SUMMARY		
Previous Balance		579.37
2 Deposits		518.20
6 Withdrawals		−612.40
Ending Balance		485.17
DEPOSITS AND CREDITS		
ATM 1205 Transfer		500.00
1230 Interest		18.20
Total (2)		518.20
WITHDRAWALS		
326 1202 Check		38.25
327 1202 Check		100.00
328 1205 Check		175.00
329 1208 Check		110.00
330 1220 Check		129.35
331 1229 Check		59.80
Total (6)		612.40

Check Register				
Balance carried forward				541.12
327	11/29/9-	A&P Groc.	−100.00	441.12
328	12/2	College	−175.00	266.12
329	12/3	Federal taxes	−110.00	156.12
ATM	12/5	from savings	500.00	656.12
330	12/15	Goldwaters	−129.35	526.77
331	12/26	LaBelles	−59.80	466.97
332	12/26	The New Look	−36.00	430.97
	12/30	Deposit	300.00	730.79
333	12/30	Bell Ford	−128.76	602.03

2. Add any necessary entries to the following check register:

CHECK NO.	DATE	CHECKS ISSUED TO OR DESCRIPTION OF DEPOSIT	AMOUNT OF CHECK	CHECK FEE (if any)	✓	AMOUNT OF DEPOSIT	BALANCE FORWARD
							466 | 97
332	12/26/9	To The New Look For Perm	36 | 00				Check or Dep. 36 | 00
							Bal. 430 | 97
	12/30	To Deposit For				300 | 00	Check or Dep. 300 | 00
							Bal. 730 | 79
333	12/30	To Bell Ford For Repairs	128 | 76				Check or Dep. 128 | 76
							Bal. 602 | 03
		To For					Check or Dep.
							Bal.
		To. For					Check or Dep.
							Bal.
		To For					Check or Dep.
							Bal.

Answers to Self-Checks

Self-Check 11A

Jody E. Campbell
3412 Seawall Ave.
Phoenix, Arizona 85301

NO. _71_

Current Date 19_90_   91-103 / 1221

PAY TO THE ORDER OF _First Federal Savings_ $ _571.85_

Five Hundred Seventy-One + 85/100 —————— DOLLARS

35TH AVE. & GLENDALE/PHOENIX
FIRST NATIONAL BANK OF ARIZONA

FOR _Mortgage Payment_   _Jody E. Campbell_

⑈1221⑈0103⑈

Self-Check 11B

CHECK NO.	DATE	CHECKS ISSUED TO OR DESCRIPTION OF DEPOSIT	AMOUNT OF CHECK	CHECK FEE (if any)	✓	AMOUNT OF DEPOSIT	BALANCE FORWARD	
							152	25
121	7/1/90	To Bell Telephone	16	50	.15	V		Check or Dep. 16	65
		For Telephone service						Bal. 135	60
122	7/10	To City Power Co.	64	22	.15	V		Check or Dep. 64	37
		For Electric service						Bal. 71	23
	7/15	To Deposit					100 00	Check or Dep. 100	00
		For						Bal. 171	23

Self-Check 11C

1. None

2. $1.29

3. $223.33

Self-Check 11D

1. $620.41 = $620.41

2. +18.20 interest
   +18¢ adjustment
   circle new balance

---

1. **Beginning with a balance of $750.25, assume you are Jody Campbell and write checks for the following transactions (15 points each).**

   No. 95, May 1, $75.12 to Consolidated Edison for electric service
   No. 96, May 5, $50.00 to Safeway Stores for groceries
   No. 97, May 9, $35.00 to Shell Oil Company for monthly statement
   Deposited $200.00 on May 20
   No. 98, May 25, $225 to Apartment Services for June rent
   No. 99, May 29, $275 to United Bank for auto payment

   Jody E. Campbell
   3412 Seawall Ave.
   Phoenix, Arizona 85301   NO. _____

                                          19____   91-103
   PAY   1221
   TO THE
   ORDER OF _____ $ _____

   _____ DOLLARS

           35TH AVE. & GLENDALE/PHOENIX
           FIRST NATIONAL BANK OF ARIZONA

   FOR _____
   ⑆1221⑈010 3⑆

   Jody E. Campbell
   3412 Seawall Ave.
   Phoenix, Arizona 85301   NO. _____

                                          19____   91-103
   PAY   1221
   TO THE
   ORDER OF _____ $ _____

   _____ DOLLARS

           35TH AVE. & GLENDALE/PHOENIX
           FIRST NATIONAL BANK OF ARIZONA

   FOR _____
   ⑆1221⑈010 3⑆

   Jody E. Campbell
   3412 Seawall Ave.
   Phoenix, Arizona 85301   NO. _____

                                          19____   91-103
   PAY   1221
   TO THE
   ORDER OF _____ $ _____

   _____ DOLLARS

           35TH AVE. & GLENDALE/PHOENIX
           FIRST NATIONAL BANK OF ARIZONA

   FOR _____
   ⑆1221⑈010 3⑆

Jody E. Campbell
3412 Seawall Ave.
Phoenix, Arizona 85301

NO. _____

19____   91-103
                1221

PAY
TO THE
ORDER OF _____ $ _____

_____ DOLLARS

35TH AVE. & GLENDALE/PHOENIX
FIRST NATIONAL BANK OF ARIZONA

FOR _____

⑈1221⑈0103⑈

Jody E. Campbell
3412 Seawall Ave.
Phoenix, Arizona 85301

NO. _____

19____   91-103
                1221

PAY
TO THE
ORDER OF _____ $ _____

_____ DOLLARS

35TH AVE. & GLENDALE/PHOENIX
FIRST NATIONAL BANK OF ARIZONA

FOR _____

⑈1221⑈0103⑈

2. Record checks 95 through 99 and the deposit on the following check register, including a service charge of 15¢ per check (25 points).

CHECK NO.	DATE	CHECKS ISSUED TO OR DESCRIPTION OF DEPOSIT	AMOUNT OF CHECK	CHECK FEE (if any)	✓	AMOUNT OF DEPOSIT	BALANCE FORWARD	
		To					Check or Dep.	
		For					Bal.	
		To					Check or Dep.	
		For					Bal.	
		To					Check or Dep.	
		For					Bal.	
		To					Check or Dep.	
		For					Bal.	
		To					Check or Dep.	
		For					Bal.	
		To					Check or Dep.	
		For					Bal.	

Name _____

Banking Records

Score _____

Bank Statement

Date	Check	Transaction	Amount	Balance
		Previous Balance		277.81
0905	707	Check	42.30−	235.51
0908	708	Check	94.62−	140.89
0912	EFT	Deposit (Payroll)	925.37	1,066.26
0914	EFT	Essex Utilities	105.65−	960.61
0918	*710	Check	128.76−	831.85
0918	ATM	Withdrawal (Olive Square)	250.00−	581.85
0919	EFT	Municipal Corp	23.19−	558.66
0920		Transfer from Savings	500.00	1,058.66
0921	*712	Check	211.35−	847.31
0922	713	Check	525.50−	321.81
0926	EFT	Deposit (Payroll)	925.37	1,247.18
0926	ATM	Withdrawal (Olive Square)	400.00−	847.18
0930		Service Charge	10.00−	837.18
0930		Interest	9.33	846.51
		New Balance		846.51

Check Register

Date	Check	Transaction	Amount	Balance
8/30	707	A&P Grocery	42.30	(235.51)
9/5	708	Windsor Garage	94.62	140.89
9/12	EFT	Payroll	925.37	1,066.26
9/14	EFT	Essex Utilities	105.65	960.61
9/15	709	Federated Stores	139.64	820.97
9/15	710	Appliance Center	128.76	692.21
9/18	ATM	Withdrawal	250.00	442.21
9/19	711	Appliance TV	79.35	362.86
9/19	712	Visa	211.35	151.51
9/20	DEP	Transfer from savings	500.00	651.51
9/20	713	Federal S&L	525.50	126.01
9/26	EFT	Payroll	925.37	1,051.38
9/26	ATM	Cash withdrawal	400.00	651.38
9/30	714	Gable Lumber Supply	105.07	546.31
10/3	715	Wright, D.D.S.	175.00	371.31

1. **Reconcile the entries in the above bank statement and check register (50 points).**

2. Continuing with the preceding problem, make the necessary entries in the following check register page (25 points).

CHECK NO.	DATE	CHECKS ISSUED TO OR DESCRIPTION OF DEPOSIT		AMOUNT OF CHECK	CHECK FEE (if any)	✓	AMOUNT OF DEPOSIT	BALANCE FORWARD 546 31		
715	10/3/9-	To	Wright, D.DS.	175 00				Check or Dep.	175	00
		For	Braces					Bal.	371	31
		To						Check or Dep.		
		For						Bal.		
		To						Check or Dep.		
		For						Bal.		
		To						Check or Dep.		
		For						Bal.		
		To						Check or Dep.		
		For						Bal.		
		To						Check or Dep.		
		For						Bal.		

3. Interest-earning accounts (25 points)

Leslie Davis had $250 in a checking account at the beginning of March, $580 from March 12 to 18, and $400 from March 19 to the end of the month. If the bank pays 5% interest on the average balance, how much interest will be credited to the account for March?

CHAPTER

12

Bank Discounting

After reading Chapter 12, you will be able to

- Explain and compute the amount of interest to be deducted and the amount actually loaned to the borrowing business.
- Determine the size of a loan to be requested so that the borrower will have access to a targeted amount of money after bank discounting.
- Describe the form and purpose of a promissory note.
- Discount interest- and non-interest—bearing notes on the basis of varying time periods.

Key Terms

discounting   promissory note
proceeds   interest-bearing note
negotiable instrument   non-interest—bearing note

In banking transactions, the word **discounting** has two meanings. First, bankers often discount loans by subtracting their interest in advance. Second, bankers routinely discount notes by paying the holders less than full value of the notes. This chapter is a continuation of the discussion of simple interest (see Chapter 9), which we begin by examining the first type of discounting.

Discounting Loans

When bankers **discount** loans they actually deduct and keep the interest from the money being loaned (illustrated in Figure 12.1). Borrowers receive the **proceeds,** which is that part of the principal that remains after the interest has been deducted.

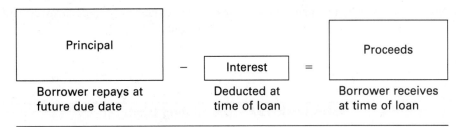

Figure 12.1   A Discounted Bank Loan

If a small business borrows $1,000 from a bank for 2 years at 9 percent simple interest, for example, the business actually receives only $820:

$$\textbf{Principal} - \textbf{Interest} = \textbf{Proceeds}$$
$$P - (PRT) = P'$$
$$1,000 - (1,000 \times 0.09 \times 2) = P'$$
$$1,000 - 180 = \$820$$

The principal is $1,000, the face value of the loan. The interest that the banker collects in advance is $180, and the **proceeds** (P'; read "P prime"), the actual amount of money that the borrower receives from the bank after discounting, is $820. The symbol P' is used for proceeds to distinguish it from the P for principal.

Rather than repay principal plus interest at the end of two years, as is done with loans that are not discounted, this borrower will repay only $1,000. The bank is not collecting interest twice. Instead, the arrangement is as though the principal of the loan were $820, with interest of $180 being added and the borrower repaying $1,000.

$$\textbf{Proceeds} + \textbf{Interest} = \textbf{Principal}$$
$$820 + 180 = \$1,000$$

When banks discount their loans by charging interest in advance, borrowers pay interest rates that are effectively higher than the stated rates. Knowing that the money the borrower actually receives (P') is $820, that the interest charge (I) is $180, and that time ($T$) is 2 years, we can use our knowledge from Chapter 9 to find that the true interest rate (R) for the preceding loan is higher than the stated 9 percent:

<table>
<tr><td align="center">Equation</td><td></td><td align="center">Formula</td></tr>
</table>

$$I = P'RT$$
$$180 = 820R(2)$$
$$\frac{180}{820(2)} = R$$
$$0.11 = 11\% = R$$

or

$$R = \frac{I}{P'T}$$
$$R = \frac{180}{820(2)}$$
$$R = 0.11 = 11\%$$

Instead of paying 9 percent interest on the money that the small business actually received from the bank, therefore, this borrower is paying 11 percent. The bank discount (the interest charge that the bank withheld from the principal of the loan) increased the true interest rate by two percentage points. Stated another way, the borrower paid interest on a loan of $1,000 but received a loan of only $820.

Self-Check 12A   Discounting Loans

1. If a business borrows $15,000 from a bank for 1 year at 15% simple interest, how much money will the business actually receive if the bank discounts the loan?

2. What is the true rate of interest being charged by the bank for this loan? (Round answer to tenths of a percent.)

3. How much must the borrower repay at the end of the 1-year loan period?

4. What are the proceeds of a 2-year loan for $12,000 that is discounted by the bank at $9\frac{1}{2}\%$?

Finding the Principal of a Discounted Loan

Knowing that a bank will collect interest in advance, leaving us with an amount less than we borrow, we may find it necessary to request a loan that is more than we actually need. If we need $10,000 cash for use in our business during the next 2 years, for example, we will have to borrow a greater amount so that after the bank has deducted the interest charge we will have proceeds of $10,000. At an annual rate of 9 percent simple interest, we will have to borrow $12,195.12:

<table>
<tr><td align="center">Equation</td><td align="center">Formula</td></tr>
</table>

$$\text{Principal} - \frac{\text{Bank}}{\text{discount}} = \frac{\text{Desired}}{\text{proceeds}} \qquad \frac{\text{Desired proceeds}}{1 - (R \times T)} = P$$

$$P - (P \times 0.09 \times 2) = 10,000 \qquad\qquad \frac{10,000}{1 - (0.09 \times 2)} = P$$

$$P - 0.18P = 10,000 \quad \text{or}$$

$$0.82P = 10,000 \qquad\qquad \frac{10,000}{1.00 - 0.18} = P$$

$$P = \$12,195.12$$

$$\frac{10,000}{0.82} = \$12,195.12$$

Principal (P) is the unknown from which we subtract the interest charge (bank discount) of $0.18P$. Thus, we subtract $0.18P$ from $1.00P$, giving us $0.82P$, which we divide into 10,000. We find that we must borrow $12,195.12 if we are to receive $10,000 proceeds (cash) after the bank has collected interest of $2,195.12 in advance.

Self-Check 12B   Finding the Principal of a Discounted Loan

---

1. If the bank charges 14% interest in advance on a 6-month loan, how much must you borrow if you are to receive $5,000 proceeds?

2. What is the interest charge on this loan?

3. How much must you repay at the end of 6 months when the loan matures?

4. If a borrower receives $7,670 as proceeds from a 6-month loan that the bank discounts at $8\frac{1}{4}\%$, what is the principal?

Discounting Negotiable Instruments

Negotiable instruments are written obligations to pay specified amounts of money in connection with which the right to collect may be transferred from one person or company to another. **Promissory notes,** like the one illustrated in Figure 12.2, are negotiable instruments in that they are written promises to pay and in that the receivers may transfer to others the right to collect the loan.

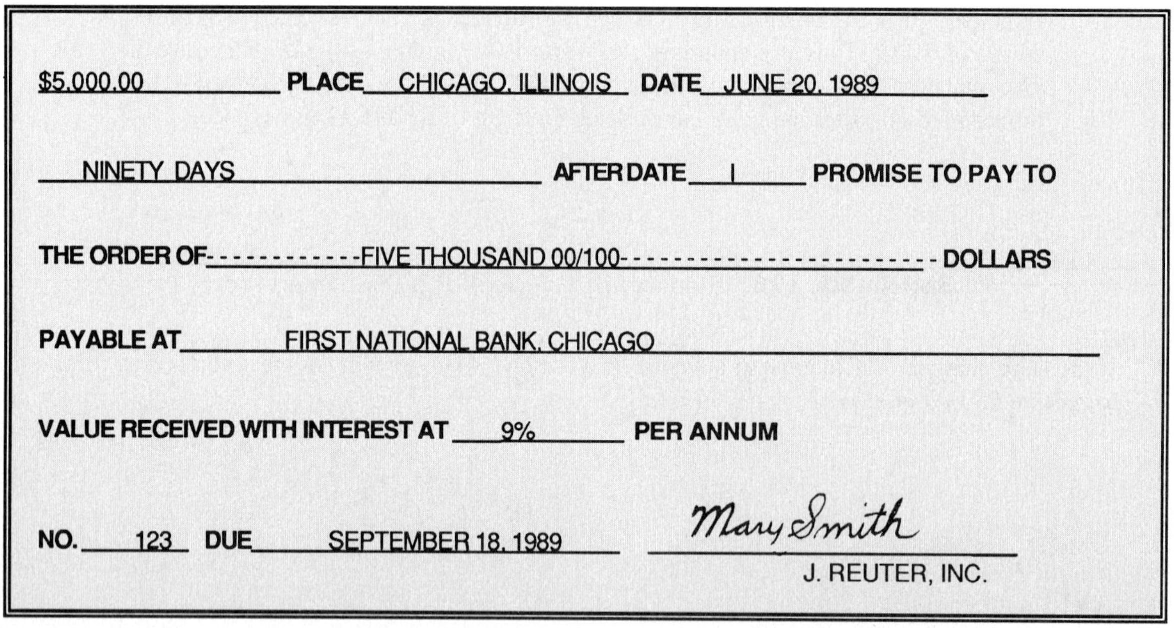

```
$5,000.00              PLACE   CHICAGO, ILLINOIS   DATE   JUNE 20, 1989


   NINETY DAYS                              AFTER DATE___I___  PROMISE TO PAY TO


THE ORDER OF- - - - - - - - - - -FIVE THOUSAND 00/100- - - - - - - - - - - - - - - - - - - - - DOLLARS


PAYABLE AT          FIRST NATIONAL BANK, CHICAGO


VALUE RECEIVED WITH INTEREST AT ____9%____  PER ANNUM


                                           Mary Smith
NO. ___123___ DUE ____SEPTEMBER 18, 1989____  _____
                                              J. REUTER, INC.
```

Figure 12.2   Promissory Note (Interest Bearing)

An **interest-bearing note** is a promise by the issuer to pay a specified amount of money plus interest by a certain date. A **non-interest–bearing note** is a promise to pay a sum of money by a specified date but with no interest added. Both types of notes are used in transactions involving the sale and purchase of goods, in which a business (the seller) extends credit to another business (the buyer).

Let's first consider an interest-bearing note. J. Reuter, Inc. is paying for $5,000 worth of merchandise bought from Marcor Corporation, and Reuter has instructed First National Bank to pay Marcor $5,000 plus 9 percent interest at the end of 90 days. The people at Marcor may either wait 90 days and collect the $5,000 plus interest, or they may discount the note at a local bank and receive immediate cash. Assuming that they decide to discount it at a bank rate of 11 percent, the *discounting of interest-bearing notes* requires a two-step procedure.

Interest-bearing note

Step 1

Find the *amount* (maturity value).

$$\text{Principal} + \text{Interest} = \text{Amount}$$
$$5,000 + (5,000 \times 0.09 \times 90/360) = A$$
$$5,000.00 + 112.50 = 5,112.50$$

Step 2

Discount the amount.

$$\text{Amount} - \text{Discount} = \text{Proceeds}$$
$$5,112.50 - (5,112.50 \times 0.11 \times 90/360) = P'$$
$$5,112.50 - 140.59 = \$4,971.91$$

Marcor receives $4,971.91, and Marcor's bank receives $5,112.50 from Reuter (through Reuter's bank) at the end of 90 days.

Let's assume instead that Marcor holds the $5,000 note for 30 days before discounting it. Rather than discounting the note for 90 days, therefore, the bank discounts it for only the last 60 days of the original 90-day loan period.

Interest-bearing note

Step 1

Find the amount (maturity value).

$$\text{Principal} + \text{Interest} = \text{Amount}$$
$$5,000 + (5,000 \times 0.09 \times 90/360) = A$$
$$5,000.00 + 112.50 = 5,112.50$$

Step 2

Discount the amount.

$$\text{Amount} - \text{Discount} = \text{Proceeds}$$

$$5{,}112.50 - (5{,}112.50 \times 0.11 \times 60/360) = P'$$

$$5{,}112.50 - 93.73 = \$5{,}018.77$$

Having held the note for 30 days, during which time interest was being earned, Marcor receives $5,018.77 from the bank. The bank, in turn, will collect $5,112.50 from Reuter's bank at the end of 60 days.

Occasionally businesses accept promissory notes on which no interest charges are assessed. *Discounting non-interest–bearing notes* requires only a one-step process. Assume, for example, that Marcor has made a special sale of a slightly inferior batch of canned goods to Reuter for $5,000 and that, as part of the purchase agreement, Marcor extends 90 days of interest-free credit to Reuter. On receipt of the non-interest–bearing note, Marcor may discount it at a bank to secure immediate cash. Assuming that discounting at 11 percent is accomplished on the same day the note is dated, Marcor realizes proceeds of $4,862.50.

Non-interest–bearing note

Step 1

Skipped because this is a non-interest–bearing note.

Step 2

$$\text{Principal} - \text{Discount} = \text{Proceeds}$$

$$5{,}000 - \left(5{,}000 \times 0.11 \times \frac{90}{360}\right) = P'$$

$$5{,}000.00 - 137.50 = \$4{,}862.50$$

Assume, instead, that Marcor does not discount the note until June 30, 10 days following its date of June 20. With only 80 days remaining in the credit period, time (T) in our equation becomes 80/360.

Non-interest–bearing note

Step 1

Skipped because this is a non-interest–bearing note.

Step 2

Discount the principal of the note.

$$5,000 - \left(5,000 \times 0.11 \times \frac{80}{360}\right) = P'$$

$$5,000.00 - 122.22 = \$4,877.78$$

——————————— **Self-Check 12C**   Discounting Negotiable Instruments ———————————

1. If a $10,000, 30-day, 8% note is discounted at $8\frac{1}{2}\%$ on the same day that it is dated, what are the proceeds?

2. If the note in Problem 1 is dated July 25, (a) when will the bank collect for the note, and (b) what amount will the bank collect?

3. If you have a 12% promissory note for $5,000 that was dated 1 month ago and has 5 months to go before maturity, what will be your proceeds if you discount the note today at $12\frac{1}{2}\%$?

4. What will be your proceeds if you have the bank discount a non-interest–bearing $600 note that matures 6 months from now at a rate of 9%?

Answers to Self-Checks

Self-Check 12A	**Self-Check 12B**	**Self-Check 12C**
1. $12,750	**1.** $5,376.34	**1.** $9,995.36
2. 17.6%	**2.** $376.34	**2.** a. August 24 b. $10,066.67
3. $15,000	**3.** $5,376.34	**3.** $5,023.96
4. $9,720	**4.** $8,000	**4.** $573

1. Discounting loans (5 points each)

a. If your company borrows $50,000 from a bank for 6 months and the bank collects $8\frac{1}{2}\%$ interest in advance, how much money will your company actually receive from the bank?

b. What is the true rate of interest paid by your company for the $50,000 loan in Problem 1.a? (Round answer to tenths of a percent.)

c. How much money must your company pay the bank upon maturity of the loan in Problem 1.a?

d. How much money will a business owner receive from a 5-year loan of $100,000 if it is discounted at $9\frac{1}{4}\%$?

e. What are the proceeds of a $750 loan for 1 year if the bank charges 9% interest in advance?

f. What is the true rate of simple interest on a $10,000 loan for 10 months on which the bank charges interest in advance of 8%? (Round answers to tenths of a percent.)

g. What are the proceeds of a 2-year bank loan for $30,000 that is discounted by the bank at 9.5% simple interest?

h. Determine the proceeds of a $1,000, 9-month loan that the bank discounts at $9\frac{1}{4}\%$ on the date of issuance.

i. In Problem 1.h, what is the actual rate of interest that the bank is charging? (Round answer to tenths of a percent.)

j. What is the amount of the bank discount on an $80,000 loan if the rate of simple interest is $12\frac{1}{2}\%$ and the term of the loan is 18 months?

k. If you need $20,000 for 9 months, how much money must you borrow from a bank that discounts the loan at 8% simple interest?

l. How much money must you repay the bank at the end of 9 months for the loan described in Problem 1.k?

m. How much interest did the bank charge in advance for the loan in Problem 1.k?

n. What are the proceeds of the loan in Problem 1.k?

o. If a bank discounts loans to small businesses at a simple interest rate of 9.75%, what must the principal of a loan be if a small-business owner is to receive exactly $23,000 to use in the business for the next 3 years?

p. If a business manager needs exactly $50,000 for 18 months for business operations, how much money must he borrow from a bank that discounts loans at a rate of $12\frac{1}{4}\%$ simple interest?

q. How much interest does a bank charge when discounting a 2-year loan of $5,000 at 8.5%?

r. If the principal of an 18-month loan is $11,000 and the bank discount is $2,640, what is the rate of discount?

s. How much interest will a bank charge in advance on a 1-year loan of $6,500 if the discount rate is $13\frac{1}{2}\%$?

t. If you need $12,500 for the purchase of a new pickup truck, for how much of a 3-year loan (principal) should you ask the banker if the loan is to be discounted at 12%?

Discounting Negotiable Instruments

1. Discounting interest-bearing notes (5 points each)

a. If a creditor owes your business $500 and has signed a note to pay this amount at the end of 6 months (180 days) with simple interest of 10%, how much money will the creditor pay you on maturity of the note?

b. If you have the bank discount the note in Problem 1.a at the end of the first 30 days at 12%, how much money will you receive from the bank?

c. How much money will the bank earn on the transaction in Problem 1.b?

d. How much interest will your company have received after having paid the bank discount in the preceding transactions?

e. How much money will the bank receive from the creditor in Problem 1.a at the end of the loan period?

2. Discounting non-interest—bearing notes (5 points each)

a. If a customer (another business) asks your company to accept a 60-day note instead of $1,200 cash for a recent purchase of your products, how much interest will your company be losing if the current value of money is 9%?

b. How much money will you receive if, immediately upon issuance of the note in Problem 2.a, you sell it to the bank at a discount rate of $9\frac{1}{2}\%$?

c. How much interest will the bank collect from your company and the writer of the note (your business customer) in Problem 2.a?

d. How much must the debtor (the business customer) in Problem 2.a pay the bank at the end of the 60 days?

e. What are the proceeds of a $750 note that the bank is discounting at 10% for 90 days?

3.   Mixture of discounting problems (5 points each)

a.   How much will it cost your company to discount a $2,500 note at the bank for 18 months at 9%?

b.   When a creditor does not pay his $3,000 debt promptly, you demand that he sign a promissory note agreeing to pay the $3,000 at the end of 2 months plus simple interest of $9\frac{1}{2}\%$. How much money should you collect at the end of the loan term?

c.   If the bank agrees to discount the note in Problem 3.b after 15 days have passed at a discount rate of 12%, how much interest is the bank charging?

d.   What are your proceeds after the bank discount in Problem 3.b?

e.   How much interest does the bank collect from the creditor (the writer of the note) in Problem 3.b on maturity?

f.   How much interest income did you end up with following the bank's discounting the note in the preceding transactions?

g.   If the company that you work for has accepted a $6,600 note for 3 months, how much will the bank pay you for the note at the end of the first 30 days if the bank discount rate is 9.5%?

h.   How much interest did your company earn before discounting the note in Problem 3.g?

i.   How much interest did the bank collect from your company for having provided the discounting service in Problem 3.g?

j.   A debt of $1,250 is due in 6 months. If the debt is settled at the end of 3 months at a discount rate of 14%, what are the proceeds?

Compound Interest

After reading Chapter 13, you will be able to

- Calculate compound interest and compound amount without the use of tables.
- Determine the number of time periods and adjust interest rates for application to compound-interest tables.
- Distinguish between compound amount, present value, sinking fund, and amortization calculations for selecting the appropriate interest tables.

Key Terms

compound interest   quarterly

compound amount   sinking fund

semiannually   amortization

In the preceding two chapters, we worked with simple interest. Unlike simple interest, **compound interest** enables depositors to earn "interest on the interest"; that is, interest on any interest that has already accumulated in their savings accounts. Computing compound interest is relatively easy because we use interest tables to simplify our calculations.

Calculating Compound Amount

The term **compound amount** refers not only to the sum of principal and interest, as in the computation of simple interest, but also to the fact that interest payments are compounded. As illustrated in Figure 13.1, we begin with a known principal, which, through an accumulation of compound interest, results in compound amount — a figure that is, of course, greater than the principal.

| Principal (known) | + Compound-interest credits = | Compound amount ? |

Figure 13.1   Compound Amount

Beginning with a lump-sum deposit, the bank pays interest that is compounded (computed and credited annually, quarterly, monthly, or daily). In knowing the principal and the compound-interest rate, we may determine compound amount.

Before learning to use compound-interest tables, you should have a basic understanding of the way compound interest works. If you deposit $100 in a savings account that pays 6 percent interest compounded annually (at the end of each year), you will have $106 (the $100 principal plus $6 interest) in your account at the end of the first year. During the second year, you will be earning interest on the $106 — not on just the original deposit of $100. At the end of the second year, therefore, you will have $112.36 in your account (the $106 plus $6.36 interest). During the third year, you will be earning interest on the new balance of $112.36, and so on.

$$\text{Principal} + \text{Interest} = \text{Amount}$$

First Year

$$P + (PRT) = \text{Amount}$$
$$100 + (100 \times 0.06 \times 1) = \text{Amount}$$
$$100 + 6 = 106$$

Second Year

$$106 + (106 \times 0.06 \times 1) = \text{Amount}$$
$$106 + 6.36 = 112.36$$

Third Year

$$112.36 + (112.36 \times 0.06 \times 1) = \text{Amount}$$
$$112.36 + 6.74 = \$119.10$$

With compound interest, therefore, we are actually computing simple interest each period (in this case, each year), using the total amount (principal plus interest) at the end of the previous period as our principal for the following time period.

Interest may also be compounded **semiannually** (twice a year), **quarterly** (4 times a year), monthly (12 times a year), weekly (52 times a year), or even daily (365 times a year). When interest is compounded annually, as in the preceding example, we do not change the interest rate or the number of time periods. When interest is compounded other than annually, however, we change the interest rate (%) and the number of time periods (n) as follows:

Compounded	Divide % by	Multiply n by
Semiannually	2	2
Quarterly	4	4
Monthly	12	12
Weekly	52	52
Daily	365	365

To illustrate, let's compute for 1 year the compound amount (the principal plus accumulated interest) for a $100 bank deposit that earns 6 percent compounded semiannually. Since the interest is to be compounded twice a year, we divide the interest rate by 2 (giving us a rate of 3%) and multiply the number of years by 2 (giving us two time periods). Since we must calculate each time period separately, T in our $I = PRT$ equation is always 1; and, of course, when we multiply another number times 1 the answer is the same as if we had not bothered to do so.

$$\overset{(P)}{} \qquad \overset{(PRT)}{}$$

Principal + Interest = Compound amount

First time period	$100 + (100 \times 0.03 \times 1) =$ $100 + 3 = 103$	End of first 6 months
Second time period	$103 + (103 \times 0.03 \times 1) =$ $103 + 3.09 = \$106.09$	End of second 6 months

As another illustration, let's find the compound amount at the end of 1 year for a bank deposit of $100 that is earning 6 percent compounded quarterly. Since the interest is compounded four times a year, the interest rate (%) is $1\frac{1}{2}$ ($6 \div 4 = 1\frac{1}{2}$) and the number of time periods (n) per year is 4 ($1 \times 4 = 4$).

$$\qquad (P) \qquad (PRT)$$

Principal + Interest = Compound amount

First time period	100 + (100 × 0.015 × 1) 100 + 1.50 = 101.50	End of first 3 months
Second time period	101.50 + (101.50 × 0.015 × 1) 101.50 + 1.52 = 103.02	End of second 3 months
Third time period	103.02 + (103.02 × 0.015 × 1) 103.02 + 1.55 = 104.57	End of third 3 months
Fourth time period	104.57 + (104.57 × 0.015 × 1) 104.57 + 1.57 = $106.14	End of fourth 3 months

During the first quarter (3 months) we were earning interest on the $100 principal. During the second quarter we were earning interest on the principal and the interest that accumulated during the first quarter, and so on. At the end of the year we had earned a total of $6.14 interest—that is, the compound amount of $106.14 less the beginning principal of $100.

—————— **Self-Check 13A** Calculating Compound Interest (without the use of tables) ——————

1. What is the compound amount of $1,500 deposited 2 years ago at a rate of $8\frac{1}{2}\%$ compounded annually?

2. How much interest will you earn in 2 years from a bank deposit of $500 if the bank pays 5% compounded semiannually?

3. Compute the amount at the end of 3 months for $100 at 12% interest compounded monthly.

Using Compound-Interest Tables

As you can see, computing compound interest without the use of tables can be very cumbersome, especially when many time periods are involved. If we had to find the compound amount for 15 years compounded monthly, for example, we would have to solve 180 individual math problems. Instead, we use tables to determine compound amounts, and Table 13.1 provides a condensed version of a table for finding the compound amount of loans and investments.

n	1%	3%	4%	6%	11%	15%	18%
1	1.010000	1.030000	1.040000	1.060000	1.110000	1.150000	1.180000
2	1.020100	1.060900	1.081600	1.123600	1.232100	1.322500	1.392400
3	1.030301	1.092727	1.124864	1.191016	1.367631	1.520875	1.643032
4	1.040604	1.125509	1.169858	1.262477	1.518070	1.749006	1.938778
5	1.051010	1.159274	1.216653	1.338226	1.685058	2.011357	2.287758
6	1.061520	1.194052	1.265319	1.418519	1.870415	2.313061	2.699554
7	1.072135	1.229874	1.315932	1.503630	2.076160	2.660020	3.185474
8	1.082857	1.266770	1.368569	1.593848	2.304538	3.059023	3.758859
9	1.093685	1.304773	1.423312	1.689479	2.558037	3.517876	4.435454
10	1.104622	1.343916	1.480244	1.790848	2.839421	4.045558	5.233836
11	1.115668	1.384234	1.539454	1.898299	3.151757	4.652391	6.175926
12	1.126825	1.425761	1.601032	2.012197	3.498451	5.350250	7.287593
13	1.138093	1.468534	1.665074	2.132928	3.883280	6.152788	8.599359
14	1.149472	1.512590	1.731676	2.260904	4.310441	7.075706	10.147244
15	1.160969	1.557968	1.800944	2.396558	4.784589	8.137062	11.973748
16	1.172579	1.604706	1.872981	2.540352	5.310894	9.357621	14.129023
17	1.184304	1.652848	1.947901	2.692773	5.895093	10.761264	16.672247
18	1.196148	1.702433	2.025817	2.854339	6.543553	12.375454	19.214436
19	1.208109	1.753506	2.106849	3.025600	7.263344	14.231772	23.007632
20	1.220019	1.806110	2.191123	3.207136	8.062312	16.366537	27.259797
21	1.232392	1.860295	2.278768	3.339564	8.949166	18.821518	32.323781
22	1.224716	1.916103	2.369919	3.603537	9.933574	21.644746	38.142061
23	1.257163	1.973587	2.464716	3.819750	11.026267	24.891458	45.007632
24	1.269735	2.032794	2.563304	4.048935	12.239157	28.625176	53.109006
25	1.282432	2.093778	2.665836	4.291871	13.585464	32.918953	62.668627
26	1.295256	2.156591	2.772470	4.549383	15.079865	37.856796	73.948980
27	1.308209	2.221289	2.883369	4.822346	16.738650	43.535315	87.259797
28	1.321291	2.287928	2.998703	5.111687	18.579901	50.065612	102.966560
29	1.334504	2.356566	3.118651	5.418388	20.623691	57.575454	121.500541
30	1.347849	2.427263	3.243398	5.743491	22.892297	66.211720	143.370638

Table 13.1 $1 at Compound Amount

To find the compound amount for a $5,000 investment for 5 years at 8 percent interest compounded semiannually, we look at the 4% column (8 ÷ 2 = 4) and read down the *n* column (*n* = number of periods interest is compounded) at the left until we find 10 time periods (5 years × 2 times each year = 10) and read across to the figure 1.480244. Since this figure gives us the compound amount of just 1 dollar (that is, $1.48), we multiply it times the amount of our investment.

$$\text{Investment} \times \begin{matrix}\textbf{Value from} \\ \textbf{Table 13.1} \\ (\% = 4, \\ n = 10)\end{matrix} = \begin{matrix}\textbf{Compound} \\ \textbf{amount}\end{matrix}$$

$$5{,}000 \quad \times \quad 1.480244 \; = \; \$7{,}401.22$$

Self-Check 13B   Using Compound-Interest Tables (Table 13.1)

1. Identify % and *n* for the following situations:

	%	n
16% compounded quarterly for 6 years		
18% compounded annually for 15 years		
12% compounded semiannually for 2 years		

2. What is the compound amount of a $200 investment for 4 years that earns 18% interest compounded annually?

3. How much interest will be earned during a 6-year period on a $10,000 investment at 12% compounded quarterly?

4. If the owners of a partnership deposit $20,000 in a bank account that pays interest of 12% compounded monthly, how much money will they have in the account at the end of 2 years?

5. For a 5-year investment of $12,000 at 12%, what is the difference between *amount* based on simple interest and *compound amount* if compounded quarterly?

Finding Present Value

In the preceding section, we knew the present value, that is, the principal or lump sum that was deposited to begin with. Now, in discussing present value as illustrated in Figure 13.2 we know the compound amount but must determine the principal.

To find the *present value of compound amount,* we refer to Table 13.2. Assume, for example, that you wish to have $5,000 available for a European vacation five years from today. If the bank is paying 6 percent interest compounded annually, how much money (principal) would you have to deposit today to total $5,000 (principal plus interest) five years from today?

n	2%	3%	4%	5%	6%	12%	15%
1	0.980392	0.979874	0.961538	0.952381	0.943396	0.892857	0.869565
2	0.961169	0.942596	0.924556	0.907029	0.889996	0.797194	0.756144
3	0.942322	0.915142	0.888996	0.863838	0.839619	0.711780	0.657516
4	0.923845	0.888487	0.845804	0.822702	0.792094	0.635518	0.571753
5	0.905731	0.862609	0.821927	0.783526	0.747258	0.567427	0.497177
6	0.887971	0.837484	0.790315	0.746215	0.704961	0.506631	0.432328
7	0.870560	0.813092	0.759918	0.710681	0.665057	0.452349	0.375937
8	0.853490	0.789409	0.730690	0.676839	0.627412	0.403883	0.326902
9	0.836755	0.766417	0.702587	0.644609	0.591898	0.360610	0.284262
10	0.820348	0.744094	0.675564	0.613913	0.558395	0.321973	0.247185
11	0.804263	0.722421	0.649581	0.584679	0.526788	0.287476	0.214943
12	0.788493	0.701380	0.624597	0.556837	0.496969	0.256675	0.186907
13	0.773033	0.680951	0.600574	0.530321	0.468839	0.229174	0.162528
14	0.757875	0.661118	0.577475	0.505068	0.442301	0.204620	0.141329
15	0.743015	0.641862	0.555265	0.481107	0.417625	0.182696	0.122894
16	0.728446	0.623167	0.533908	0.458112	0.393646	0.163122	0.106865
17	0.714163	0.605016	0.513373	0.436297	0.371364	0.145644	0.092926
18	0.700159	0.587395	0.493628	0.415521	0.350344	0.130040	0.080805
19	0.686431	0.570286	0.474642	0.395734	0.330513	0.116107	0.070265
20	0.672971	0.553676	0.456387	0.376889	0.311805	0.103667	0.061100
21	0.659776	0.537549	0.438834	0.358942	0.294155	0.092560	0.053131
22	0.646839	0.521893	0.421995	0.341850	0.277505	0.082643	0.046201
23	0.634156	0.506692	0.405726	0.325571	0.261797	0.073788	0.040174
24	0.621721	0.491934	0.390121	0.310068	0.246979	0.065882	0.034934
25	0.609531	0.477606	0.375117	0.295303	0.232999	0.058823	0.030378
26	0.597579	0.463695	0.360689	0.281241	0.219810	0.052521	0.026415
27	0.585862	0.450189	0.346817	0.267848	0.207368	0.046894	0.022970
28	0.574375	0.437077	0.333477	0.255094	0.195630	0.041869	0.019974
29	0.563112	0.424346	0.320651	0.242946	0.184557	0.037383	0.017369
30	0.552071	0.411987	0.308319	0.231377	0.174110	0.033378	0.015103

Table 13.2   Present Value

Principal (present value) ? + Compound-interest credits = Compound amount (known)

Figure 13.2   Present Value of Compound Amount

$$\text{Compound amount} \times \begin{array}{c} \text{Value from} \\ \text{Table 13.2} \\ (\% = 6, \\ n = 5) \end{array} = \begin{array}{c} \text{Principal} \\ \text{(present} \\ \text{value)} \end{array}$$

$$\$5,000 \times 0.747258 = \$3,736.29$$

A deposit of \$3,736.29 at the present time at 6 percent compounded annually would "grow" to \$5,000.00 within five years. At the existing interest rate, therefore, \$3,736.29 is the present value of \$5,000.00. We may double-check our answer by using Table 13.1 to find the compound amount of \$3,736.29, to see if \$3,736.29 will, in fact, increase to \$5,000 within the five-year period:

$$\text{Principal} \times \begin{array}{c} \text{Value from} \\ \text{Table 13.1} \\ (\% = 6, \\ n = 5) \end{array} = \begin{array}{c} \text{Compound} \\ \text{amount} \end{array}$$

$$\$3,736.29 \times 1.338226 = \$5,000.00$$

Self-Check 13C   Finding the Present Value of Compound Amounts (Table 13.2)

---

1. How much money must you deposit today, at 12% compounded semiannually, if you expect the deposit to increase to \$10,000 within 2 years from today?

2. What is the present value of a payment of \$40,000 that is to be received 5 years from now, if money is worth 20% compounded quarterly?

3. In Problem 2, what is the principal, and how much interest will accumulate on the principal during the 5 years?

4. If, as a business person, another business owes you $20,000 that is payable 7 years from today, how much money would you be willing to accept today as payment in full—assuming that you could deposit the money in an account that pays 8% compounded quarterly?

Sinking Funds

A **sinking fund,** as illustrated in Figure 13.3, consists of a series of deposits that, with accumulated interest, reaches a targeted amount of money by a specified date.

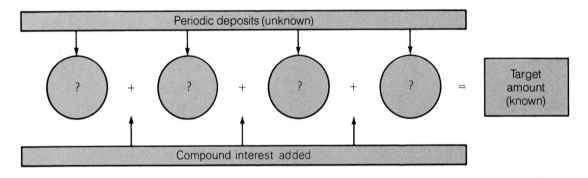

Figure 13.3   Sinking Fund

In sinking-fund problems we know the end amount but must determine the size of the periodic deposits that will (with added interest) equal the targeted amount at the end of the term. If a business that has just borrowed $20,000 must repay that amount at the end of five years, how much money must be deposited in a sinking fund each month if the deposits will earn interest of 16 percent compounded quarterly? Using Table 13.3, we find that the business must deposit $671.64 each month:

$$\begin{array}{ccc} & \text{Value from} & \\ \text{Amount} & \text{Table 13.3} & \text{Periodic} \\ \text{needed} \;\times\; & (\% = 4, n = 20) \;=\; & \text{payment} \\ \$20{,}000 \;\times\; & 0.033582 & = \;\$671.64 \end{array}$$

The monthly deposits of $671.64 along with the interest earned on each deposit, will provide the needed $20,000 at the end of five years.

n	1/2%	1%	4%	5%	6%	12%	15%
1	1.000000	1.000000	1.000000	1.000000	1.000000	1.000000	1.000000
2	0.498753	0.497512	0.490196	0.487805	0.485437	0.471698	0.465116
3	0.331672	0.330022	0.320349	0.317209	0.314110	0.296349	0.287977
4	0.248133	0.246281	0.235490	0.232012	0.228592	0.209234	0.200265
5	0.198010	0.196040	0.184627	0.180975	0.177396	0.157410	0.148316
6	0.164596	0.162548	0.150762	0.147018	0.143363	0.123226	0.114237
7	0.140729	0.138628	0.126610	0.122820	0.119135	0.099118	0.090360
8	0.122829	0.120690	0.108528	0.104722	0.101036	0.081303	0.072850
9	0.108907	0.106740	0.094493	0.090690	0.087022	0.067679	0.059574
10	0.097771	0.095582	0.083291	0.079505	0.075868	0.056984	0.049252
11	0.088659	0.086454	0.074149	0.070389	0.066793	0.048415	0.041069
12	0.081066	0.078849	0.066552	0.062825	0.059277	0.041437	0.034481
13	0.074642	0.072415	0.060144	0.056456	0.052960	0.035677	0.029110
14	0.069136	0.066901	0.054669	0.051024	0.047585	0.030871	0.024688
15	0.064364	0.062124	0.049941	0.046342	0.042963	0.026824	0.021017
16	0.060189	0.057945	0.045820	0.042270	0.038952	0.023390	0.017948
17	0.056506	0.054258	0.042199	0.038699	0.035445	0.020457	0.015367
18	0.053232	0.050982	0.038993	0.035546	0.032357	0.017937	0.013186
19	0.050303	0.048052	0.036139	0.032745	0.029621	0.015763	0.011336
20	0.047667	0.045415	0.033582	0.030243	0.027185	0.013879	0.009761
21	0.045282	0.043431	0.031280	0.027996	0.025005	0.012240	0.008417
22	0.043114	0.040864	0.029199	0.025971	0.023046	0.010811	0.007266
23	0.041135	0.038886	0.027309	0.024137	0.021279	0.009560	0.006278
24	0.039321	0.037073	0.025587	0.022471	0.019679	0.008463	0.005430
25	0.037652	0.035407	0.024012	0.020953	0.018227	0.007500	0.004699
26	0.036112	0.033869	0.022567	0.019564	0.016904	0.006652	0.004070
27	0.034686	0.032446	0.021239	0.018292	0.015697	0.005904	0.003526
28	0.033362	0.031124	0.020013	0.017123	0.014593	0.005244	0.003057
29	0.032139	0.029895	0.018880	0.016046	0.013580	0.004660	0.002651
30	0.030979	0.028748	0.017830	0.015051	0.012649	0.004144	0.002300

Table 13.3 Sinking-Fund

Self-Check 13D   Sinking Funds (using Table 13.3)

---

1. How much money must be invested each year at 15% compounded annually, if $50,000 is needed 15 years from now?

2. How much money must you save each month if you wish to have a $6,000 European trip 2 years from now, assuming that the bank pays you 6% compounded monthly?

3. If a corporation must retire a $5 million bond 20 years from now, how much money must the company deposit every year in an account that pays interest of 6% compounded annually?

Amortization

Amortization, as illustrated in Figure 13.4, is the opposite of sinking funds in that we begin with a lump sum and identify the size of payments that must be made to reduce the lump sum to zero at the end of the term. Part of each payment is used to pay the interest that has accumulated since the preceding payment, with the balance being used to reduce the principal—just as we computed simple interest on partial payments in Chapter 10.

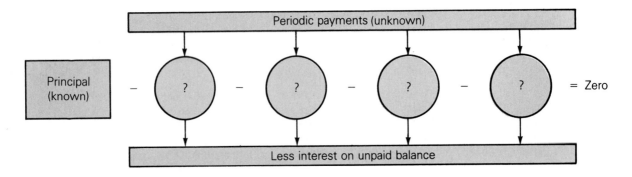

Figure 13.4   Amortization

If, for example, two partners purchase a building for $100,000, they might pay $10,000 cash and give the bank a mortgage for the $90,000 balance. Referring to Table 13.4, we may calculate the monthly payment that will be required to pay off the mortgage. Assuming a two-year mortgage at 12 percent interest, the partners must make monthly payments of $4,236.57 to pay off the loan in two years.

$$\text{Principal} \times \begin{matrix}\text{Value from}\\ \text{Table 13.4}\\ (\% = 1, n = 24)\end{matrix} = \begin{matrix}\text{Monthly}\\ \text{payment}\end{matrix}$$

$$90,000 \quad \times \quad 0.047073 \quad = \$4,236.57$$

The mortgage will be reduced to zero at the end of the two-year period (following the 24th payment), and the partners wil have paid $11,677.68 interest (101,677.68 − 90,000.00 = $11,677.68).

n	1/2%	1%	4%	5%	6%	12%	15%
1	1.005000	1.010000	1.040000	1.050000	1.060000	1.120000	1.150000
2	0.503753	0.507512	0.530196	0.537805	0.545437	0.591698	0.615116
3	0.336672	0.340022	0.360349	0.367209	0.374110	0.416349	0.437977
4	0.253133	0.256281	0.275490	0.282012	0.288591	0.329234	0.350265
5	0.203010	0.206040	0.224627	0.230975	0.237396	0.277410	0.298316
6	0.169595	0.172548	0.190762	0.197-17	0.203363	0.243226	0.264237
7	0.145729	0.148628	0.166610	0.172820	0.179135	0.219118	0.240360
8	0.127829	0.130690	0.148528	0.154722	0.161036	0.201303	0.222850
9	0.113907	0.116740	0.134493	0.140690	0.147022	0.187679	0.209574
10	0.102771	0.105582	0.123291	0.129505	0.135868	0.176984	0.199252
11	0.093659	0.096454	0.114149	0.120389	0.127893	0.168415	0.191069
12	0.086066	0.088849	0.106552	0.112825	0.119277	0.161437	0.184481
13	0.079642	0.082415	0.100144	0.106456	0.112960	0.155677	0.179110
14	0.074136	0.076901	0.094669	0.101024	0.107585	0.150871	0.174688
15	0.069364	0.072124	0.089941	0.096242	0.102963	0.146824	0.171017
16	0.065189	0.067945	0.085820	0.092270	0.098952	0.143390	0.167948
17	0.061506	0.064258	0.082199	0.088699	0.095445	0.140457	0.165367
18	0.058232	0.060982	0.078993	0.085546	0.092357	0.137937	0.163186
19	0.055303	0.058052	0.076139	0.082745	0.089621	0.135763	0.161336
20	0.052666	0.055415	0.073582	0.080243	0.087185	0.133879	0.159761
21	0.050282	0.053030	0.071280	0.077996	0.085005	0.132240	0.158417
22	0.048114	0.050864	0.069199	0.075971	0.083046	0.130811	0.157266
23	0.046135	0.048886	0.067309	0.074137	0.081278	0.129560	0.156278
24	0.044321	0.047073	0.065587	0.072471	0.079679	0.128463	0.155430
25	0.042652	0.045407	0.064012	0.070952	0.078227	0.127500	0.154699
30	0.035979	0.038748	0.057830	0.065051	0.072649	0.124144	0.152300
35	0.031216	0.034004	0.053577	0.061072	0.068974	0.122317	0.151135
40	0.027646	0.030456	0.050523	0.058278	0.066472	0.121304	0.150562
45	0.024871	0.027705	0.048262	0.056262	0.064701	0.120726	0.150279
50	0.022654	0.025513	0.046550	0.054777	0.063444	0.120417	0.150139

Table 13.4   Amortization

Self-Check 13E   Amortization (using Table 13.4)

1. What is the annual payment on a $150,000 computer at 15% interest on a 10-year payment schedule?

2. In Problem 1, how much interest will have been paid at the end of the 10-year period?

3. An employee of Zorid Corporation bought a used car for $2,250 and financed it through the employees' credit union at a rate of 12% on the unpaid balance. What size payments must be made each month to pay off the loan in 18 months?

4. In Problem 3, how much interest will the employee have paid over the 18-month period?

Answers to Self-Checks

Self-Check 13A

1. $1,765.84

2. $551.90

3. $103.03

Self-Check 13B

1. %: 4, 18, 6
    n: 24, 15, 4

2. $387.76

3. $10,327.94

4. $25,394.70

5. $2,473.32

Self-Check 13C

1. $7,920.94

2. $15,075.56

3. $24,924.44

4. $11,487.50

Self-Check 13D

1. $1,050.85

2. $235.93

3. $135,925

Self-Check 13E

1. $29,887.80

2. $148,878

3. $137.21

4. $219.78

Name _____

Compound Interest

Score _____

---

1. **Calculating the compound amount (without the use of tables) (5 points each)**

a. What is the compound amount of a 2-year investment of $500 at interest of 12% compounded annually?

b. In Problem 1.a, how much interest accumulated during the 2-year period?

c. With a principal of $1,000 and interest of $8\frac{1}{2}\%$ compounded annually, what will be the compound amount at the end of 5 years?

d. How much interest will be earned during a 1-year period on an investment of $250 and interest of 5% compounded quarterly?

e. In Problem 1.d, what will the compound amount be at the end of 1 year?

f. If the interest rate is $9\frac{1}{2}\%$ compounded semiannually, what will the compound amount be at the end of 2 years on an investment of $5,000?

g. What will the amount be after 3 months if $500 is invested at 6% compounded monthly?

h. If you deposited $1,500 in a savings institution that pays 12% compounded quarterly, how much money will you have in your account at the end of the first quarter?

i.   In Problem 1.h, how much money will you
have in your account at the end of the
second quarter?

j.   If the investment is $1,000, the term is
2 years, and the rate is 8% compounded
annually, what is the amount?

2.   Calculating the compound amount (for use with a table) (5 points each)

Identify the % and n to complete the accompanying table:

%	n

a.   12% interest compounded semiannually for
15 years

a.

b.

b.   16% compounded annually for 30 years

c.

c.   12% compounded semiannually for 10 years

d.

d.   9% compounded quarterly for 6 years

e.

e.   11 percent compounded semiannually for
$1\frac{1}{2}$ years

3.   Calculating the compound amount (using Table 13.1) (5 points each)

a.   What is the compound amount at the end of
7 years of a $500 investment at 16% interest
compounded quarterly?

b.   How much interest will $100 accumulate
over a 10-year period at an interest rate of
12% compounded semiannually?

c.   What is the difference between a 5-year
investment of $1,000 that earns 6%
compounded annually and a similar
investment compounded semiannually?

d.   What is the compound amount of a 15-year
investment of $5,000 at interest of 8%
compounded semiannually?

e.   Find the compound amount on $1,600 for
2 years at a rate of 12% compounded
monthly.

1. A mixture (5 points each)

a. How much interest will a 6-year investment of $1,500 earn at a rate of 16% compounded quarterly?

b. How much money must be deposited at this time if the investor is to have $1,250 available at the end of 7 years and the interest rate is 8% compounded semiannually?

c. If the compound amount is $16,500 and the interest rate for a 6-year period is 16% compounded quarterly, what is the present value?

d. How much money must owners of a business save each year to accumulate $50,000 within a 5-year period, if they can earn 15% interest on the savings compounded annually?

e. If the financial managers at Amax signed an agreement promising to make monthly payments for the next 2 years to repay a $150,000 loan at 12% interest, what is the size of each payment?

f. If Janet Meyers finances $12,000 of the cost of a used delivery truck for her new business for 2 years at an amortized interest rate of 12%, what are her monthly payments?

g. In Problem 4.d, what amount of her total payments will have gone to pay interest on the loan?

h. The managers at Marco Steel Works paid $50,000 cash for a new building and signed a 20-year mortgage for the balance that carried an interest rate of 6%. What is the size of their annual payments on the $200,000 building?

i. In Problem 4.b, what was the total interest paid?

j. How much money will an investor have in his bank account at the end of 10 years if he deposits $500 today at 6% compounded semiannually?

2. Identify percent (%), time periods (n), and type of problem (T) (5 points each)

a. If $1,500 is deposited in a bank account today at interest of 10% compounded semiannually, how much money will be in the account at the end of 10 years?

%_____

n _____

T _____

b. If $15,000 is needed 10 years from now, how much must be deposited each year at 5% compounded annually?

%_____

n _____

T _____

c. How much must you invest today at 12% compounded semiannually if you wish to have $40,000 15 years from now?

%_____

n _____

T _____

d. How much money must a business save every 3 months at an interest rate of 16% compounded quarterly if the business is to have $17,500 available for the purchase of new equipment 5 years from now?

%_____

n _____

T _____

e. How much interest will a $25,000 deposit accumulate over a 7-year period at 20% compounded quarterly?

%_____

n _____

T _____

f. Ron and Karen Phillips purchased a house for $84,000, paid 10% down, and financed the balance at 12% for 30 years. What is their monthly payment, excluding taxes and insurance?

%_____

n _____

T _____

g. How much money should a business deposit in the bank today at 12% compounded quarterly if savings of $25,000 at the end of the next 5 years is the goal?

%_____

n _____

T _____

h. What are the monthly payments on a $16,000 automobile, assuming a down payment of $2,500, a 4-year loan, and interest of 9% monthly?

%_____

n _____

T _____

i. If you placed $5,000 today in an investment that pays 16% compounded quarterly, what will be the total value of your investment at the end of 4 years?

%_____

n _____

T _____

j. A business now has $45,000 in a savings account that earns 8% compounded quarterly. How much was deposited 7 years ago to have increased to this amount?

%_____

n _____

T _____

Mathematics of Banking

1. Simple interest problems (5 points each)

a. Find the exact interest on a loan of $600 at 9% for 30 days.

b. If a borrower writes a check for $3,388.50 in full payment of a $2,700 loan at 8 1/2 percent approximate interest, what was the term of the loan?

c. If you borrowed $1,100 from a friend for 9 months at 8% simple interest, how much would you still owe at the end of 3 months, after just having made a partial payment of $400?

d. What percent interest is the borrower paying on a 3-year loan of $2,400 on which $810 interest is paid? (Round to hundredths.)

2. Banking records (15 points)

The monthly bank statement shows an ending balance of $230.81 and a service charge of $1.50. The statement does not show a deposit of $125.00 that you made two days ago, nor does it list four checks that you wrote last week totaling $169.38. Balance the statement with your checkbook balance of $187.93.

3. Credit transactions (15 points)

If the balance in your charge account at a department store is $55 at the beginning of November and you charge purchases of $135 on the 12th, $110 on the 18th, and $82 on the 25th, what is your average daily balance for the 30-day billing period?

4. Bank discounting (10 points each)

a. How much must you borrow to realize proceeds of $20,000, if the bank charges 12% interest in advance on a 2-year loan?

b. If you discount a 90-day, 9%, $10,000 note at the bank at a 10% rate of interest, 60 days after receiving it, how much money will you receive from the bank?

5. Compound interest

a. Referring to the partial table following, determine the amount at the end of 1 year of a $7,000 investment at 12% interest compounded quarterly.

n	1%	3%	4%	6%	11%	15%	18%
1	1.010000	1.030000	1.040000	1.060000	1.110000	1.150000	1.180000
2	1.020100	1.060900	1.081600	1.123600	1.232100	1.322500	1.392400
3	1.030301	1.092727	1.124864	1.191016	1.367631	1.520875	1.643032
4	1.040604	1.125509	1.169859	1.262477	1.518070	1.749006	1.938778
5	1.051010	1.159274	1.216653	1.338226	1.685058	2.011357	2.287758

Identify percent (%), time periods (n), and type of problem (T) (5 points each)

b. What will be the total amount in a bank account at the end of 20 years on a $12,000 deposit that earns an annual rate of 8%?

% _____

n _____

T _____

c. If a business must repay a $35,000 loan 15 years from now, how much must the business set aside each year if it receives interest of 12% compounded annually?

% _____

n _____

T _____

d. If a business deposits $25,000 in a savings account that earns 12% interest compounded quarterly, how much interest will it receive during the next 5 years?

% _____

n _____

T _____

e. You wish to finance over a 5-year period a $150,000 combine that you have just sold to a farmer. After the farmer has made a 10% down payment, what will be the monthly payments at 18%?

% _____

n _____

T _____

f. If $16,000 will be needed 6 years from now, how much money must be invested today at 16% compounded quarterly?

% _____

n _____

T _____

PART

4

Mathematics of Marketing

14. Manufacturers' Prices and Discounts

Trade Discounts
Cash Discounts
Extended Charges

15. Transport Costs, Commissions, and Invoices

Transport Costs and Commissions
Sellers' Invoices

16. Retailers' Costs, Markups, and Prices

Markup Based on Cost
Markup Based on Price
Markdowns
Finding the Percent Markup
Finding Cost and Price

CHAPTER 14

Manufacturers' Prices and Discounts

After reading Chapter 14, you will be able to

- Explain and compute trade discounts from list prices of manufacturers.
- Use a shortcut method for allowing a series of discounts.
- Determine the effective rate of multiple discounts.
- Define and apply cash discounts that manufacturers extend to wholesalers and retailers for paying promptly.
- Calculate the balance due on receiving a partial payment.
- Assess extended charges for tardy payment.

Key Terms

list price	terms
trade discount	invoice
effective discount	ROG (receipt of goods)
multiple discount	EOM (end of month)
net price	partial payment
equivalent (true) discount	extended charges
cash discount	

Marketing includes a lot of business mathematics relating to manufacturers — the prices they charge, the discounts they give, and the penalties they impose. The process is complicated somewhat because manufacturers often publish several prices for a single product, depending on the quantities purchased, the terms of payment, and other considerations.

Trade Discounts

When manufacturers sell products to retailers such as grocery and department stores, they may charge a single price for a product. This **list price** is the manufacturers' price that generally appears on a price list along with prices for many other products. For example, Del Monte Corporation may offer to sell 24/8 sliced beets to grocery stores for $6.50 per case. The "24/8" means that each case contains 24/8 ounce cans; and the price of $6.50 is the list price. If a grocer orders 500 cases of this item, the charge is $3,250:

$$\textbf{Units} \times \textbf{Price} = \textbf{Cost}$$
$$\textbf{500} \times \textbf{6.50} = \textbf{\$3,250}$$

A **trade discount** is a reduction in price that manufacturers offer their business customers. Many manufacturers have periodic sales on selected products. Instead of calling them sales, however, they refer to the reductions in price as trade discounts. For instance, Del Monte Corporation may offer to sell 24/8 sliced beets to grocers at a 10 percent discount off the list price during the next 30 days, resulting in a cost of $2,925 to a grocer who purchases 500 cases during that period. By buying the beets at a discount, the grocer saves $325.

Step 1	**Step 2**
6.50 list price	6.50 list price
×0.10 discount	−0.65 discount
0.6500 discount	5.85 net price

Step 3

500 units
× 5.85 net price
$2,925.00 grocer's cost

An easier approach to figuring the retailer's cost is to realize that if a manufacturer is offering a 10 percent discount on an item, the retailer is actually paying only 90 percent of the list price (100% − 10% = 90%). The calculation can then be reduced to two steps.

Step 1	**Step 2**

6.50 list price
×0.90 (1.00 − 0.10)
5.8500 net price

500 units
×   **5.85** net price
$2,925.00 grocer's cost

In addition to the practice of manufacturers offering sale prices through trade discounts, they sometimes offer trade discounts as a way of avoiding temporary price reductions. Rather than lower the price of a particular television set from $750 to $675, for example, the television manufacturer may issue a discount sheet to retailers making the $750 television sets subject to a 10 percent discount. Although the net price to the retailer is $675, there is a psychological tendency for them to think of the product as being a $750 television set that has been discounted, rather than a set that costs only $675. As a common practice, manufacturers also offer trade discounts for purchases of large quantities of products.

Multiple discounts consist of two or more discounts being applied to the list price of a product. Assume, for example, that a manufacturer lists television sets at $750 each with a standard 10 percent discount for purchases of 25 or more sets and an additional discount of 5 percent for purchases of 50 or more sets. The **net price** (the price after trade discounts have been deducted) is found by applying the 10 percent discount to the list price of $750 and then applying the 5 percent discount to the net cost following the first discount.

$$750.000 \times 0.90 = 675.00$$
$$675.00 \times 0.95 = 641.25$$

or

$$750 \times 0.9 \times 0.95 = \$641.25$$

We can derive the same answer by computing each discount separately, but the process takes considerably more time. We also may perform the multiplication in any order, such as multiplying 750 or 0.95 and the product by 0.90 or multiplying 0.90 times 0.95 and the product times 750.

We cannot add the 10 percent and 5 percent discounts and say that the **equivalent (true) discount** is 15 percent, because the discount of 5 percent is not applied against the list price. Instead, the second discount of 5 percent is applied to the net price following the first discount. To figure the equivalent (true) discount, therefore, we (1) take the difference between the list price and the net price and (2) divide that difference by the list price. Using the price of the television set in the previous example, we find that the equivalent discount is $14\frac{1}{2}$ percent:

Step 1

$$\text{List} - \text{Net} = \$ \text{ Discount}$$
$$750.00 - 641.25 = 108.75$$

Step 2

$$\$ \text{ Discount} \div \text{List} = \text{Equivalent discount}$$
$$108.75 \div 750.00 = 0.145 = 14\frac{1}{2}\%$$

In the second step of figuring the equivalent discount, we are actually asking: What percentage is the actual dollar discount of the list price? So we divide the dollar discount by the list price. The equivalent discount is always a slightly lower percent than the sum of the chain discounts.

We can also compute the equivalent discount of a chain of discounts without relating the discounts to a particular list price. With a trade discount of 10 percent, the retailer is actually paying only 90 percent of any list price $(1.00 - 0.10 = 0.90)$. With a trade discount of 5 percent, the retailer is paying only 95 percent of any list price $(1.00 - 0.05 = 0.95)$. To find the equivalent discount, we multiply these two percents and subtract the answer (the product) from 1.

$$\text{Multiply:} \quad 0.90 \times 0.95 = 0.855$$

$$\text{Subtract:} \quad 1.00 - 0.855 = 0.145 = 14\frac{1}{2}\%$$

Self-Check 14A   Trade Discounts

1. What is the net price of a carton of canned pet food that lists for $7.50 and carries a 5% discount?

2. What is the net price of an item that lists for $20 with chain discounts of 10%, 8%, and 5%?

3. What is the single trade discount that is equivalent to the chain discounts in Problem 2? (Round answer to tenths of a percent.)

4. If a manufacturer offers multiple discounts of 5%, 3%, and 1%, what is the actual (true, equivalent) rate of discount? (Round answer to tenths of a percent.)

5. If a product lists at $129 and is subject to a trade discount of $12\frac{1}{2}\%$, what is the amount of the discount? (Round answer to even cents.)

Cash Discounts

Unlike trade discounts, which are discounts off the list prices of products, **cash discounts** are reductions in price that manufacturers give their business customers for paying promptly. In the canned-food industry, for example, canners commonly give **terms** of 2/10, n/30 (read "two ten, net thirty"). The "2/10" means that buyers may deduct 2 percent from the price of the canned goods purchased if they pay for the goods within 10 days from the date of the **invoice** (the bill that sellers mail to buyers). The "n/30" means that when buyers do not pay within the discount period (10 days) they must pay the net amount (full cost following any trade discounts) within 30 days from the date that the seller issues the invoice — without taking any cash discount.

If Tillie Lewis Foods bills (invoices) 1,000 cases of canned goods to Safeway Stores on March 1 at $10 per case, with terms of 2/10, n/30, Safeway Stores may deduct 2 percent when paying the invoice if they make payment to Tillie Lewis within 10 days from the date of the invoice (March 1 + 10 = March 11):

$$1,000 \text{ cases} \times \$10 = \$10,000$$
$$\text{Less } 2\% \qquad\qquad - \quad 200$$
$$\overline{\qquad\qquad\qquad\qquad \$\ 9,800}$$

If Safeway fails to make payment by March 11, the n/30 indicates that Safeway must pay the entire amount of the invoice ($10,000) within 30 days from the date of the invoice (by March 31). Notice that in figuring discount and due dates, the date of the invoice is *not* counted.

Some sellers use such terms as **ROG (receipt of goods)** and **EOM (end of month)**. If terms are 2/10 ROG and the goods are received by the buyer on March 1, for example, the buyer may deduct 2 percent of the value of the goods purchased if payment is made to the seller by March 11 (within 10 days after the buyer's receipt of the goods), regardless of the date of the invoice. This provision is important for goods that are being shipped long distances.

If terms are 2/10 EOM, on an invoice dated anytime from January 1 through 25, the buyer may deduct 2 percent of the value of the products purchased if he makes payment to the seller by February 10, that is, within 10 days after the end of the current month. If the invoice is dated after January 25 (that is, from January 26 to 31), the buyer has an extra month to pay, so that the cash discount could be deducted if payment were made by March 10.

Some sellers offer a choice of cash discounts, such as 3/10, 2/20, n/30, which enables buyers to deduct 3 percent if payment is made within 10 days from the date of invoice or just 2 percent if payment is made between the tenth and twentieth days. No discount is allowed if payment is made after the twentieth day, and the invoice becomes delinquent after the thirtieth day.

Figuring the cash discount is complicated somewhat when buyers make **partial payments**. Although commercial buyers generally are eager to earn cash discounts by paying promptly, they sometimes find themselves short of cash. It is not unusual, therefore, for a buyer to send part of the money owed as a way of earning at least part of the cash discount. If we (the seller) mail the Mom & Pop Grocery Company an invoice on June 10 for $700 with terms of 2/10, n/30 and we receive a partial payment of $350 on June 18, we must credit the partial payment for the cash discount. Since the discount is 2 percent, the $350 actually represents 98 percent (100% − 2% = 98%) of some unknown amount. We can take either of two approaches to finding this unknown amount:

Equation

$$0.98x = 350$$
$$x = 350 ÷ 0.98$$
$$x = \$357.14$$

Formula

$$\frac{\text{Partial payment}}{1.00 - \% \text{ discount}} = \frac{350}{1.00 - 0.02} = \frac{350}{0.98}$$
$$= \$357.14$$

This buyer has, in effect, paid $357.14 of his bill, but has deducted the 2 percent discount in doing so. The balance due is $342.86 (700.00 − 357.14 = 342.86), which becomes due (with no further discounting) on July 10—30 days from the date of the invoice. Note, however, that some firms allow cash discounts only when invoices are paid in full.

Self-Check 14B   Cash Discounts

1. How much money should a seller expect to receive from a buyer for a sale of canned goods invoiced on August 15, totaling $1,500 with terms of 2/10, n/30, if payment is made on: a. August 20; b. August 30.

2. If, in Problem 1, the buyer sends a check on August 20 for $1,000, how much money is still owed?

3. If Artic Fashions buys $4,500 worth of merchandise on January 5 under terms of 1/10, EOM, by what date must Artic pay the invoice to be entitled to the cash discount?

4. Under terms of 2/10 EOM, what is the last day that a discount can rightfully be taken for invoices dated: a. July 3? b. July 27?

Extended Charges

Rather than offer cash discounts, which are rewards that manufacturers extend to commercial buyers for paying promptly, manufacturers often use **extended charges** to penalize buyers for not paying promptly. If a manufacturer sells 1,000 wire coils on March 1 at 25¢ per coil and terms of "net 10 days + 1% in 30 days," for example, the buyer would pay as follows:

If paid within 10 days

$$1,000 \times 0.25 = \$250.00$$

If paid within 30 days

$$1,000 \times 0.25 = 250.00$$
$$250 \times 0.01 = \underline{2.50}$$
$$\$252.50$$

And the buyer would be instructed on the invoice as follows:

Invoice due date 3/11/91	$250.00
Extended time charges	2.50
Pay this amount by 4/1/91	$252.50

If the buyer pays for the coils by March 11 (within 10 days) he pays $250.00. If he pays after 10 days but within 30 days he must pay an additional charge of $2.50. The bill becomes delinquent if payment is not made by the 30th day after the invoice is issued.

You might be wondering why some businesses offer cash discounts to their business customers for paying promptly and others simply penalize customers for paying late. This decision depends on patterns within industries that have been long established, and if a manufacturer were to impose extended charges while competing companies were offering cash discounts, that manufacturer could lose a lot of business.

Self-Check 14C Extended Charges

1. If the invoice is dated June 10 for goods valued at $1,000 with terms of net 10 days + 1% in 30 days, how much money must the buyer pay if payment is made on June 19?

2. How much must the buyer pay if payment is made July 10?

3. When will the invoice become delinquent?

Self-Check 14A

1. $7.13

2. $15.73

3. 21.4% or 21.3%

4. 8.8%

5. $16.13

Self-Check 14B

1. a. $1,470
   b. $1,500

2. $479.59

3. February 10

4. August 10
   September 10

Self-Check 14C

1. $1,000

2. $1,010

3. July 11

1. Straight sales with no discounts (5 points each)

a. What is the total value of 75 packages of electronic parts if the manufacturer charges $1.17 for each package?

b. Compute the total cost to the buyer of 16 coils @ $3.25 each and 12 springs @ $1.15 each.

c. How much should a manufacturer charge for 15 gross of pencils that sell for $12\frac{1}{2}$¢ per pencil?

d. Find the total value of 1,500 cases of canned peaches @ $12.50 each and 1,500 cases of canned pears @ $11.00 each.

e. Calculate the total cost of the following items: 500 wire coils @ 39¢ each and 250 steel coils @ $15\frac{1}{2}$¢ each.

2. Single trade discounts (5 points each)

a. What is the net cost of an item that is selling for $25 and is being discounted at 10%?

b. If the manufacturer's list price for an item is $37.50, what is the net price following a discount of 8%?

c. If the list price of a clock is $60 and the trade discount is 30%, what is the actual selling price?

d. How much must a retailer pay the manufacturer for a $26 item that is being discounted at 5%?

e. If one manufacturer is offering margarine at $12 per case, less a trade discount of 15%, and another manufacturer is offering a similar quality product at a straight $11 per case, which offer would you accept? (Show your calculations.)

3.   Chain discounts (5 points each)

a. What is the net price of an item that lists for $80 and is subject to multiple discounts of 5% and 3%?

b. If an item lists for $375, what is the net price following discounts of 12% and 5%?

c. What is the actual price of a $25 item that has been discounted at rates of 10% and 12%?

d. If water glasses are shown on a price list at $8.50 per dozen, subject to discounts of 5% and $7\frac{1}{2}\%$, what is the actual price of a single glass? (Do not round answer.)

e. If the list price of a china closet is $850, what is the net price following multiple trade discounts of 20%, 10%, and 3%?

4.   Equivalent discounts (round to tenths of a percent) (5 points each)

a. What discount is equivalent to those listed in Problem 3.a?

b. What single discount is the same as the multiple discounts listed in Problem 3.e?

c. What single discount is equivalent to chain discounts of 8%, 5%, and 2%?

d. What is the true discount of chain discounts of 12%, 10%, and 5%?

e. Which multiple discounts would you rather apply to your purchase, 15% and 5%, or 5% and 15%?

Cash Discounts and Extended Charges

1. Cash discounts (5 points each)

a. If an invoice of $500 is dated September 30 with terms of 2/10, n/30, how much must the buyer pay if payment is made October 9?

b. If an invoice for $750 is dated April 10 with terms of 1/10, n/30, how much may the buyer deduct when making payment April 20?

c. If an invoice for $275.50 is dated August 15 with terms of 3/10, n/30, in what amount should the buyer write the check if payment is made on August 30?

d. What is the last day that payment can be made on an invoice dated June 25 with terms of 2/10, n/30, if the cash discount is to be secured?

e. If a buyer pays on June 30 an $850 invoice dated June 1 with terms of 3/10, n/30, how much did the extra 20 days of credit cost him?

f. If an invoice for $116.25 is dated January 10 with terms of 3/10, 2/20, n/30, how much should the buyer remit on January 20?

g. If an invoice for $226.22 is dated January 20, with terms of 2/10, 1/20, n/30, what should the amount of the check be if payment is made February 5?

h. What is the last day that the cash discount may be taken for an invoice dated May 7 with terms of 2/10 EOM?

i. What is the last day that the cash discount may be taken for an invoice dated October 4 with terms of 2/10 ROG, providing that shipment is not received until October 15?

j. What is the amount of the cash discount if payment is made on August 29 for a $1,600 invoice dated August 1 with terms of 3/10, 2/20, n/30?

2. Extended charges (5 points each)

a. If terms are net 10 days + 1% in 30 days on a $900 invoice dated July 10, how much must be paid if payment is made July 19?

b. In Problem 2.a, how much must be paid if payment is made after July 20?

c. What is the extended charge for a $350 invoice dated November 1 with terms of net 10 days + 1% in 30 days if payment is made November 29?

3. Partial payments (5 points each)

a. If partial payment of $100 is made on June 15 for a $200 invoice dated June 5 with terms of 2/10, n/30, how much is still owed?

b. If partial payment of $250 is made on August 15 for a $500 invoice dated August 3 with terms of 2/10, n/30, what is the balance due?

c. If an invoice is dated September 10 for $900 with terms of 3/10, 2/20, n/30, by how much should the bill be reduced by a partial payment of $500 made on September 29?

4. Two partial payments (10 points each)

a. What is the balance due on an $800 invoice dated February 2 with terms of 2/10, 1/20, n/30, if a $200 partial payment is made February 11 and a $300 partial payment is made February 20?

b. What is the balance due on a $300 invoice dated December 5, if partial payment of $100 is made on January 5 and a second $100 partial payment is made on January 15? Terms of sale are 2/10 EOM.

CHAPTER
15

Transport Costs, Commissions, and Invoices

After reading Chapter 15, you will be able to

- Explain and apply transportation charges under varying terms of sale.
- Calculate the total charges for a shipment of products involving discounts, commissions, and transportation charges.
- Explain the reasons that manufacturers use one form of discount instead of another.
- Explain the meaning of "free on board" and compute related freight charges.
- Prepare and interpret all common elements of sellers' invoices.

Key Terms

FOB plant   commission
FOB origin   invoice
FOB destination   collect on delivery (COD)

The material in this chapter explains the mathematical transactions manufacturers need to transport their products to wholesalers and retailers. Manufacturers either ship their products collect, with buyers paying the freight charges, or they pay the freight charges themselves. And for many invoices that manufacturers mail to their commercial customers, they must pay a commission to the broker (selling agent) who made the sale.

Transport Costs and Commissions

Costs for transporting products from the seller's plant to the buyer's warehouse may be payable by either the seller or the buyer, depending on the terms of sale. If a sale is made **FOB plant** or **FOB origin,** the buyer must pay the transportation costs. The letters FOB stand for "free on board." If, instead, a sale is made **FOB destination,** the seller must pay the freight costs.

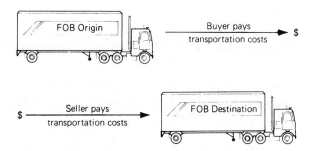

You should understand, however, that sellers often prepay all shipments as a matter of practice, and then add the transportation costs to the invoice even when the terms of sale are FOB origin.

Additionally, many manufacturers pay **commissions** to brokers who actually sell their products. Unlike transportation costs, however, commissions are seldom paid by the buyer or shown on the **invoice,** (the bill that the seller presents to the buyer). In fact, the buyer may be totally unaware that a broker's commission is involved in the transaction. To illustrate the effects of transportation costs and commissions, consider the following example:

Transaction

If Canners Co-op ships 1,000 cartons of canned peaches to Buyers Warehouse at a price of $15 per carton, less a 10% trade discount and with shipping costs of $125, how much will Buyers Warehouse have to pay for the transaction, assuming that a broker's commission of 3% is involved and that the terms of sale are FOB origin?

Solution

1,000 × 15 =	$15,000
Less 10% discount	1,500
Net amount	$13,500
Plus freight charges	125
Total charges	$13,625

Buyers Warehouse (receiver of the goods) will pay $13,625 to Canners Co-op. Canners Co-op (seller of the goods) will pay a commission of $405 (13,500 × 0.03) to the broker at the end of the month, along with the commissions on any other sales by the broker during the month.* Notice that the commission is paid on the net amount of the invoice ($13,500), following the discount but before adding the freight charges. Freight charges are always excluded when figuring commissions or discounts. Accordingly, a cash discount, if one were offered, would also be based on the net amount of $13,500—following the trade discount but before the freight is added.

Self-Check 15A   Transport Costs and Commissions

---

1. How much will the buyer be required to pay for the purchase of 100 bundles of steel rods that sell for $65 per bundle? Freight charges total $350, FOB destination, and the broker's commission is 2%.

2. How much commission did the broker earn from the transaction in Problem 1?

3. If the total amount of an invoice is $14,900, including shipping costs of $895, what is the amount of broker's commission at a rate of $2\frac{1}{2}\%$?

4. In Problem 3, what size check must the buyer send to the producer if payment is made within the discount period—assuming a cash discount of 2%?

---

*Although some brokers perform a buying function, this discussion is limited to only those brokers who sell products for their principals.

Sellers' Invoices

Now that we have discussed prices, trade discounts, cash discounts, extended charges, and transportation costs, let's consider these elements together in several different forms of invoices. Although invoice forms vary widely among companies, they have many of the common elements reflected in the sample invoices presented here. In Figure 15.1, Montiel Supply Company is the seller and Baldour Industries is the buyer. Notice that provision is made for two addresses: The seller typically mails an invoice to the "sold to" address, but often sends the merchandise to a different "ship to" location.

As shown, it is important that Montiel show Baldour's purchase order number, because many buyers will not pay invoices that do not include this identification. Shipment was actually made on February 13 via Central Couriers, a trucking company, and terms are 2/10, n/30, as related to the invoice date and number at the top right of the invoice. Notice in the listing of items that only 24 of the fourth item were shipped and that 6 were back-ordered for later shipment. Both the list prices and the net (after discount) prices are shown.

The net amount ($542.34), shipping cost ($19.84), and the sum of these two amounts ($562.18) are entered at the bottom of the invoice. A cash discount of $10.85 (2% of 542.34) is shown at the right, as the amount to be deducted by the buyer if the invoice is paid by February 25, the tenth day following the invoice date of February 15 (15 + 10 = 25). As explained earlier, this is a situation in which the seller has paid the shipping costs of $19.84 and passed the charge on to the buyer by adding that amount to the invoice.

As a second illustration, consider the contents of The Conodec Corporation's invoice, shown in Figure 15.2, to see if you can identify and understand all of the entries. The "sold to" and "ship to" addresses differ in this instance. Terms of sale are **collect on delivery (COD),** and that Crystaline Corp. (the buyer) must pay the shipping charges (FOB Los Angeles, the city from which the merchandise is being shipped). The net amount of the invoice ($8,235.00) is restated at the bottom of the invoice, along with shipping charges and a COD fee that the buyer must pay, for a total of $8,267.85. The $4.35 fee is to cover the cost of having the driver who delivers the merchandise secure a check for $8,267.85 — before making delivery — and the cost to Emery (the transportation company) in issuing a check to Conodec Corporation for $8,235.00, the value of the merchandise.

MONTIEL SUPPLY COMPANY

1649 Circle Drive, N.W.
Buchanan, Michigan 49107
(616) 697-8131

INVOICE NO.
95113
INVOICE DATE
2/15/89

SOLD TO: Baldour Industries, Inc.   **SHIP TO:**   Same
501 Wickham Road
Melbourne, FL 32901

ACCOUNT NO: 58012

PURCHASE ORDER	SHIPPING DATE	SHIPPED VIA	TERMS OF SALE
16309	2/13/89	Central Couriers	2/10, n/30

UNITS ORDERED	UNITS SHIPPED	BACK ORDERED	ITEM NUMBER AND DESCRIPTION	LIST PRICE	NET PRICE	NET AMOUNT
12	12		310 ROM DRILL PRESS 10% discount	14.79	13.31	159.72
6	6		322 ROM MOTO TOOL 10% discount	29.61	26.65	159.90
6	6		410 ROM MOTO TOOL 10% discount	37.02	33.32	199.92
30	24	6	586 ROM 1/32 COLET	.95	.95	22.80

AMOUNT OF SALE	SHIPPING COST	PAY THIS AMOUNT	LESS DISCOUNT: $10.85
$ 542.34	$19.84	$ 562.18	IF PAID BY: 2/25/89

FOR PROPER CREDIT—RETURN REMITTANCE COPY WITH PAYMENT
Subject to terms and condition on this and reverse side of invoice

Figure 15.1 Sample Invoice

THE CONODEC CORPORATION

3299 SAN FERNANDO ROAD
LOS ANGELES CA 90065
(213) 258-7777 258-7778

PLEASE RECORD ACCOUNT
NUMBER ON YOUR CHECK
ACCOUNT NUMBER
034775

INVOICE NO.
006915

INVOICE DATE
8/22/89

SOLD TO:	SHIPPED TO:
CRYSTALINE CORP 300 WEST MADISON STREET CHICAGO IL 60606	CRYSTALINE CORP 6512 WEST JACKSON BLVD CHICAGO IL 60606

ORDER DATE	SHIPPING DATE	SHIPPED BY	CUST. ORD. NO.	FOB	TERMS
8-18-89	8-21-89	EMERY	A-12319	LA	COD

QUANTITY	DESCRIPTION	PRICE	AMOUNT
300	1 MM BULK PACK DRILL BITS	5.25	1,575.00
400	1.25 MM BULK PACK DRILL BITS	6.15	2,460.00
400	1.5 MM BULK DRILL BITS	10.50	4,200.00
			8,235.00

COLLECT ON DELIVERY	
MERCHANDISE	$ 8,235.00
SHIPPING	28.50
COD FEE	4.35
TOTAL	$ 8,267.85

ANY RETURNED MERCHANDISE SUBJECT
TO A 10 PERCENT RESTOCKING CHARGE

Figure 15.2 Sample Invoice

Self-Check 15B Sellers' Invoices

Use the following information to complete the invoice: Customer's purchase order is 29134, and the invoice number is 17311 dated June 5, 1990. The buyer is Cutlass Distributors at 1633 West Avenue, Chicago, Illinois, for shipment to their South Chicago warehouse at 15211 Beeline Highway. Shipment was made on June 4 via Milne Trucking Company, and freight costs are included in the prices charged, so that no separate freight charge need be shown on the invoice. The zip code for the Chicago addresses is 60607.

HARVILL & HANCOCK 816 Fifth Avenue New York, NY 10025			**Invoice Date**
Sold to:		**Ship to:**	

Purchase Order	Routing	Date Shipped	Terms:	

Quantity	Product Description	Price	Amount
983	032 × 6 × 36 silver sheet	0.213	
590	020 × 6 × 36 silver sheet	0.218	

Total Units	**Pay this amount by** _____ **Extended payment time extra 1%** **Total due in 30 days**	_____ _____ _____

Answers to Self-Checks

Self-Check 15A

1. $6,500

2. $130

3. $350.13

4. $14,619.90

Self-Check 15B

Amounts: $209.38; $128.62
Total units 1573
Amount to be paid: $338.00 by 6/15/90
Extended payment: $3.38
Total due in 30 days: $341.38

Transportation Costs and Commissions

1. **Transport costs and commissions (10 points each)**

a. If 1,000 units are shipped, with each unit weighing $22\frac{1}{2}$ pounds, what is the freight charge @ $1.35 per cwt?

b. If the net amount of an invoice is $1,200 and the freight cost is $150, what is the amount of the cash discount at 2/10, n/30 if the buyer makes payment within the discount period?

c. If the total amount of the goods sold is $800, with trade discounts of 10% and 5%, how much is the cash discount under terms of 2/10, 1/20, n/30 if the buyer makes payment 15 days after the date of the invoice?

d. If the value of the merchandise is $1,000, including $50 freight charges, how much may the buyer deduct for his cash discount if he makes payment within the discount period under terms of 2/10 EOM?

e. What is the net amount of an invoice for 500 items at $15 each with trade discounts of 5%, 3%, and 2%, and brokerage of 2%?

f. If merchandise costing $1,500 is subject to a trade discount totaling $150, how much will the broker earn at a commission rate of 3%?

g. How much must a retailer pay for 1,600 cases of canned goods priced at $15 per case, with each case weighing 31 pounds and freight costs of $1.85 per cwt FOB origin? The broker earns a commission of 2%, terms are 2/10, n/30, and the buyer makes payment within the discount period. Also, the seller prepays the freight charges and adds the cost to the invoice.

2.   Refer to the following invoice segment (5 points each)

Quantity	Description	Price	Amount
250	24/8 oz ABC stewed tomatoes	9.50	
	Less trade discount of 5%		

Add freight charges of 6,250 lb @ $2.25 cwt

Pay this amount by _____
If paid by _____ deduct
and pay this amount

a.   What is the dollar amount of the trade discount?

b.   What are the total freight charges?

c.   What is the net amount of this invoice?

d.   If the date of the invoice is August 10, 1990 and terms are 2/10, n/30, how much must the buyer pay if payment is made on or before August 20?

e.   If the rate of commission is 3%, how much must the seller pay the broker?

f.   Complete this partial invoice by entering your answers in the appropriate places.

1. Complete the following invoice (40 points)

Sold To	J.D. Smith Company 334 West Thomas Road Phoenix, AZ 85013	**CENTRAL SALES COMPANY** 11 Parkington Road Benson, Indiana 46204
Ship To	same	

Invoice No.	26141
Invoice Date	3/1/90

Purchase Order 16161	Terms 1/15, n/30	Shipped via Yellow Freight	☐ FOB Origin ☒ FOB Destination

Ordered	Shipped	Backordered	Number and Description	Price	Amount
12	12		120 Drill Presses	13.31	
3	3		322 Universal Stand	8.64	
6	6		802 Moto Tool	26.65	
6	6		830 Moto Tool	33.32	
36	24	12	482 Check Colet	0.50	
1	1		856 Merchandiser	165.92	
			⎾ CASH DISCOUNT ⏋		
			Deduct $ If paid by		
▲ Total	▲ Total	▲ Total			▲ Total Amount

2. Invoices (60 points)

Use the following data to complete the invoice: Sold to A. C. Jones, Inc., 1321 North Central Ave., Philadelphia, Pennsylvania 19104 and shipped via the Santa Fe Railway on February 13 to the same company at 14205 Buckeye Road, Philadelphia, PA 19106, 1,000 cases 48/2 SEA STAR tuna @ $18.50 per case with a trade discount of 50¢ per case and weighing 27 pounds per case. Freight charges are $2.75 per cwt, FOB origin and prepaid by West Bank. The selling broker is Gerber Bros., Inc., who earns a 3% commission. The buyer's purchase order number is S33341 and terms of sale are $1\frac{1}{2}/10$, n/30. The invoice number is 13205, the invoice date is February 15, and the product number is 22361.

WEST BANK SEAFOOD CORPORATION
223 West Seafood Lane
San Diego, CA 92101

SEA STAR

WHITE CAP

| Invoice No. |
| Invoice Date |

Sold To ⌐   ⌐   Ship To ⌐

| Selling broker | Transportation company | Shipping date |

| Customer purchase order | Terms of sale | |

Cases	Size	Description	Number	Price	Amount

☐ FOB Destination   Net value ▶

▲
Total Cases   ☒ **FOB** San Diego
_____ lb @ _____ cwt   Freight ▶

Cash Discount ▶   Deduct   if paid by _____   Total ▶

Retailers' Costs, Markups, and Prices

After reading Chapter 16, you will be able to

- Compute retail markups and explain the elements involved.
- Apply markups based on cost and on price.
- Determine cost, markup, or price, when any two of these three variables are known.
- Calculate the percent that markup is of cost and of price.
- Find the sale prices on items that have been marked down.

Key Terms

cost
markup
retail price

markup on cost
markup on price
markdown

Retailers, such as grocery and department stores, buy goods from manufacturers for resale to individuals like you and me—the ultimate consumers. When retailers pay the invoices that manufacturers mail to them, the manufacturers' prices become the retailers' costs for the items purchased.

If Appliance Mart (a retailer) buys new refrigerators from General Electric (a manufacturer) at a price of $450 each, for example, the General Electric price of $450 becomes the **cost** per unit to Appliance Mart. Appliance Mart must then add an amount (called a **markup**) to the cost to cover the expense of selling the refrigerator and to provide the store with a profit. The **retail price** that Appliance Mart charges its customers is the sum of the store's cost (the manufacturer's price) and the added markup. To determine the retail price of an item, we add the retailer's cost and markup. Figure 16.1 illustrates these relationships.

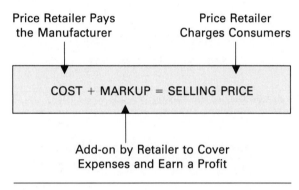

Figure 16.1   Retail Pricing

If, on the other hand, we know the selling price and the cost of an item, we can find the markup by subtracting cost from the selling price:

Finding Markup

Cost + Markup = Price

Markup = Price − Cost

or

$$M = P - C$$

As discussed in Chapter 4, we switch cost ($+C$) to the right of the equation and change its sign (to a $-C$).

Similarly, if we know the price and the markup, we can find cost by subtracting markup from the selling price:

Finding Cost

Cost + Markup = Price

Cost = Price − Markup

or

$$C = P - M$$

To determine cost, we switch markup $(+M)$ to the right of the equation and change its sign (to a $-M$).

Markup Based on Cost

Some retailers compute their markup on the cost of items purchased for resale. If an item cost $10 and the retailer wishes to add a **markup on cost** of 10 percent, for instance, the selling price is $11:

$$\text{Cost} \times 10\% = \text{Markup}$$
$$\$10 \times 0.10 = \quad \$1$$
$$\text{Cost} + \text{Markup} = \text{Price}$$
$$\$10 + \quad \$1 \quad = \$11$$

A shortcut method of computing the selling price is to multiply the cost times "1 plus the percent markup":

$$\text{Cost} \times (1 + \% \text{ Markup}) = \text{Price}$$
$$\$10 \times \quad (1.00 + 0.10) \quad = \text{Price}$$
$$\$10 \times \quad \quad 1.10 \quad \quad = \$11$$

Self-Check 16A   *Markup Based on Cost*

1. If the price is $12 and the cost $8.50, what is the amount of markup?

2. If the cost is $1.65 and the markup based on cost is $5\frac{1}{2}\%$, what is the selling price?

3. Using the shortcut method, find the selling price of an item that cost $27 and carries a markup on cost of 15%.

4. If the selling price of an item is $69.45 and the markup is $12.45, what is the retailer's cost?

5. If a retailer pays a manufacturer $1,250 each for personal computers, to which a markup of $275 is added, what is the retail price?

Markup Based on Price

Many retailers like to base their markup on the prices that they charge. Unlike markups based on cost, in which we know the cost, we must now find the price. To illustrate, assume that a retailer pays $150 for a piece of furniture and that he wants to earn a **markup on price** of 45 percent. We may use a simple equation to find the price to be charged, or we may memorize a formula:

Equation	*Formula*

$$\text{Cost} + \text{Markup} = \text{Price} \qquad \frac{\text{Cost}}{1 - \text{Markup}} = \text{Price}$$

$$150 + 0.45P = P \qquad\qquad \frac{150}{1.00 - 0.45} = \text{Price}$$

$$150 = P - 0.45P$$

$$150 = 0.55P \qquad\qquad \frac{150}{0.55} = \$272.73$$

$$\$272.73 = P$$

Using the first approach, we begin with the equation Cost + Markup = Price. We enter the cost of $150 and make price ($P$) the unknown. Because we know that markup is to be 45 percent of price, we show it as 45 percent of the unknown price ($0.45P$). We gather the terms by moving the $+0.45P$ to the right of the equal sign and changing the sign. Then, remembering the P is the same as $1P$, we subtract ($1.00P - 0.45P = 0.55P$) and divide the difference into the cost ($150 \div 0.55 = 272.73$).

Using the formula approach, we divide the cost by 1 minus the percentage markup. Although the formula may appear easier than the equation, the formula approach requires memorization.

At this point, you may be wondering why some retailers choose cost as the basis for adding a markup and some retailers choose price. The decision is generally based on custom. A retailer may price frozen dinners on the basis of markup as a percent of cost, for instance, because that approach has become traditional within the frozen food industry.

Self-Check 16B Markup Based on Price

1. If cost is $16.00 and markup is $2.50, what is price?

2. Find the markup and the price on an item that costs $80, for a retailer who wishes to earn a markup of 15% on the price.

3. If the markup on price is 20% and cost is $15.50, what is the price?

4. If the retail price is $26.50 and the markup on price is 12%, what is the retailer's cost for the item?

5. A bookstore paid $12.95 each for 50 copies of a bestseller, to which a markup of 20% on price was added. What was the amount of the markup on each book?

Markdowns

Markdowns are reductions in retail prices. Retailers occasionally lower the prices of their goods as a way of increasing sales, and they generally base the reductions on the selling price. A retailer may decide to lower the $95 selling price of a bicycle by 15 percent of the selling price, for example, which would result in a new price of $80.75.

$$\text{Price} \times \% = \text{Markdown}$$
$$95.00 \times 0.15 = 14.25$$
$$\text{Price} - \text{Markdown} = \text{New price}$$
$$95.00 - 14.25 = \$80.75$$

A shortcut method of figuring markdowns is to subtract the percentage of the price reduction from 1 and multiply the difference by the price:

$$1.00 - 0.15 = 0.85$$
$$95.00 \times 0.85 = \$80.75$$

Self-Check 16C   Markdowns

---

1. If a retailer decides to mark down men's shirts that are selling for $14.99 by 12%, what price must he charge?

2. If the managers of a department store reduce all prices within a department by 15%, by how much should a $4.95 item be reduced?

3. What is the new price on skirts that were previously priced at $38 each following a markdown on price of 23%?

4. If your supervisor directs you to mark prices to reflect a markdown of 20%, what prices would you mark on items that were priced at $79.50, $129.95, and $59.00?

Finding the Percent Markup

As discussed earlier in this chapter, retailers may base their markups on either the cost or the price of the products being sold. Although retailers may know the cost of an item and the price they are charging for it, they also need to know the percent of the markup. Knowing the percent markup is important because costs and expenses change. Current prices may cover costs and expenses plus a reasonable profit, but if costs or expenses increase, as they have in recent years, knowing the percent markup makes it easier for retailers to establish new prices. Consider the following example:

$$\text{Cost} + \text{Markup} = \text{Price}$$
$$10 + 5 = \$15$$

To find the percent that markup is of cost, we divide markup by cost:

$$\textbf{Markup} \div \textbf{Cost} = \textbf{\% Markup on cost}$$
$$5 \div 10 = 0.50 = 50\%$$

We are actually asking what percent 5 is of 10, so we divide 5 by 10. Correspondingly, we find the percent that markup is of price by dividing markup by price:

$$\textbf{Markup} \div \textbf{Price} = \textbf{\% Markup on price}$$
$$5 \div 15 = 0.333 = 33\frac{1}{3}\%$$

To summarize, we find the percent of markup based on cost by dividing markup by cost, and we find the percent of markup based on price by dividing markup by price.

Self-Check 16D   Finding the Percent Markup

---

1. If an item that is selling for $250 carries a markup of $60, what is the percent markup based on price?

2. If an item that costs $45 is priced at $60, what percent is markup of cost? (Round answer to tenths of a percent.)

3. If the cost is $2.16 and the markup is 54¢, what is the percent markup based on price?

4. If a retailer pays $48 for a pair of shoes, to which he adds a 25% markup on price, what is the markup on cost? (Round answer to tenths of a percent.)

5. If a retailer pays 69¢ a pound for apples, to which a markup of 15¢ per pound is added, what is the markup as a percent of cost? (Round answer to tenths of a percent.)

Finding Cost and Price

Retailers often must use the type of retail mathematics that we have been discussing to find (1) the prices that they are willing and able to pay the manufacturers for products and (2) the prices that they must charge to cover the expenses of selling and to make a certain percent profit. Remember that the retailer's markup must be high enough to cover expenses and to provide a reasonable profit.

If a retailer knows that to compete with other stores he can sell a certain product for just $4.99, for example, how much can he afford to pay a manufacturer for the product and still realize a 15 percent markup on cost? Recalling that the manufacturer's price for a product is the retailer's cost, we make cost (C) the unknown. And because the retailer desires a markup that is 15 percent of cost, we make markup $0.15C$.

<table>
<tr><td align="center">Equation</td><td align="center">Formula</td></tr>
<tr><td>Cost + Markup = Price</td><td rowspan="2">$\dfrac{\text{Price}}{1.00 + \text{Markup}} = \text{Cost}$</td></tr>
<tr><td>$C \;+\; 0.15C \;=\; 4.99$</td></tr>
<tr><td>$1.15C = 4.99$ or</td><td>$\dfrac{4.99}{1.00 + 0.15} = \text{Cost}$</td></tr>
<tr><td>$C = 4.99 \div 1.15$</td><td></td></tr>
<tr><td>$C = \$4.34$</td><td>$\dfrac{4.99}{1.15} = \$4.34$</td></tr>
</table>

Finding the unknown cost (C) to be $4.34, we calculate markup at 65¢ ($4.34 \times 0.15 = 0.65$). We can then check our answer by entering the cost and markup amounts into our equation:

$$\text{Cost} + \text{Markup} = \text{Price}$$
$$4.34 + \quad 0.65 \quad = \$4.99$$

Because 4.34 plus 0.65 equals $4.99, we know that the retailer can pay as much as $4.34 for the item, sell it for $4.99, and earn a markup of 65¢, which is the desired 15 percent of cost.

Another computation that retailers often must make is to find the price to charge when markup is based on price. If the cost of a product is $140 and the retailer desires a markup of 11 percent based on price, for example, we follow the same procedure that we used in the second part of this chapter for finding markup based on price:

<table>
<tr><td align="center">Equation</td><td align="center">Formula</td></tr>
<tr><td>Cost + Markup = Price</td><td>$\dfrac{\text{Cost}}{1.00 - \text{Markup}} = \text{Price}$</td></tr>
<tr><td>$140 \;+\; 0.11P \;=\; P$</td><td></td></tr>
<tr><td>$140 = P - 0.11P$ or</td><td>$\dfrac{140}{1.00 - 0.11} = \text{Price}$</td></tr>
<tr><td>$140 = 0.89P$</td><td></td></tr>
<tr><td>$140 \div 0.89 = P$</td><td>$140 \div 0.89 = \$157.30$</td></tr>
<tr><td>$\$157.30 = P$</td><td></td></tr>
</table>

Finding the unknown price (P) to be $157.30, we calculate markup at $17.30 (157.30 $\times$ 0.11 = 17.30). We then check the answer by entering the price and markup amounts into our equation:

$$\text{Cost} + \text{Markup} = \text{Price}$$
$$140.00 + 17.30 = \$157.30$$

To earn an 11 percent markup on price for an item costing $140.00, therefore, the retailer must charge a price of $157.30.

Self-Check 16E   Finding Cost and Price

---

1. How much can a retailer afford to pay for a product that can be priced at $9.50, if he must have a markup of 23% of cost to cover expenses and to provide the desired profit margin?

2. If the manufacturer charges $12 each for neckties, what price must the retailer charge if he is to realize a markup of 25% based on price?

3. If a retailer adds a 32% markup on cost to derive a selling price of $56.10, what amount did the retailer pay for the item?

Answers to Self-Checks

Self-Check 16A	**Self-Check 16B**	**Self-Check 16C**	**Self-Check 16D**	**Self-Check 16E**
1. $3.50	1. $18.50	1. $13.19	1. 24%	1. $7.72
2. $1.74	2. $14.12, $94.12	2. 74¢	2. 33.3%	2. $16
3. $31.05	3. $19.38	3. $29.26	3. 20%	3. $42.50
4. $57.00	4. $23.32	4. $0.80 $63.60 $103.96 $47.20	4. 33.3%	
5. $1,525	5. $3.24		5. 21.7%	

Markup and Markdown

1. Markup based on cost (5 points each)

a. If the cost is $250 and the markup based on cost is 12%, what is the selling price?

b. Find the selling price of an item that costs $16 and carries a markup on cost of 15%.

c. If markup based on cost is 23%, and cost is $64, what is the selling price?

2. Markup based on price (5 points each)

a. If a retailer pays $68 each for a certain style of women's dress, how much markup must he add to this cost if he desires a 50% markup based on price?

b. If the markup on price is 25% and the cost is $14.60, what is the selling price?

c. What is the retail price of an office machine that costs the retailer $325 if the markup on price is 35%?

3. Markdowns (5 points each)

a. If a retailer marks down blouses that are selling for $36 by 15%, what is the new price?

b. What is the reduced price of a $650 refrigerator that is marked down by $7\frac{1}{2}$%?

c. At what price should a retailer sell a can of peaches if a price of 60¢ per can is to be reduced by 15%?

4. **Mixture of markup and markdown problems (5 points each)**

a. If a retailer buys a filing cabinet from the manufacturer for $65 and adds a markup of 25% of the selling price, what is the selling price?

b. What is the price of an $85 bedspread that has been marked down 10%?

c. What is the retail price of a loaf of bread that costs the retailer 90¢, if the retailer adds a markup of 15% of the cost?

d. Find the retail price of a chair that the manufacturer sells for $375 if the retailer is to realize a markup of 40% on his cost.

e. If the markup on the price of a new stereo system is 35% and the retailer's cost for the system is $850, what is the retailer's price?

f. Find the retail price of alarm clocks that the manufacturer sells for $7.50 each, so that the retailer will realize a markup on cost of 16%.

g. A retailer has been selling tires at a price of $75 each. For how much will he sell them after marking them down 5%?

h. If a retailer pays $450 for a mattress and boxspring combination and expects to earn a markup of 28% based on price, what price should he charge for the item?

i. How much should a retailer charge for an electric toaster if he desires an 8% markup based on cost and the toaster cost $21.50?

j. Find the markup and the selling price for carpeting that costs the retailer $23 per square yard, if the markup on selling price is to be 20%.

k. If a retailer reduces the price of women's purses from $35 to $29.75, what is the percent markdown?

Percent Markup, Cost, and Price

1. Percent markup (round answers to tenths) (5 points each)

a. If a piece of furniture is selling for $495, what is the markup based on cost if cost is $250?

b. If a used car costs the dealer $4,500 and he adds a markup of $500, what percent is his markup of the selling price?

c. In Problem 1.b, what percent is the dealer's markup on cost?

2. Retailer's cost (5 points each)

a. What price did a retailer pay for CB radios that he sells for $125, if his markup on cost is 20%?

b. How much can a retailer afford to pay for CB radios that he can sell for $99.99 if he is to realize a 15% markup on cost?

c. What is the cost of an item that sells for $18.50 after a markup of $3.50 has been added to cost?

3. Retailer's price (5 points each)

a. If the manufacturer charges the retailer $45 each for ping-pong tables, what price must the retailer charge his customers to realize a 15% markup on price?

b. If the manufacturer charges $825 for color TVs, what price must the retailer charge to earn a markup of 22% of the price?

c. Find the retail price of an item that costs the retailer $33, if the markup on price is 6%.

4.   Mixture of percent and cost-price problems (5 points each)

a. If a bookstore is selling a new book for $15
and the markup is 20% of the price, how
much did the bookstore pay the publisher for
the book?

b. If a new book that is priced at $18.00 carries
a markup of $3.60, what percent is the
markup based on cost?

c. If a bookstore is selling a $15 book that is
marked up 20% on cost, what did the book
cost the bookstore?

d. If a bookstore is selling a $12.00 book
(publisher's price) to students for $14.50,
what percent is the markup of the price?
(Round to 1 place.)

e. In Problem 4.d, what is the percent markup
based on cost? (Round to 2 places.)

f. If, after adding a markup of 15¢, the price of
toothpaste is 95¢, what percent is the markup
of cost? (Round to tenths.)

g. What should the retail price be for packages
of rubber gloves if the retailer pays the
manufacturer $1.50 per package and marks
the gloves up 12% of the price?

h. If a dealer buys men's ties for $8.50 each
and adds a markup of 40% on cost, what
percent is his markup of the price? (Round
to tenths.)

i. If a competing retailer is selling carpeting at
$19.95 per yard, after having added a
markup of 20% of his cost, how much did he
pay the manufacturer for the carpeting?

j. Determine the cost of a new motor bike that
is selling for $250, if the retailer is adding a
markup of 25% of his cost.

k. If a retailer buys a product from the
manufacturer for 36¢ and marks up the item
by 4¢, what is the retailer's price?

Mathematics of Marketing

1. Manufacturer's prices and discounts (5 points each)

a. What is the net price of a case of auto polish (in cans) that lists for $15.50 per case with a trade discount of 8% per case?

b. If the manufacturer sells a box of wrenches at a price of $24.25, a price that is subject to trade discounts of 5% and 10%, what is the amount of the discount?

c. In Problem 1.b, what is the equivalent (actual) percentage of discount? (Round answer to tenths of a percent.)

d. If a manufacturer makes a sale totaling $2,500, with terms of $1\frac{1}{2}/10$, n/30, how much money should the buyer remit if payment is made within the discount period?

e. In Problem 1.d, if the buyer sends a $1,000 check to the manufacturer within the discount period, how much will he still owe the manufacturer?

2. Transport costs, commissions, and invoices (5 points each)

a. How much money must a canning company pay a broker for selling $750 worth of merchandise, if the commission rate is 3%? The $750 includes freight charges of $50.

b. If the value of a purchase is $1,500, including freight charges of $250, how much money may the buyer deduct for his cash discount, providing that he makes payment within the discount period and terms are 2/10 EOM?

c. How much money must the buyer (the receiver of goods) pay the transportation company if freight charges are $550, FOB destination?

d. What are the transportation costs for a shipment of 1,250 units weighing 31 pounds each at a rate of $5.50 cwt?

e. At a commission rate of 3%, how much money will a broker earn for sales totaling $2,150, including freight charges of $150?

3. Retailers' costs, markups, and prices (5 points each)

a. If the cost is $16.75 and the markup based on cost is 18%, what is the selling price?

b. If the markup on selling price is 23% and the cost is $4.25, what is the selling price?

c. If the selling price is $4.99 and the cost is $3.25, what is the amount of the markup?

d. If the prices of all men's shirts are reduced by 25%, what is the new price of a shirt that was priced at $25?

e. If a microwave oven that sells for $550 carries a markup of $150, what is the percent markup based on price? (Round answer to tenths of a percent.)

f. In Problem 3.e, what is the percent markup based on cost? (Round answer to tenths of a percent.)

g. If a used car dealer can sell a 3-year-old Plymouth for $2,500, how much can he afford to pay for the car and still earn a markup on his costs of 25%?

h. If a retailer pays the manufacturer $46.50 for a lady's shoe and adds a 36% markup on cost, what is the retailer's selling price?

i. A jeweler pays a Japanese manufacturer $86.00 each for a new style of men's watch and sells it for $180.60. What is the percent markup based on price? (Round answer to tenths of a percent.)

j. In Problem 3.i, what is the percent markup based on cost?

PART

5

Mathematics of Accounting

17. Payroll Records

Prorating Salaries
Calculating Gross Pay
Figuring Deductions
Payroll Records

18. Business Taxes

Employee Taxes
Excise and Sales Taxes
Corporate Income Tax
Property Taxes

19. Depreciation Schedules

Straight-Line Depreciation
Accelerated Cost Recovery
Real Estate

20. Inventory Valuation

Inventory Records
Specific Identification
Average Cost
FIFO and LIFO

Payroll Records

After reading Chapter 17, you will be able to

- Prorate annual salaries on the basis of weekly, biweekly, semimonthly, and monthly paydays.
- Calculate gross pay on the basis of both regular and overtime rates, as well as earnings based on piecework schedules.
- Figure payroll deductions such as federal income taxes and Social Security contributions, using both percentage methods and tables.
- Compute net (take-home) pay following deductions.
- Maintain and cross-check payroll records.

Key Terms

overtime

piecework

commission

gross pay

federal income tax

net pay

Social Security

Federal Insurance Contribution
    Act (FICA)

take-home pay

This chapter is important for two reasons. First, you should be able to double-check your employer to make certain that your pay and the deductions from your pay are correct. Second, you may become directly involved with payroll. Secretaries and office managers often maintain payroll records in small companies. Many students find employment in the payroll departments of large companies, and students who achieve positions in the personnel departments of large companies often become involved in payroll preparation.

Prorating Salaries

Many companies place their nonunion employees on salary. Rather than paying office workers hourly rates, for example, a company might pay them monthly or annual salaries. The payment of monthly or annual salaries does not mean that employees must wait that long to receive their pay; actual payment may be made weekly or biweekly (every 2 weeks). To prorate Maria Rodriguez's annual salary of $22,000 into biweekly payments, we determine the weekly salary and multiply by 2.

$$\frac{\text{Annual}}{\text{salary}} \div \text{Weeks} = \frac{\text{Weekly}}{\text{salary}}$$
$$\$22,000 \div 52 = \$423.08$$

$$\frac{\text{Weekly}}{\text{salary}} \times 2 \text{ Weeks} = \frac{\text{Biweekly}}{\text{salary}}$$
$$\$423.08 \times 2 = \$846.16$$

Or, knowing that there are 26 two-week periods in a year, we may simply divide the annual salary by 26:

$$\frac{\text{Annual}}{\text{salary}} \div 26 \text{ Periods} = \frac{\text{Biweekly}}{\text{salary}}$$
$$\$22,000 \div 26 = \$846.15$$

Notice that the two answers differ by one cent. Such differences occur frequently when prorating salaries because we must round our answers to the cents (hundredths) position.

Assume, instead, that Maria is paid on a semimonthly (twice a month) basis. To prorate her $22,000 annual salary on a semimonthly basis, we find the monthly salary and divide by 2. Or, knowing that paydays twice each month result in 24 paydays a year ($2 \times 12 = 24$), we simply divide the annual salary by 24:

$$\frac{\text{Annual}}{\text{salary}} \div \text{Months in a year} = \frac{\text{Monthly}}{\text{salary}}$$
$$\$22,000 \div 12 = \$1,833.33$$

$$\frac{\text{Monthly}}{\text{salary}} \div \text{Twice a month} = \frac{\text{Semimonthly}}{\text{salary}}$$
$$\$1,833.33 \div 2 = \$916.67$$

or

$$\begin{array}{ccccc} \text{Annual} & & & & \text{Semimonthly} \\ \text{salary} & \div & \text{24 Periods} & = & \text{salary} \\ \$22,000 & \div & 24 & = & \$916.67 \end{array}$$

You may wonder why the biweekly salary ($846.16) differs from the semi-monthly salary ($916.67). The differences exist because there are more than 4 weeks in a month. Only February has exactly 4 weeks (28 days, except during leap year); all other months have either 30 or 31 days. This point is important to remember when computing payroll.

Self-Check 17A   Prorating Salaries
---

1. If Jonathan Mead earns an annual salary of $18,500, what is his semimonthly salary?

2. If, in Problem 1, Mead were to be paid every other Friday instead, what amount would be due him?

3. Rhonda Jackson has just been employed at an annual salary of $24,250. What is her salary on a biweekly basis?

4. Continuing with Problem 3, what would Jackson's income be on a semimonthly basis?

Calculating Gross Pay

Gross pay is the total amount of wages that employers pay employees before deducting federal and state income tax, Social Security payments, and employee contributions to programs such as health insurance, retirement plans, and union dues. Wages are usually hourly rates. If employees earn $5.50 per hour, for example, they will earn $220 for a 40-hour week ($5.50 \times 40 = 220$). When employees work longer than 40 hours per week, the additional time worked is called **overtime**, and the rate of overtime is usually $1\frac{1}{2}$ times the regular rate. At 5.50 per hour for regular time, therefore, employees will earn $8.25 per hour for overtime ($5.50 \times 1\frac{1}{2} = 8.25$).

To illustrate further, assume that Stephen Keating worked 8 hours on Monday, 10 hours on Tuesday, 9 hours on Wednesday, 10 hours on Thursday, and 8 hours on Friday. We compute the weekly wage in four steps:

Step 1

Total the hours.

$$8 + 10 + 9 + 10 + 8 = 45$$

Step 2

Compute regular pay.

40 hours × $5.50 = $220.00

Step 3

Compute overtime pay.

5 hours × $8.25 = $41.25

Step 4

Compute total pay.

$220.00 + $41.25 = $261.25

The employer has paid a penalty of $13.75 for this employee's working overtime (time in excess of 40 hours per week). Instead of paying the regular rate of $5.50 per hour for the 5 hours overtime, the employer has paid an extra $2.75 for each overtime hour ($2.75 × 5 = $13.75).

When a **piecework** program is in effect, earnings are figured on the number of units (pieces) that a worker produces. For example, a worker may earn 50¢ for every shirt on which cuffs are sewn, so that an employee who attaches cuffs to 482 shirts during a 40-hour week will gross $241.

$$\textbf{Units × Rate = Weekly pay}$$
$$482 \times 0.50 = \$241.00$$

Similarly, many salespeople work on a **commission** basis, under which earnings are usually based on the total value of sales. An employee working under a commission of $6\frac{1}{2}$ percent, for instance, would receive on sales of $18,615.00 a commission of $1,209.98.

$$\textbf{Sales × Rate = Commission}$$
$$18,615 \times 0.065 = \$1,209.98$$

Employers sometimes guarantee new employees a minimum salary, to provide a degree of security until they have had time to build sales to a level at which they can earn liveable incomes on commissions.

Self-Check 17B   Calculating Gross Pay

Calculate gross pay in the following situations, assuming that overtime is paid at $1\frac{1}{2}$ times the regular rate for time worked in excess of 40 hours per week.

1. What is the total pay for a person who works 43 hours during the week at a rate of $6.75 per hour?

2. If an employee receives a guaranteed monthly salary of $500 plus a commission of $2\frac{1}{2}$% of monthly sales totaling $25,200, what is that person's gross pay for the one month?

3. What is the total pay for an employee who produces 121 items during the week at a piecework rate of $0.56?

4. If a real estate agent sells a property for $110,500 and receives a partial commission of 2%, what is the amount received?

Figuring Deductions

Employers may either use the percentage method to figure the amount of **federal income tax** to withhold from the earnings of their employees, or they may use tax tables.

The **percentage method,** which is especially useful for computerized payroll, involves a two-step process:

Step 1

Deduct from gross pay an amount for any withholding allowances claimed, as provided in Table 17.1.

Step 2

Determine the tax by applying the adjusted gross pay to Table 17.2.

Table 17.1 provides for a withholding allowance of $37.50 for each allowance from weekly pay, $75.00 from biweekly pay, $81.25 from semimonthly pay, and so on.

Payroll Period	One With- holding Allowance
Weekly.............................	$ 37.50
Biweekly...........................	75.00
Semimonthly......................	81.25
Monthly...........................	162.50
Quarterly..........................	487.50
Semiannually.....................	975.00
Annually..........................	1,950.00
Daily or miscellaneous (each day of the payroll period)	7.50

Table 17.1 Deductions for Withholding Allowances

For an employee with biweekly gross pay of $675 and three withholding allowances (two adults and a child), we deduct $225 (75 × 3 = 225).

$$\textbf{Gross pay} - (\textbf{3} \times \textbf{75}) = \textbf{Taxable amount}$$
$$675 \quad - \quad 225 \quad = \quad \$450$$

In the second step, we take the taxable amount to Table 17.2, which also categorizes the entries according to payroll period (weekly, biweekly, etc.). We move downward to the biweekly payroll period (the second category on the page), where the rates at right are for married taxpayers. Because the $450 is over $117 but not over $1,262, the tax rate is 15 percent of any excess over $117.

Percentage Calculation

$$450 - 117 = 333.00$$
$$333 \times 0.15 = \$49.95$$

If we wish to avoid the calculations involved with the percentage method, we may refer to Table 17.3, which is one page of a multipage table obtained from the IRS. In the preceding situation, we refer to this table for married employees with biweekly paydays. To figure the tax deduction for a married employee who grosses $675 every other week and who has three allowances, we look down the two columns at left until we find the row that reads "at least 660 but less than 680" and then read across to the column for three allowances (see the row across the top of the table) and find a tax deduction of $49.

Because the table deals with only even dollars, the deduction figured with the percentage method turns out to be 95¢ higher than the deduction found using Table 17.3. Slight differences will be experienced between the two methods, but adjustments are made at the end of the year, with the employee either making an additional payment or receiving a refund. (For a complete set of tax tables that are revised every January, request Circular E from the local Internal Revenue Service.)

If the Payroll Period With Respect to an Employee Is Weekly

(a) SINGLE person—including head of household:

If the amount of wages (after subtracting withholding allowances) is:		The amount of income tax to be withheld shall be:	
Not over $20		.0	
Over—	But not over—		of excess over—
$20	—$363 .	. 15%	—$20
$363	—$850 .	. $51.49 plus 28%	—$363
$850	—$1,953 .	. $187.72 plus 33%	—$850
$1,953 .	. . . . .	. $551.55 plus 28%	—$1,953

(b) MARRIED person—

If the amount of wages (after subtracting withholding allowances) is:		The amount of income tax to be withheld shall be:	
Not over $59		.0	
Over—	But not over—		of excess over—
$59	—$631	. 15%	—$59
$631	—$1,441	. $85.82 plus 28%	—$631
$1,441	—$3,559	. $312.78 plus 33%	—$1,441
$3,559 .	. . . .	. $1,011.55 plus 28%	—$3,559

If the Payroll Period With Respect to an Employee Is Biweekly

(a) SINGLE person—including head of household:

If the amount of wages (after subtracting withholding allowances) is:		The amount of income tax to be withheld shall be:	
Not over $40		.0	
Over—	But not over—		of excess over—
$40	—$727 .	. 15%	—$40
$727	—$1,700 .	. $102.98 plus 28%	—$727
$1,700	—$3,905 .	. $375.44 plus 33%	—$1,700
$3,905 .	. . . .	. $1,103.09 plus 28%	—$3,905

(b) MARRIED person—

If the amount of wages (after subtracting withholding allowances) is:		The amount of income tax to be withheld shall be:	
Not over $117		.0	
Over—	But not over—		of excess over—
$117	—$1,262	. 15%	—$117
$1,262	—$2,883	. $171.63 plus 28%	—$1,262
$2,883	—$7,118	. $625.56 plus 33%	—$2,883
$7,118 .	. . . . .	. $2,023.11 plus 28%	—$7,118

If the Payroll Period With Respect to an Employee Is Semimonthly

(a) SINGLE person—including head of household:

If the amount of wages (after subtracting withholding allowances) is:		The amount of income tax to be withheld shall be:	
Not over $44		.0	
Over—	But not over—		of excess over—
$44	—$788 .	. 15%	—$44
$788	—$1,842 .	. $111.56 plus 28%	—$788
$1,842	—$4,230 .	. $406.73 plus 33%	—$1,842
$4,230 .	. . . .	. $1,195.02 plus 28%	—$4,230

(b) MARRIED person—

If the amount of wages (after subtracting withholding allowances) is:		The amount of income tax to be withheld shall be:	
Not over $127		.0	
Over—	But not over—		of excess over—
$127	—$1,367	. 15%	—$127
$1,367	—$3,123	. $185.94 plus 28%	—$1,367
$3,123	—$7,711	. $677.69 plus 33%	—$3,123
$7,711 .	. . . .	. $2,191.70 plus 28%	—$7,711

If the Payroll Period With Respect to an Employee Is Monthly

(a) SINGLE person—including head of household:

If the amount of wages (after subtracting withholding allowances) is:		The amount of income tax to be withheld shall be:	
Not over $88		.0	
Over—	But not over—		of excess over—
$88	—$1,575 .	. 15%	—$88
$1,575	—$3,683 .	. $223.13 plus 28%	—$1,575
$3,683	—$8,461 .	. $813.46 plus 33%	—$3,683
$8,461	. . . . .	. $2,390.03 plus 28%	—$8,461

(b) MARRIED person—

If the amount of wages (after subtracting withholding allowances) is:		The amount of income tax to be withheld shall be:	
Not over $254		.0	
Over—	But not over—		of excess over—
$254	—$2,733	. 15%	—$254
$2,733	—$6,246	. $371.88 plus 28%	—$2,733
$6,246	—$15,422	. $1,355.38 plus 33%	—$6,246
$15,422 .	. . . .	. $4,383.40 plus 28%	—$15,422

Table 17.2 Percentage Method of Withholding

And the wages are–		And the number of withholding allowances claimed is–										
At least	But less than	0	1	2	3	4	5	6	7	8	9	10
		The amount of income tax to be withheld shall be–										
$0	$120	$0	$0	$0	$0	$0	$0	$0	$0	$0	$0	$0
120	125	1	0	0	0	0	0	0	0	0	0	0
125	130	2	0	0	0	0	0	0	0	0	0	0
130	135	2	0	0	0	0	0	0	0	0	0	0
135	140	3	0	0	0	0	0	0	0	0	0	0
140	145	4	0	0	0	0	0	0	0	0	0	0
145	150	5	0	0	0	0	0	0	0	0	0	0
150	155	5	0	0	0	0	0	0	0	0	0	0
155	160	6	0	0	0	0	0	0	0	0	0	0
160	165	7	0	0	0	0	0	0	0	0	0	0
165	170	8	0	0	0	0	0	0	0	0	0	0
170	175	8	0	0	0	0	0	0	0	0	0	0
175	180	9	0	0	0	0	0	0	0	0	0	0
180	185	10	0	0	0	0	0	0	0	0	0	0
185	190	11	0	0	0	0	0	0	0	0	0	0
190	195	11	0	0	0	0	0	0	0	0	0	0
195	200	12	1	0	0	0	0	0	0	0	0	0
200	205	13	2	0	0	0	0	0	0	0	0	0
205	210	14	2	0	0	0	0	0	0	0	0	0
210	215	14	3	0	0	0	0	0	0	0	0	0
215	220	15	4	0	0	0	0	0	0	0	0	0
220	225	16	5	0	0	0	0	0	0	0	0	0
225	230	17	5	0	0	0	0	0	0	0	0	0
230	235	17	6	0	0	0	0	0	0	0	0	0
235	240	18	7	0	0	0	0	0	0	0	0	0
240	245	19	8	0	0	0	0	0	0	0	0	0
245	250	20	8	0	0	0	0	0	0	0	0	0
250	260	21	9	0	0	0	0	0	0	0	0	0
260	270	22	11	0	0	0	0	0	0	0	0	0
270	280	24	12	1	0	0	0	0	0	0	0	0
280	290	25	14	3	0	0	0	0	0	0	0	0
290	300	27	15	4	0	0	0	0	0	0	0	0
300	310	28	17	6	0	0	0	0	0	0	0	0
310	320	30	18	7	0	0	0	0	0	0	0	0
320	330	31	20	9	0	0	0	0	0	0	0	0
330	340	33	21	10	0	0	0	0	0	0	0	0
340	350	34	23	12	0	0	0	0	0	0	0	0
350	360	36	24	13	2	0	0	0	0	0	0	0
360	370	37	26	15	3	0	0	0	0	0	0	0
370	380	39	27	16	5	0	0	0	0	0	0	0
380	390	40	29	18	6	0	0	0	0	0	0	0
390	400	42	30	19	8	0	0	0	0	0	0	0
400	410	43	32	21	9	0	0	0	0	0	0	0
410	420	45	33	22	11	0	0	0	0	0	0	0
420	430	46	35	24	12	1	0	0	0	0	0	0
430	440	48	36	25	14	3	0	0	0	0	0	0
440	450	49	38	27	15	4	0	0	0	0	0	0
450	460	51	39	28	17	6	0	0	0	0	0	0
460	470	52	41	30	18	7	0	0	0	0	0	0
470	480	54	42	31	20	9	0	0	0	0	0	0
480	490	55	44	33	21	10	0	0	0	0	0	0
490	500	57	45	34	23	12	0	0	0	0	0	0
500	520	59	48	36	25	14	3	0	0	0	0	0
520	540	62	51	39	28	17	6	0	0	0	0	0
540	560	65	54	42	31	20	9	0	0	0	0	0
560	580	68	57	45	34	23	12	0	0	0	0	0
580	600	71	60	48	37	26	15	3	0	0	0	0
600	620	74	63	51	40	29	18	6	0	0	0	0
620	640	77	66	54	43	32	21	9	0	0	0	0
640	660	80	69	57	46	35	24	12	1	0	0	0
660	680	83	72	60	49	38	27	15	4	0	0	0
680	700	86	75	63	52	41	30	18	7	0	0	0
700	720	89	78	66	55	44	33	21	10	0	0	0
720	740	92	81	69	58	47	36	24	13	2	0	0
740	760	95	84	72	61	50	39	27	16	5	0	0
760	780	98	87	75	64	53	42	30	19	8	0	0
780	800	101	90	78	67	56	45	33	22	11	0	0
800	820	104	93	81	70	59	48	36	25	14	3	0
820	840	107	96	84	73	62	51	39	28	17	6	0
840	860	110	99	87	76	65	54	42	31	20	9	0

Table 17.3   Table for Married Persons with a Biweekly Payroll Period

Wages at least	But less than	Tax to be withheld	Wages at least	But less than	Tax to be withheld	Wages at least	But less than	Tax to be withheld	Wages at least	But less than	Tax to be withheld
51.07	51.20	3.84	63.72	63.85	4.79	76.37	76.50	5.74	89.02	89.15	6.69
51.20	51.34	3.85	63.85	63.99	4.80	76.50	76.64	5.75	89.15	89.29	6.70
51.34	51.47	3.86	63.99	64.12	4.81	76.64	76.77	5.76	89.29	89.42	6.71
51.47	51.60	3.87	64.12	64.25	4.82	76.77	76.90	5.77	89.42	89.55	6.72
51.60	51.74	3.88	64.25	64.39	4.83	76.90	77.04	5.78	89.55	89.69	6.73
51.74	51.87	3.89	64.39	64.52	4.84	77.04	77.17	5.79	89.69	89.82	6.74
51.87	52.00	3.90	64.52	64.65	4.85	77.17	77.30	5.80	89.82	89.95	6.75
52.00	52.14	3.91	64.65	64.79	4.86	77.30	77.44	5.81	89.95	90.08	6.76
52.14	52.27	3.92	64.79	64.92	4.87	77.44	77.57	5.82	90.08	90.22	6.77
52.27	52.40	3.93	64.92	65.05	4.88	77.57	77.70	5.83	90.22	90.35	6.78
52.40	52.53	3.94	65.05	65.18	4.89	77.70	77.83	5.84	90.35	90.48	6.79
52.53	52.67	3.95	65.18	65.32	4.90	77.83	77.97	5.85	90.48	90.62	6.80
52.67	52.80	3.96	65.32	65.45	4.91	77.97	78.10	5.86	90.62	90.75	6.81
52.80	52.93	3.97	65.45	65.58	4.92	78.10	78.23	5.87	90.75	90.88	6.82
52.93	53.07	3.98	65.58	65.72	4.93	78.23	78.37	5.88	90.88	91.02	6.83
53.07	53.20	3.99	65.72	65.85	4.94	78.37	78.50	5.89	91.02	91.15	6.84
53.20	53.33	4.00	65.85	65.98	4.95	78.50	78.63	5.90	91.15	91.28	6.85
53.33	53.47	4.01	65.98	66.12	4.96	78.63	78.77	5.91	91.28	91.42	6.86
53.47	53.60	4.02	66.12	66.25	4.97	78.77	78.90	5.92	91.42	91.55	6.87
53.60	53.73	4.03	66.25	66.38	4.98	78.90	79.03	5.93	91.55	91.68	6.88
53.73	53.87	4.04	66.38	66.52	4.99	79.03	79.17	5.94	91.68	91.82	6.89
53.87	54.00	4.05	66.52	66.65	5.00	79.17	79.30	5.95	91.82	91.95	6.90
54.00	54.13	4.06	66.65	66.78	5.01	79.30	79.43	5.96	91.95	92.08	6.91
54.13	54.27	4.07	66.78	66.92	5.02	79.43	79.57	5.97	92.08	92.22	6.92
54.27	54.40	4.08	66.92	67.05	5.03	79.57	79.70	5.98	92.22	92.35	6.93
54.40	54.53	4.09	67.05	67.18	5.04	79.70	79.83	5.99	92.35	92.48	6.94
54.53	54.67	4.10	67.18	67.32	5.05	79.83	79.97	6.00	92.48	92.61	6.95
54.67	54.80	4.11	67.32	67.45	5.06	79.97	80.10	6.01	92.61	92.75	6.96
54.80	54.93	4.12	67.45	67.58	5.07	80.10	80.23	6.02	92.75	92.88	6.97
54.93	55.06	4.13	67.58	67.71	5.08	80.23	80.36	6.03	92.88	93.01	6.98
55.06	55.20	4.14	67.71	67.85	5.09	80.36	80.50	6.04	93.01	93.15	6.99
55.20	55.33	4.15	67.85	67.98	5.10	80.50	80.63	6.05	93.15	93.28	7.00
55.33	55.46	4.16	67.98	68.11	5.11	80.63	80.76	6.06	93.28	93.41	7.01
55.46	55.60	4.17	68.11	68.25	5.12	80.76	80.90	6.07	93.41	93.55	7.02
55.60	55.73	4.18	68.25	68.38	5.13	80.90	81.03	6.08	93.55	93.68	7.03
55.73	55.86	4.19	68.38	68.51	5.14	81.03	81.16	6.09	93.68	93.81	7.04
55.86	56.00	4.20	68.51	68.65	5.15	81.16	81.30	6.10	93.81	93.95	7.05
56.00	56.13	4.21	68.65	68.78	5.16	81.30	81.43	6.11	93.95	94.08	7.06
56.13	56.26	4.22	68.78	68.91	5.17	81.43	81.56	6.12	94.08	94.21	7.07
56.26	56.40	4.23	68.91	69.05	5.18	81.56	81.70	6.13	94.21	94.35	7.08
56.40	56.53	4.24	69.05	69.18	5.19	81.70	81.83	6.14	94.35	94.48	7.09
56.53	56.66	4.25	69.18	69.31	5.20	81.83	81.96	6.15	94.48	94.61	7.10
56.66	56.80	4.26	69.31	69.45	5.21	81.96	82.10	6.16	94.61	94.75	7.11
56.80	56.93	4.27	69.45	69.58	5.22	82.10	82.23	6.17	94.75	94.88	7.12
56.93	57.06	4.28	69.58	69.71	5.23	82.23	82.36	6.18	94.88	95.01	7.13
57.06	57.20	4.29	69.71	69.85	5.24	82.36	82.50	6.19	95.01	95.14	7.14
57.20	57.33	4.30	69.85	69.98	5.25	82.50	82.63	6.20	95.14	95.28	7.15
57.33	57.46	4.31	69.98	70.11	5.26	82.63	82.76	6.21	95.28	95.41	7.16
57.46	57.59	4.32	70.11	70.24	5.27	82.76	82.89	6.22	95.41	95.54	7.17
57.59	57.73	4.33	70.24	70.38	5.28	82.89	83.03	6.23	95.54	95.68	7.18
57.73	57.86	4.34	70.38	70.51	5.29	83.03	83.16	6.24	95.68	95.81	7.19
57.86	57.99	4.35	70.51	70.64	5.30	83.16	83.29	6.25	95.81	95.94	7.20
57.99	58.13	4.36	70.64	70.78	5.31	83.29	83.43	6.26	95.94	96.08	7.21
58.13	58.26	4.37	70.78	70.91	5.32	83.43	83.56	6.27	96.08	96.21	7.22
58.26	58.39	4.38	70.91	71.04	5.33	83.56	83.69	6.28	96.21	96.34	7.23
58.39	58.53	4.39	71.04	71.18	5.34	83.69	83.83	6.29	96.34	96.48	7.24
58.53	58.66	4.40	71.18	71.31	5.35	83.83	83.96	6.30	96.48	96.61	7.25
58.66	58.79	4.41	71.31	71.44	5.36	83.96	84.09	6.31	96.61	96.74	7.26
58.79	58.93	4.42	71.44	71.58	5.37	84.09	84.23	6.32	96.74	96.88	7.27
58.93	59.06	4.43	71.58	71.71	5.38	84.23	84.36	6.33	96.88	97.01	7.28
59.06	59.19	4.44	71.71	71.84	5.39	84.36	84.49	6.34	97.01	97.14	7.29
59.19	59.33	4.45	71.84	71.98	5.40	84.49	84.63	6.35	97.14	97.28	7.30
59.33	59.46	4.46	71.98	72.11	5.41	84.63	84.76	6.36	97.28	97.41	7.31
59.46	59.59	4.47	72.11	72.24	5.42	84.76	84.89	6.37	97.41	97.54	7.32
59.59	59.73	4.48	72.24	72.38	5.43	84.89	85.02	6.38	97.54	97.67	7.33
59.73	59.86	4.49	72.38	72.51	5.44	85.02	85.16	6.39	97.67	97.81	7.34
59.86	59.99	4.50	72.51	72.64	5.45	85.16	85.29	6.40	97.81	97.94	7.35
59.99	60.12	4.51	72.64	72.77	5.46	85.29	85.42	6.41	97.94	98.07	7.36
60.12	60.26	4.52	72.77	72.91	5.47	85.42	85.56	6.42	98.07	98.21	7.37
60.26	60.39	4.53	72.91	73.04	5.48	85.56	85.69	6.43	98.21	98.34	7.38
60.39	60.52	4.54	73.04	73.17	5.49	85.69	85.82	6.44	98.34	98.47	7.39
60.52	60.66	4.55	73.17	73.31	5.50	85.82	85.96	6.45	98.47	98.61	7.40
60.66	60.79	4.56	73.31	73.44	5.51	85.96	86.09	6.46	98.61	98.74	7.41
60.79	60.92	4.57	73.44	73.57	5.52	86.09	86.22	6.47	98.74	98.87	7.42
60.92	61.06	4.58	73.57	73.71	5.53	86.22	86.36	6.48	98.87	99.01	7.43
61.06	61.19	4.59	73.71	73.84	5.54	86.36	86.49	6.49	99.01	99.14	7.44
61.19	61.32	4.60	73.84	73.97	5.55	86.49	86.62	6.50	99.14	99.27	7.45
61.32	61.46	4.61	73.97	74.11	5.56	86.62	86.76	6.51	99.27	99.41	7.46
61.46	61.59	4.62	74.11	74.24	5.57	86.76	86.89	6.52	99.41	99.54	7.47
61.59	61.72	4.63	74.24	74.37	5.58	86.89	87.02	6.53	99.54	99.67	7.48
61.72	61.86	4.64	74.37	74.51	5.59	87.02	87.16	6.54	99.67	99.81	7.49
61.86	61.99	4.65	74.51	74.64	5.60	87.16	87.29	6.55	99.81	99.94	7.50
61.99	62.12	4.66	74.64	74.77	5.61	87.29	87.42	6.56	99.94	100.00	7.51
62.12	62.26	4.67	74.77	74.91	5.62	87.42	87.55	6.57			
62.26	62.39	4.68	74.91	75.04	5.63	87.55	87.69	6.58			
62.39	62.52	4.69	75.04	75.17	5.64	87.69	87.82	6.59			
62.52	62.65	4.70	75.17	75.30	5.65	87.82	87.95	6.60			
62.65	62.79	4.71	75.30	75.44	5.66	87.95	88.09	6.61			
62.79	62.92	4.72	75.44	75.57	5.67	88.09	88.22	6.62			
62.92	63.05	4.73	75.57	75.70	5.68	88.22	88.35	6.63			
63.05	63.19	4.74	75.70	75.84	5.69	88.35	88.49	6.64			
63.19	63.32	4.75	75.84	75.97	5.70	88.49	88.62	6.65			
63.32	63.45	4.76	75.97	76.10	5.71	88.62	88.75	6.66			
63.45	63.59	4.77	76.10	76.24	5.72	88.75	88.89	6.67			
63.59	63.72	4.78	76.24	76.37	5.73	88.89	89.02	6.68			

Wages	Taxes
100	$7.51
200	15.02
300	22.53
400	30.04
500	37.55
600	45.06
700	52.57
800	60.08
900	67.59
1,000	75.10

Table 17.4   Social Security Employee Tax Table (partial)

Deductions for **Social Security** contributions (officially referred to as **Federal Insurance Contributions Act** or **FICA**) are also taken from tables, like the partial listing in Table 17.4. To find the deductible contribution for the previously mentioned employee who earns $675 each payday, we refer to the lower right corner at the end of the table and find that the deduction for $600 is $45.06. For the remaining $75 we locate the columns in the table that read "Wages at least 74.91 but less than 75.04" to find a contribution of $5.63, resulting in a total FICA deduction of $50.69.

	Gross Pay	FICA
First	$600	45.06
Remaining	75	5.63
	$675	$50.69

Because the table is based on an FICA rate of 7.51 percent, we may avoid use of the table by simply multiplying gross pay times the rate.

$$675.00 \times 0.0751 = \$50.69$$

Doubling this figure to allow for matching funds by the employer, we find that the total Social Security contribution for this one employee is $101.38 (50.69 $\times$ 2 = 101.38). At the time of this publication, the FICA contribution is withheld on only the first $48,000 of an employee's earnings each year. (Because the government has plans to change FICA rates every other year beyond the year 1990, you should check the annual IRS publications of *Circular E* for current withholding tables.)

Net or **take-home pay** consists of the amount of money that is left after deductions are subtracted from gross pay.

$$\text{Gross pay} - \text{Deductions} = \text{Net pay}$$
$$675.00 - (49.00 + 50.69) =$$
$$675.00 - 99.69 = \$575.31$$

Ignoring any other deductions that the employer may make for such items as pension benefits, health insurance, and union dues, this employee will receive a check for $575.31.

Self-Check 17C Figuring Deductions

---

1. Using the percentage method, what is the federal income tax to be withheld from a single employee's semimonthly gross pay of $1,050? The employee claims only one allowance.

2. Using Table 17.3, what amount of tax should be withheld from the biweekly pay of $640 for a married employee who claims four withholding allowances?

3. Using the percentage method, compute the amount of FICA to be withheld from the pay of an employee with gross pay of $945.26.

4. Using Table 17.4, determine the amount of FICA to be withheld from an employee with gross pay of $383.85.

5. Referring to Problem 4, what is the total Social Security contribution that the employer must pay to the federal government?

Payroll Records

Business people combine gross pay, deductions withheld, and net pay to form a payroll record similar to the form illustrated in Figure 17.1. The federal taxes and FICA deductions listed here were computed by the percentage methods.

Payroll for week of: 1/18/90					For branch office: Newtown				
Withholding Allowances	Hours Worked	Hourly Rate	Regular Pay	Overtime Rate	Overtime Pay	Gross Pay	Federal Taxes	FICA	Net Pay
1 S*	40	5.12	204.80	7.68		204.80	22.09	15.38	167.33
3 M	43	5.12	204.80	7.68	23.04	227.84	8.45	17.11	202.28
2 M	40	6.80	272.00	10.20		272.00	20.70	20.43	230.87
0 S	45	6.85	274.00	10.275	51.38	325.38	45.81	24.44	255.13
1 S	25	4.70	117.50	7.05		117.50	9.00	8.82	99.68
4 M	40	8.90	356.00	13.35		356.00	22.05	26.74	307.21
Totals			1429.10		74.42	1503.52	128.10	112.92	1262.50

*M = Married; S = Single

Figure 17.1   Payroll Record

After computing gross and net pay for each employee, we total the columns. Then, to check our accuracy, we add total regular and overtime pay to make certain that they agree with the total for gross pay. We then subtract from total gross pay the bottom totals for federal tax and FICA to make sure that the difference agrees with our bottom total for net pay. If these figures agree, we know that our addition within the payroll record has been accurate.

Self-Check 17D   Payroll Records

Using the appropriate tables, complete the following payroll record. Assume that each employee is married and is paid every other week.

Allowances Claimed	Hours Worked	Hourly Rate	Regular Pay	Overtime Rate	Overtime Pay	Gross Pay	Federal Taxes	FICA	Net Pay
3	40 40	6.20							
4	43 42	6.80							
1	40 40	6.25							
2	43 43	6.70							
0	35 28	4.70							
Totals									

Answers to Self-Checks

Self-Check 17A

1. $770.83

2. $711.54

3. $932.69

4. $1,010.42

Self-Check 17B

1. $300.38

2. $1,130

3. $67.76

4. $2,210

Self-Check 17C

1. $162.17

2. $35

3. $70.99

4. $28.83

5. $57.66

Self-Check 17D

Total net pay = $2,124.90

ASSIGNMENT 17A

Payroll Records

1. Gross pay (5 points each)

a. If Anita Rudgers earns an annual salary of $11,518, what is her gross biweekly salary?

b. What is Norma Babbit's semimonthly gross earnings if her annual salary is $9,750?

c. If Joseph Crocker grosses $820 every 2 weeks, what is his annual salary?

d. What is the monthly gross pay of a salesperson who receives a flat salary of $1,500 plus $2\frac{1}{2}\%$ of his monthly sales of $51,200?

e. What is the gross pay during an 8-hour period for a seamstress who turns out 48 men's ties at a piecework rate of $0.45 per tie?

2. Deductions (5 points each)

a. Using the appropriate table, determine the amount of federal income tax to be withheld from an employee's biweekly gross pay of $560. The employee has two withholding allowances.

b. Using the percentage method, find the amount of federal income tax to be withheld from a married employee's semimonthly pay of $1,025. The employee has four allowances.

c. Using the appropriate table, find the amount of Social Security contribution to be withheld from an employee's gross pay of $483.16.

d. Using the percentage method, determine the amount of FICA to be withheld from an employee's gross pay of $1,200.

e. Using the tables, calculate the net pay for a married employee with two allowances and a biweekly gross income of $765.50.

3. Payroll records (50 points)

Use the appropriate tables to complete the following payroll records. All nine employees are married. Note also that time worked in excess of 40 hours per week is paid at $1\frac{1}{2}$ times the regular rate. Cross-check your totals.

Biweekly Payroll Beginning January 1, 1990

Employee Name	Allowances	Week	M	T	W	T	F	S	Total	Regular Rate	Regular Pay	Overtime Rate	Overtime Pay	Gross Pay	Federal Tax	FICA	Net Pay
Allen, June	0	1	8	8	10	10	10		46	4.00	320.00	6.00	42.00	362.00	37.00	27.19	297.81
		2	8	8	8	8	9		41								
Brinks, Tony	2	1	8	9	9	9	8			4.00							
		2	8	9	9	8	9										
Clemmins, David	3	1	8	8	8	8	8			4.45							
		2	8	8	8	8	8										
Jones, Cal	1	1	8	8	8	8	8	4		4.00							
		2	8	8	8	8	8	2									
Keller, Brenda	2	1	8	8	8	8	8			4.50							
		2	8	8	8	8	8										
Rickert, Sidney	4	1	8		8	8	8			4.40							
		2	8	9	8	9	8										
Shapiro, Rudy	1	1	4	4	4	8	4			3.90							
		2	4	4	4	8	4										
Speck, Winston	2	1	8	8	8	8	8	8		4.00							
		2	8	8	8	8	6										
Spillars, Nancy	1	1	8	9	9	8	8			4.05							
		2	8	9	9	8	10										

1. Gross pay (5 points each)

a. If Roger Sterling earns an annual salary of $24,500, what is his gross biweekly salary?

b. If Leslie Williams grosses $850 semimonthly, what is her annual salary?

c. If Rhonda Dalidas grosses $620 every 2 weeks, what is her annual salary?

d. How much money will a salesperson gross from a 2% commission on the sale of a new automobile priced at $17,500?

e. What is the gross pay for 1 week for an employee who produces 1,120 grommets at a piecework rate of 28 cents per unit?

2. Deductions (5 points each)

a. Using Table 17.3, compute the amount of federal income tax to be withheld from the biweekly gross pay of $475, provided the employee is married and has only 2 allowances.

b. Using the percentage method, determine the amount of federal tax to be withheld from the weekly pay of a married employee who has earnings of $630 and claims 5 allowances.

c. Using Table 17.4, determine the amount of FICA to be withheld from an employee's gross income of $465.

d. What is the net pay of a married employee with 2 allowances and a biweekly income of $590? Use the appropriate tables rather than the percentage method.

e. If an employee's net pay is $325.25, after deductions of $31.10 for federal taxes and $15.59 for Social Security, what is the employee's gross pay for the period?

3. Payroll records (50 points)

Using the percentage methods for computing federal tax and FICA, complete the following payroll records. Note that time worked in excess of 40 hours per week is paid at $1\frac{1}{2}$ times the regular rate. Cross-check your totals. (M = Married, S = Single)

Biweekly Payroll Beginning January 1, 1990

Employee Name	Allowances	Week	M	T	W	T	F	S	Total	Regular Rate	Regular Pay	Overtime Rate	Overtime Pay	Gross Pay	Federal Tax	FICA	Net Pay
Abel, DeAnn	0 (S)	1	10	8	8	8	8			6.00							
		2	10	8	8	8	9										
Brown, James	2 (M)	1	8	8	8	8	8			6.00							
		2	8	8	8	8	8										
Frazer, Carl	3 (M)	1	8	8	8	8	8			6.20							
		2	8	8	8	8	8	4									
Inman, Rob	1 (S)	1	8	8	8	8	8			6.40							
		2	8	8	8	8	8										
Moreno, Rose	2 (S)	1	10	10	8	8	8			6.25							
		2	10	10	8	8	8										
Redmon, W. T.	4 (M)	1	8	8	8	8	8			7.50							
		2	8	8	8	8	8										
Smith, Ben	1 (S)	1	8	8	8	8	8	2		6.75							
		2	8	8	8	8	8	2									
Thomas, S. T.	2 (M)	1	8	8	8	8	8			6.00							
		2	8	8	8	8	8										
Winston, Beth	1 (S)	1	4	4	4	4	4	4		5.10							
		2	4	4	4	4	4	4									

CHAPTER

18

Business Taxes

After reading Chapter 18, you will be able to

- Determine the matching FICA taxes that companies must pay.
- Compute federal and state unemployment taxes.
- Identify the amount of excise tax that manufacturers pay and the amounts of sales tax that retailers collect from consumers.
- Calculate federal corporate taxes.
- Figure property taxes on the basis of assessed valuation.

Key Terms

Federal Unemployment Tax (FUT)   partnership
State Unemployment Tax (SUT)   corporation
excise tax   property tax
sales tax   assessed valuation
sole proprietorship   mill

Business people function as both tax collectors and taxpayers. As tax collectors, they withhold federal and state taxes from employees and collect sales taxes from customers. As taxpayers, businesses pay federal and state taxes on their profits, excise taxes on some products, local taxes on their properties, and several types of state and federal taxes in connection with their employees.

Employee Taxes

As discussed in Chapter 17, employers must collect *Social Security* contributions from employees through payroll deduction. *Federal Insurance Contribution Act (FICA)* is the legal title for this program, which provides benefits to insured people who have retired or become disabled, as well as to family survivors in the event of the insured person's death. The Act also provides funding for the Medicare program.

The size of the payroll deduction depends on the current FICA rate, a figure that Congress has been increasing regularly. The rate at the time of this publication, and the rate that applies to all problems within this chapter, is 7.51 percent of the first $48,000 of gross earnings each year. If Bill James earns $500 during the current pay period, bringing his yearly earnings for the year to $12,250, the employer withholds $37.55.

$$\frac{\text{Gross}}{\text{pay}} \times 7.51\% = \frac{\text{FICA}}{\text{contribution}}$$

$$500 \times 0.0751 = \$37.55$$

If, however, Connie Steward earns $2,500 during the current pay period, bringing her total income so far this year to $48,200, only $2,300 of that amount is subject to FICA withholding.

$$\frac{\text{Income}}{\text{to date}} - \frac{\text{Income}}{\text{limit}} = \frac{\text{Nontaxable}}{\text{amount}}$$

$$48,200 - 48,000 = \$200$$

$$\frac{\text{Taxable}}{\text{amount}} \times \frac{\text{FICA}}{\text{rate}} = \frac{\text{FICA}}{\text{withholding}}$$

$$2,300 \times 0.0751 = \$172.73$$

Because Connie Steward's gross pay of $2,500 places her $200 beyond the taxable limit of $48,000, we apply the FICA rate only to the balance (2,500 − 200 = $2,300). As with the $200, any future income received by Connie during this taxable year will be free of FICA withholding.

Employers must also make matching FICA payments to the federal government. For each dollar withheld for FICA from employee paychecks, employers must contribute an additional dollar. The current cost of Social Security, therefore, is 15.02 percent (7.51 percent withheld from the employee's paycheck plus 7.51 percent paid by the employer).

Taxpayers who are self-employed must pay 12.3 percent. A self-employed person who realizes profits during January of $5,500, for instance, would make an FICA contribution of $676.50.

Business profits × 12.3% = FICA contribution

5,500 × 0.123 = $676.50

As with employees who are subject to FICA withholding, self-employed persons make FICA contributions on only the first $48,000 of annual earnings.

Most employers must also pay **Federal Unemployment Tax (FUT)** and **State Unemployment Tax (SUT).** The current SUT rate in most states is 5.4 percent of the first $7,000 earned in each year. The FUT rate is 6.2 percent, but, because states may deduct the state rate of up to 5.4 percent, the actual federal rate is 0.8 percent.

On the $500 Bill James earns in the current pay period, his employer must pay an unemployment tax of $31.

$$
\begin{aligned}
\text{SUT: } 500 \times 0.054 &= 27.00 \\
\text{FUT: } 500 \times 0.008 &= \underline{4.00} \\
&\ \$31.00
\end{aligned}
$$

The employer of Connie Steward would pay no FUT or SUT for the current period, because her gross pay had long ago exceeded the annual maximum $7,000 of taxable income.

Self-Check 18A   Employee Taxes

---

1. If an employee's gross pay for the first payday in January is $880, what amount of FICA must the employer remit to the government?

2. In Problem 1, how much FUT and SUT must the employer remit?

3. If an employee earns $600 during the current pay period, which brings his or her year-to-date earnings to $7,300, what amount must the employer remit to the government for FICA, FUT, and SUT— including any amounts withheld from the employee's earnings?

4. The owner and operator of a small business received profits of $3,800 during March. What related amount should have been paid to the government as a contribution to Social Security?

Excise and Sales Taxes

Businesses also pay **excise taxes** to federal and local governments on certain items that they sell. Table 18.1 presents a partial listing of federal excise taxes that manufacturers must pay. If a manufacturer sells a bus to a transportation company for $100,000, for example, the manufacturer must pay an excise tax of $5,000:

$$\text{Price} \times \text{Rate} = \text{Tax}$$
$$\$100,000 \times 0.05 = \$5,000$$

Similarly, if a tire manufacturer sells tires weighing 50,000 pounds, the manufacturer must pay an excise tax of $2,500:

$$\text{Pounds} \times \text{Rate} = \text{Tax}$$
$$50,000 \times 0.05 = \$2,500$$

Businesses do not actually pay taxes, of course, because all taxes are included in the prices that they charge. Therefore, businesses are really tax collectors; their customers are the taxpayers.

Item	Rate
Trucks, buses, and trailers that weigh more than 10,000 pounds	5% of price
Tires	5¢ per pound
Gasoline	4¢ per gallon
Fishing equipment	10% of price
Pistols and revolvers	10% of price
Liquor	$12.50 per gallon

Table 18.1 Excise Tax Schedule

State and local governments force some businesses to collect one tax directly from their customers — the **sales tax** — which ranges from a low of $2\frac{1}{2}$ percent to a high of 8 percent, depending on the state in which the business is operating. For a 4 percent sales tax, businesses generally charge the tax on all customer purchases according to the schedule in Table 18.2.

Amount of Sale	Tax Collected
1–10¢	1¢
11–40¢	2¢
41–70¢	3¢
71–$1	4¢

Table 18.2   4% Sales Tax Schedule

The sales clerk would collect 2¢ tax on an item costing 35¢, for example, and 10¢ for the purchase of goods costing $2.35:

$$\$2.00 \times 0.04 = 0.08$$
$$\text{Tax on } 35\text{¢} = 0.02$$
$$= 0.10$$

Similarly, the sales tax on a $15,000 automobile would be $600:

$$\text{Price} \quad \times \text{Rate} = \text{Tax}$$
$$\$15,000 \times 0.04 = \$600$$

Self-Check 18B   Excise and Sales Taxes

1. If fishing equipment sells for $65.95, how much excise tax has been paid to the federal government on that amount?

2. How much sales tax would a customer pay on a $160 purchase in a state that has a tax rate of 4%?

3. How much would you collect from a customer who has purchased several items totaling $26.65, if all of the items are subject to a sales tax of 4%?

4. If a customer purchased items totaling $130.00, including a sales tax of 4%, what amount should be refunded for a returned item priced at $19.99?

Corporate Income Tax

Sole proprietorships (unincorporated businesses owned by one person) and **partnerships** (unincorporated businesses owned by more than one person) do not pay income taxes on their business income. Instead, the owners report business income on their individual tax returns (their Form 1040s).

Corporations, which are incorporated businesses that are usually owned by many people, must pay federal and state taxes on their incomes on the basis of the rates listed in Table 18.3.

		Income ($)	Rate (%)	Maximum Amount				
0	to	50,000	15%	50,000	×	0.15	=	7,500
50,001	to	75,000	25%	25,000	×	0.25	=	6,250
75,001	to	100,000	34%	25,000	×	0.34	=	8,500
100,001	to	335,000	39%	235,000	×	0.39	=	91,650
								113,900
$335,000 and over: flat rate of			34%	335,000	×	0.34	=	113,900

Table 18.3 Corporate Tax Rates

To illustrate, a corporation with net income (profit) of $20,000 would pay federal tax of $3,000.

$$\text{Net income} \times \text{Rate} = \text{Corporate tax}$$
$$20,000 \quad \times \ 0.15 \ = \quad \$3,000$$

The federal tax obligation for a corporation with net income of $80,000 would be $15,450.

$$\text{Net income} \times \text{Rate} = \text{Corporate tax}$$

50,000	× 0.15 =	$ 7,500
25,000	× 0.25 =	6,250
5,000	× 0.34 =	1,700
$80,000		$15,450

Federal income tax for a corporation with net income of $210,000 would be $65,150.

Net income	× Rate	= Corporate tax
50,000	× 0.15 =	$ 7,500
25,000	× 0.25 =	6,250
25,000	× 0.34 =	8,500
110,000	× 0.39 =	42,900
$210,000		$65,150

The 39 percent rate is actually the sum of 34 percent and a surcharge of 5 percent. Assessment of the surcharge enables the government to recover some of the tax breaks (lower rates) intended for small companies as their profits exceed $100,000. A corporation with taxable income of $200,000 is actually paying less than the 34 percent rate because of the lower rates paid on the first $75,000.

Net income	× Rate	= Corporate tax
50,000	× 0.15 =	$ 7,500
25,000	× 0.25 =	6,250
25,000	× 0.34 =	8,500
100,000	× 0.39 =	39,000
$200,000		$61,250

Then, to find the actual percent of income being paid in taxes we divide taxes by taxable income.

$$BR = P$$
$$200,000R = 61,250$$
$$R = 61,250 \div 200,000$$
$$R = 30.6\%$$

As shown at the bottom of Table 18.3, corporations with $335,000 or more in taxable income pay a flat rate of 34 percent. A corporation with profits of $525,318 would pay a federal income tax of $178,608.12.

Net income	× Rate	= Corporate tax
525,318	× 0.34 =	$178,608.12

Corporations usually compute taxes on the basis of even dollars, however, which would convert the amount due to $178,608.

Self-Check 18C   Corporate Income Tax

---

1.   How much federal income tax must a corporation pay on profits of $18,525?

2. What is the federal income tax obligation on corporate profits of $70,725?

3. How much federal income tax must a partnership pay on profits of $60,300?

4. What is the federal income tax on corporate profits of $450,000?

5. Compute the federal income tax on net income of $125,750 for a corporation.

Property Taxes

The kinds of tax and the amount of tax that businesses must pay on their properties vary from state to state, but most businesses are required to pay **property tax**—or local (state and county) taxes on any real property (land and buildings) that they own. Local governments employ people (called assessors) who establish the value of each piece of land and of each building within the community. Businesses must then pay a property tax on all or part of the **assessed valuation.**

If the tax rate is $0.03222 per dollar value of a piece of property that is assessed at $50,000, for example, the business must pay a property tax of $1,611:

$$\text{Assessed value} \times \text{Rate} = \text{Tax}$$
$$\$50,000 \times 0.03222 = \$1,611$$

If, instead, the government taxes the business on only 25 percent of the assessed valuation, the business pays $402.75:

$$\text{Assessed value} \times \text{Percentage} = \text{Taxable amount}$$
$$\$50,000 \times 0.25 = \$12,500$$
$$\text{Taxable amount} \times \text{Rate} = \text{Tax}$$
$$\$12,500 \times 0.03222 = \$402.75$$

Some city and county governments quote tax rates **on each $100 of assessed valuation,** making it necessary for us to divide the assessed valuation by 100 before multiplying by the rate. For a business property with an assessed value of $150,000 and a tax rate of $1.45 per $100 of assessed valuation, for instance, the property tax would be $2,175.

$$\frac{\text{Assessed value}}{100} \times \frac{\text{Rate}}{\text{per } \$100} = \frac{\text{Tax}}{\text{obligation}}$$

$$\frac{150,000}{100} \times 1.45 = \$2,175.00$$

Because the rate is on every $100 of valuation, we divide the assessed valuation by 100 to find that there are 1,500 increments of $100.

Some local governments establish tax rates in terms of mills, with a **mill** being 1/10 of a penny or, stated another way, 1/1,000 of a dollar, in which case we must divide the assessed value by 1,000 before multiplying. If the $150,000 property in the preceding example were subject to a rate of 14.5 mills, the computation would be as follows:

$$\frac{\text{Assessed value}}{\text{value}} \times \frac{\text{Rate}}{\text{in mills}} = \frac{\text{Tax}}{\text{obligation}}$$

$$\frac{150,000}{1,000} \times 14.5 = \$2,175$$

The two situations are the same, except that one rate is per $100 of assessed valuation and the other is per $1,000 of assessed valuation.

Self-Check 18D Property Taxes

---

1. What is the tax on property with an assessed value of $125,000, if the tax rate is $0.0125 on 50% of the assessed value?

2. What is the semiannual payment on a business property that is assessed at $490,000 if the tax rate is $0.025 on 40% of the assessed valuation?

3. What is the tax on a property that has an assessed value of $200,000, if the property rate is $0.525 per $100 of assessed valuation?

───────────────────── **Answers to Self-Checks** ─────────────────────

Self-Check 18A

1. $132.18

2. $54.56

3. $108.72

4. $467.40

Self-Check 18B

1. $6.60

2. $6.40

3. $27.72

4. $20.79

Self-Check 18C

1. $2,778.75

2. $12,681.25

3. None

4. $153,000

5. $32,292.50

Self-Check 18D

1. $781.25

2. $2,450

3. $1,050

1. **Employee taxes (5 points each)**

a. Use Table 17.4 to compute the employer's FICA contribution for an employee with earnings of $900.

b. Use the percentage method to compute the FICA contribution for the same employee who earned $900 during the one pay period.

c. How much FUT and SUT should the employer pay for the employee who has gross pay of $900 during a biweekly period?

d. How much FICA must a self-employed person pay on business profits of $4,250 under the percentage method?

e. If a married employee earns $760 during the first 2 weeks of March, bringing the total earnings for the year to $3,100, what is the total cost of the employee to the employer for the biweekly pay period, not including any fringe benefits that the employee may receive?

2. **Sales and excise taxes (5 points each)**

a. How much excise tax must a manufacturing company pay to the federal government on sales of fishing equipment totaling $5,600?

b. If the sales tax is 6%, how much tax must you pay for the purchase of a new automobile that sells for $9,500?

c. If General Motors Corporation sells 12 large trucks to a dealer at a price of $75,000 per truck, how much money must the company pay to the federal government in excise taxes on the sale?

d. How much excise tax must Shell Oil Company pay on sales of 1 million gallons of gasoline?

e. If your state charges a sales tax of 5% and the next state charges only 3%, how much more would you have to pay for an $11,000 car than a person living in the next state would have to pay?

3. Corporate income tax (5 points each)

a. What is the federal corporate tax on net income of $20,222?

b. If a small corporation earns profits of just $68,200, how much tax would be paid to the federal government?

c. What is the federal corporate tax on net income of $1,250,332?

d. What corporate tax must be paid on net income of $150,212?

e. In Problem 3.d, what actual percentage of net income is the company paying to the federal government? Round your answer to tenths of a percent.

4. Property tax (5 points each)

a. If the tax rate is $1.234 for each $100 of assessed valuation, what is the tax on a property that is assessed at $40,000?

b. If the tax rate is 17.17 mills, what is the tax on a property that is assessed at $150,000?

c. If the tax rate is $0.011113 on 50% of each dollar of assessed valuation, what is the tax on a property that is assessed at $80,000?

d. The property tax on an office building is $1.65 per each $100 of assessed valuation. What is the tax if the office building is assessed at $265,000?

e. If the tax rate is 16.67 mills and a business pays $316 tax on its property, what is the assessed value of the property?

1. **Employee taxes (5 points each)**

   a. Refer to Table 17.4 to determine the amount of FICA that an employer must pay in relation to an employee's gross pay of $282.

   b. Use the percentage method to compute the employer FICA contribution on gross pay of $1,080.

   c. An employee earns $775 during the current pay period, bringing her yearly earnings to $18,000. Use Table 17.4 to find the total employee-employer FICA contribution.

   d. What amount of FICA contribution must a sole proprietor pay on net income (profit) of $35,100 — assuming a current rate of 12.3 percent?

   e. If an employee earns $250 for last week's work, bringing yearly earnings to $7,100, how much money will be deducted from the paycheck for FICA, FUT, and SUT?

2. **Sales and excise taxes (5 points each)**

   a. What is the amount of excise tax on each revolver that sells for $250?

   b. If you pay $27.30 for an item and the price includes a 5% sales tax, what was the price of the item before the tax was added?

   c. If a customer buys items costing 65¢, 25¢, 95¢, and $2.55, how much sales tax should be added to the purchase price, using the 4% schedule in Table 18.2?

   d. Using the 4% schedule in Table 18.2, what amount of sales tax should a store charge on the sale of items totaling $16.16?

e. How much excise tax must a tire manufacturer pay on the sale of a railcar load of
tires weighing 75,000 pounds?

3. Corporate income tax (5 points each)

a. What is the corporate tax on net income of
$1,050,000?

b. If two owners receive $25,000 each in profits
from their business, which is a partnership,
how much federal tax must be paid?

c. What is the federal corporate tax on net
income of $46,511.10?

d. If a corporation had a total income of
$489,000 and costs and expenses totaling
$424,000, how much money must be paid to
the federal government for income tax?

e. Determine the tax to be paid by a corporation
with taxable income of $125,000. Show your
computations for each applicable tax rate.

4. Property tax (5 points each)

a. What is the amount of property tax that is
due on a building that has an assessed value
of $135,000 and a tax rate of $0.0125?

b. If a property has an assessed value of
$650,000 and a tax rate of $0.75 per $100 of
assessed valuation, what amount of property
tax must be paid?

c. If a property is assessed at a value of
$250,000 by the county and is taxed at 35%
of the assessed value at a rate of 12.5 mills,
what is the annual tax obligation?

d. If the county has a property tax of $3.65 per
$100 valuation, how much tax must a
small-business owner pay on property
assessed at $65,000?

e. In Problem 4.d, how much tax must the
owner pay if the rate is applied to only 25%
of the assessed valuation?

Depreciation Schedules

After reading Chapter 19, you will be able to

- Describe and apply the straight-line and accelerated-cost-recovery methods of depreciation.
- Compute annual depreciation expenses for business assets other than real estate on the basis of current straight-line and accelerated-cost-recovery methods.
- Calculate annual depreciation expenses for both residential and nonresidential properties.

Key Terms

profit

depreciation

business assets

straight-line depreciation

half-year convention

book value

accelerated cost recovery

200-percent declining balance

150-percent declining balance

real estate

mid-month convention

The **profit** of a business is the amount of money that is left over from income received from the sale of goods or services, after having paid for the cost of producing those goods or services and after having paid for any related expenses. One related expense that isn't actually paid, but must be deducted from income when calculating profit, is **depreciation,** the decline in value of business assets. Through the use of depreciation schedules, the Internal Revenue Service permits businesses to avoid paying taxes on profits equaling the purchase value of certain business assets.

Business assets are the typewriters, computers, vehicles, machinery, buildings, and other properties that businesses use to earn income. To say that a company has earned a certain amount of profits without deducting a depreciation expense for the wear and tear on company assets, therefore, would result in an overstatement of profits.

Realizing that business assets eventually wear out or become obsolete, the Internal Revenue Service (IRS) permits businesses to deduct depreciation (decrease-in-value) expenses each year from the income on which they must pay taxes. In effect, this provision permits businesses to recover tax-exempt amounts from future income equal to the original purchase prices of their assets.

Following drastic changes in the rules in both 1981 and 1987, the current methods of depreciation are straight-line and accelerated cost recovery. The straight-line method results in an equal distribution of depreciation expense over the economic life of an asset, whereas the accelerated cost recovery results in higher depreciation expenses during the early life of an asset and lower amounts during later years.

Straight-Line Depreciation

To find the yearly depreciation expense under **straight-line depreciation,** we divide the value of the asset by the number of years involved. For a $10,000 asset that is to be depreciated over a five-year period, the yearly expense that may be deducted from the income of a business as tax-free income is a constant $2,000.*

Installation cost	÷	Number of years	=	Annual depreciation expense
$10,000	÷	5	=	$2,000

Because business people do not necessarily purchase equipment at the beginning of a year, however, the IRS imposes a **half-year convention,** which treats all assets as if they were bought at midyear. Regardless of the month of purchase of the previously mentioned $10,000 asset, the allowable depreciation expense for the first year is only $1,000 — just half of the yearly expense. As shown in Table 19.1, the business claims $1,000 the first year, $2,000 for each of the following four years, and $1,000 (a carry-over from the first year) the sixth year.

---

*Effective with 1986 tax law, salvage value is no longer a consideration in compiling depreciation schedules.

Year	Depreciation Expense	Accumulated Depreciation	Book Value
1	1,000	1,000	9,000
2	2,000	3,000	7,000
3	2,000	5,000	5,000
4	2,000	7,000	3,000
5	2,000	9,000	1,000
6	1,000	10,000	0

Table 19.1   Straight-line Depreciation Schedule for an Asset Costing $10,000

Notice that the **book value** is the difference remaining each year after the depreciation expense is deducted from the original value (first year) or the book value of the preceding year. For the first year it was $10,000 (the original value) minus $1,000. For the second year, it was $9,000 (the book value for the first year) minus $2,000. Business managers may elect to use straight-line depreciation for any asset. Once having chosen straight-line, however, they may not switch to another method.

--- **Self-Check 19A**   Straight-Line Depreciation ---

1. What is the depreciation expense the first year of ownership, using the straight-line method, for an asset that cost $38,500 and has a 12-year life?

2. In Problem 1, what is the depreciation expense for the second year?

3. In Problems 1 and 2, what is the book value at the end of the second year?

4. If a property is depreciated on the basis of straight-line over a period of $27\frac{1}{2}$ years, what is the yearly depreciation expense, assuming an initial cost of $150,000? (Round your answer to even dollars.)

Accelerated Cost Recovery

As mentioned earlier, **accelerated cost recovery** enables business people to claim relatively high amounts of depreciation expense on an asset during the earlier years of its ownership and progressively lower amounts during the latter years. We begin by referring to Table 19.2 to identify the class of the particular asset to be depreciated.

Class (years)	Description	Method
3	4 years or less (such as tractor units for highway use)	200% DB
5	5–9 years (autos, trucks, computers, typewriters)	200% DB
7	10–15 years (all other assets including office furniture)	200% DB
10	16–19 years (water vessels such as barges and tugs)	200% DB
15	20–24 years (municipal wastewater treatment plants)	150% DB
20	25 years or more (farm buildings, municipal sewers)	150% DB
27.5	Residential rental property (houses and apartments)	27.5-year SL
31.5	Nonresidential rental property (office buildings, warehouses)	31.5-year SL

Note: DB = declining balance; SL = straight line

Table 19.2   Classes of Assets

At the left of the table is the number of years that an asset can be depreciated. Regardless of whether an automobile or truck has a useful life of five to nine years, for example, because the asset falls within Class 5 we depreciate it over a five-year period. Assets within the first four categories are subject to 200-percent declining balance, and those in Classes 15 and 20 are subject to the 150-percent declining-balance method. The last two categories involve real estate, which is discussed later in this chapter.

Let's begin with discussion of **200-percent declining balance.** For office furniture costing $50,000, a Class 7 asset, we find the depreciation expense for the first year and resulting book value in a five-step process.

Step 1

Divide 1 by the number of years shown in Table 19.2.

1 ÷ 7 = 0.1429 (rounded to four places)

Step 2

Double the resulting figure in Step 1.

0.1429 × 2 = 0.2858

Step 3

Find yearly depreciation by multiplying asset value by the resulting figure in Step 2.

50,000 × 0.2858 = 14,290

Step 4

Determine depreciation for the first year by applying the half-year convention.

14,290 × 1/2 = 7,145

Step 5

Find book value by subtracting first-year depreciation from the beginning value.

50,000 − 7,145 = 42,855

In Step 1 we find the rate of 0.1429 by dividing 1 by 7 years. In Step 2, we multiply the rate derived in Step 1 by 2 (200%) and find the applicable depreciation rate to be 0.2858. In Step 3 we multiply the cost of the asset (including installation charges, if any) by the 0.2858 percent rate and identify the amount of yearly depreciation expense to be $14,290.

Then, because the half-year convention applies to the first year, no matter which month the asset is purchased, we take one-half of the yearly depreciation to find that $7,145 may be claimed the first year. These results are summarized in Table 19.3, which shows the depreciation expense and book value for seven years with a carryover to the eighth year because of the half-year convention that applied the first year.

Year	Previous Book Value	Depreciation Expense	Year-End Book Value
1	50,000.00 × 0.2858 × 1/2	7,145.00	42,855.00
2	42,855.00 × 0.2858	12,247.96	30,607.04
3	30,607.04 × 0.2858	8,747.49	21,859.55
4	21,859.55 × 0.2858	6,247.46	15,612.09
5	15,612.09 × 0.2858	4,461.94	11,150.15
6	11,150.15 × 0.40 ⎫	4,460.06	6,690.09
7	11,150.15 × 0.40 ⎬ 100%	4,460.06	2,230.03
8	11,150.15 × 0.20 ⎭	2,230.03	—

Table 19.3   Ten-Year Depreciation Schedule Using 200-Percent Declining Balance

Because we could keep multiplying the remaining book value by 0.2858 for many years and not depreciate the asset to zero, we apply the straight-line method for the last two years (6 and 7) and for the carryover year (8). For the sixth year, we take

40 percent of the fifth-year book value. For the seventh year, we take 40 percent of the fifth-year book value. For the eighth (carryover) year, we take 20 percent of the fifth-year book value.

Now notice in Table 19.2 that Classes 15 and 20 call for **150-percent declining balance.** The computation of depreciation for these two classes is the same as for 200-percent declining balance, except for Step 2. If we're depreciating a $50,000 farm building, for instance, we divide 1 by 20 (Class 20) and multiply the answer by 1.5 (150%) rather than by 2 (200%).

Step 1

Divide 1 by the number of years as shown in Table 19.2.

$$1 \div 20 = 0.05$$

Step 2

Multiply the resulting figure in Step 1 by 1.5 (that is, by 150%).

$$0.05 \times 1.5 = 0.075$$

Step 3

Find the first-year depreciation by multiplying the asset value by the resulting figure in Step 2.

$$50,000 \times 0.075 = 3,750$$

Step 4

Apply the half-year convention by taking one-half of the yearly depreciation expense.

$$3,750 \times 0.5 = 1,875$$

Step 5

Find the book value by subtracting the first-year depreciation from the beginning value.

$$50,000 - 1,875 = 48,125$$

We then take 7.5 percent of $48,125 to find the second year's depreciation, and so on, until reaching the end of the eighteenth year ($20 - 2 = 18$). We find the depreciation expense for the last two years (19 and 20) by multiplying the eighteenth year book value by 40 percent for each year. Finally, we find the depreciation for the twenty-first (carryover) year by multiplying the eighteenth-year book value by 20 percent.

Self-Check 19B   Accelerated Cost Recovery
---

1. Find the depreciation expense over a 5-year period for a $28,000 asset that a business acquires on March 5, 1990.

2. What is the first-year depreciation of a Class 15 asset costing $150,000?

Real Estate

Thus far, we have been discussing methods for depreciating business assets other than real estate. The term **real estate** refers to land, buildings, and anything permanently attached to the buildings. Raw land or land associated with buildings cannot be depreciated, however.

As shown in the bottom two categories of Table 19.2, real estate is classified as either *residential rental property* (such as houses and apartments) or *nonresidential rental property* (such as office buildings and warehouses). The straight-line method is applied exactly as explained at the beginning of this chapter but with one major exception: The month of purchase is taken into consideration.

Regardless of the day of purchase, we apply the **mid-month convention;** that is, we treat the purchase as though it were made at the middle of the month. We count 1/2 of the first month, as well as all the months that follow within the first year of ownership.

Residential rental property takes the 27.5-year straight-line method. If a person buys a duplex on January 28 for $200,000, the depreciation is calculated as follows:

Step 1

Find the yearly expense by dividing the value by 27.5 years.

200,000 ÷ 27.5 = 7,272.73

Step 2

Determine the monthly expense by dividing the yearly expense by 12 months.

7,272.73 ÷ 12 = 606.06

Step 3

Determine the first month's expense by taking 1/2 of the monthly expense.

$$606.06 \times \frac{1}{2} = 303.03$$

Step 4

Determine the first year's expense for the half month and any remaining months.

$$606.06 \times \frac{1}{2} = 303.03 \text{ (January)}$$

$$606.06 \times 11 = \underline{6,666.66} \text{ (February–December)}$$

$$\$6,969.69$$

In Step 1 we figure the yearly depreciation expense by dividing the asset value by $27\frac{1}{2}$ years. In Step 2 we derive the monthly depreciation expense by dividing the annual (7,272.73) by the number of months in a year (12). In Step 3, because of the mid-month convention, we claim depreciation for $\frac{1}{2}$ of a month just as though the asset were purchased at the middle of January rather than January 28. Adding that amount (\$303.03) to depreciation for the remaining 11 months of the year (\$606.06 $\times$ 11 = \$6,666.66), we have a total first-year expense of \$6,969.69 for the first year of ownership.

Notice in Table 19.4 that, after annual depreciation of \$7,272.73 for each year (second year through twenty-seventh year), the balance remaining includes one-half year (27.5 years − 27 years = 0.5 year) and half a month of depreciation for the year of purchase.

Year	Depreciation Expense	Book Value	Year	Depreciation Expense	Book Value
1	6,969.69	193,030.31	16	7,272.73	83,939.36
2	7,272.73	185,757.58	17	7,272.73	76,666.63
3	7,272.73	178,484.85	18	7,272.73	69,393.90
4	7,272.73	171,212.12	19	7,272.73	62,121.17
5	7,272.73	163,939.39	20	7,272.73	54,848.44
6	7,272.73	156,666.66	21	7,272.73	47,575.71
7	7,272.73	149,393.93	22	7,272.73	40,302.98
8	7,272.73	142,121.20	23	7,272.73	33,030.25
9	7,272.73	134,848.47	24	7,272.73	25,757.52
10	7,272.73	127,575.74	25	7,272.73	18,484.79
11	7,272.73	120,303.01	26	7,272.73	11,212.06
12	7,272.73	113,030.28	27	7,272.73	3,939.33
13	7,272.73	105,757.55	28	3,939.33	—
14	7,272.73	98,484.82	29		
15	7,272.73	91,212.09	30		

Table 19.4 Straight-Line Depreciation Schedule for a Residential Property Costing \$200,000

Depreciation for nonresidential property, such as office buildings and warehouses, is calculated in the same manner as residential property, except it is figured over a 31.5-year period. The mid-month convention applies to both types of property.

Self-Check 19C   Real Estate
---

1. What is the yearly depreciation expense for residential rental property purchased on March 2 for $250,000?

2. In Problem 1, what is the monthly depreciation expense?

3. In Problem 1, what is the depreciation expense for the first month of ownership?

4. In Problem 1, what is the depreciation for the first year of ownership?

5. In Problem 1, what is the book value at the end of the first year?

6. If an investor pays $500,000 for an office building on July 5, what depreciation expense may be claimed for the first year of ownership?

Answers to Self-Checks

Self-Check 19A	Self-Check 19B	Self-Check 19C
1. $1,604.17	1.	1. $9,090.91

Self-Check 19B

1.

Year	Depreciation
1990	5,600.00
1991	8,960.00
1992	5,376.00
1993	3,225.60
1994	3,225.60
1995	1,612.80

2. $7,500

Self-Check 19A

1. $1,604.17

2. $3,208.33

3. $33,687.50

4. $5,455

Self-Check 19C

1. $9,090.91

2. $757.58

3. $378.79

4. $7,197.01

5. $242,802.99

6. $7,275.13

Depreciation Schedules

1. Straight-line depreciation (5 points each)

a. What amount of depreciation expense can an accountant claim for the first year of ownership of a computer that cost $60,000, assuming that the unit has an estimated 6-year economic life?

b. In Problem 1.a, what is the depreciation expense for the second year?

c. In Problem 1.a, what is the book value at the end of the second year?

2. Real estate (10 points each)

a. What is the depreciation expense for the first year of ownership of a nonresidential property costing $300,000 that is being depreciated over 31.5 years? The purchase agreement was signed on August 18.

b. In Problem 2.a, what is the book value at the end of the second year?

3. Accelerated cost recovery (5 points each)

a. Find the first-year's depreciation expense for a delivery truck purchased on June 12 at a total price of $23,500.

b. In Problem 3.a, what is the book value at the end of the first year of ownership?

c.   In Problem 3.a, what is the depreciation
     expense for the second year of ownership?

d.   Compute the first-year depreciation for a
     municipal waste water treatment plant valued
     at $1,500,000.

e.   In Problem 3.d, what is the book value at the
     end of the second year of ownership?

4. Depreciation schedule (50 points)

Complete a straight-line schedule for a 10-year asset that costs $124,668.

Year	Depreciation Expense	Book Value
1		
2		
3		
4		
5		
6		
7		
8		
9		
10		
11		

Show your first- and second-year computations in the following space.

Depreciation Schedules

1. **Straight-line depreciation (5 points each)**

   a. If the owner of a small business buys a used delivery truck for $12,500, what amount of depreciation expense may be claimed for the vehicle for the first year of ownership? Assume that the truck has a useful economic life of 5 years.

   b. In Problem 1.a, what is the depreciation expense for the second year?

   c. In Problem 1.a, what is the book value at the end of the second year?

2. **Real estate (10 points each)**

   a. What is the depreciation expense for the first year of ownership of a residential property costing $750,000 that is being depreciated over 27.5 years? The new owner purchased the property on February 3.

   b. In Problem 2.a, what is the book value at the end of the second year?

3. **Accelerated cost recovery (5 points each)**

   a. Using accelerated cost recovery, find the first-year's depreciation expense for a microcomputer purchased April 16 at a total price of $1,750. Assume that the computer has an estimated economic life of 5 years.

   b. In Problem 3.a, what is the book value at the end of the first year of ownership?

   c. In Problem 3.a, what is the depreciation expense for the second year of ownership?

d. Find the first-year depreciation expense for
a farm building, assuming a 20-year schedule
and a purchase price of $120,000.

e. In Problem 3.d, what is the book value at the
end of the second year of ownership?

4.   Depreciation schedule (50 points)

Complete a 200% declining balance schedule for a Class 10 asset that costs $84,200.

Year	Depreciation Expense	Book Value
1		
2		
3		
4		
5		
6		
7		
8		
9		
10		
11		

Show your first- and second-year computations in the following space.

Inventory Valuation

After reading Chapter 20, you will be able to

- Maintain and interpret inventory records.
- Determine the value of products remaining in stock on the basis of cost or market, whichever is lower.
- Calculate the value of products remaining in stock on the basis of specific identification and average cost.
- Calculate inventory valuation on the basis of "first-in, first-out" and "last-in, first-out" and explain the advantages and disadvantages of each approach.

Key Terms

inventory

inventory control department

ending inventory

specific identification

cost

market

average cost method

first in, first out (FIFO)

last in, first out (LIFO)

The word **inventory** refers to stored products. Most manufacturing companies make at least some of their products ahead of time; that is, before the products are shipped to customers or even before customer orders are received. Similarly, the many businesses that buy goods for resale, rather than manufacture them, must store the products until they are actually sold to customers. If accountants are to determine the amount of profits earned or losses incurred, they must first assign a value to those products that remain unsold at the end of the accounting term.

Inventory Records

Employees in **inventory control departments** must keep records of inventory so that employees in the product distribution departments will know the number of items that are available for sale and so that production people will know when to replenish a particular item. Also, accountants must be able to determine periodically the approximate value of inventories so that they can calculate the cost of products that have been sold. (This procedure is explained in Chapter 21.)

The abbreviated inventory record in Figure 20.1 is typical of those used in many businesses. This company made four purchases of 24/8 oz SJ tomatoes (24 eight-ounce cans in each case) during the year (columns 2, 3, and 4), each at a slightly higher price than for the previous purchase. As shown at the right side of the card (columns 5 and 6), the company made eight sales of this item during the year, resulting in 2,200 units remaining in stock at the end of the year (column 7). Note in column 7 that purchases are added and that sales are subtracted.

Inventory Record						
Item Number 24714				Warehouse B		
Description 24/8 oz SJ Tomatoes				City San Pedro		
1	2	3	4	5	6	7
Date	Purchase Order No.	Quantity Received	Unit Cost	Sales Order No.	Quantity Sold	Quantity Remaining
1/5/90	14650	3,000	8.00			3,000
1/7/90				P30141	200	2,800
1/10/90				P32462	500	2,300
2/28/90				P34617	1,000	1,300
3/15/90	14685	2,000	8.20			3,300
4/15/90				P35112	2,000	1,300
6/25/90				P36281	500	800
8/15/90	15113	3,500	8.30			4,300
8/30/90				P37294	1,100	3,200
10/1/90				P37861	1,500	1,700
11/18/90	15798	2,500	8.35			4,200
12/12/90				P38611	2,000	2,200

Figure 20.1   Inventory Record

Self-Check 20A   Inventory Records

Complete the inventory record to include the following transactions:

P.O. No.	Date	Quantity	Price	S.O. No.	Date	Quantity
14210	Feb. 5	1,000	7.40	S16101	Feb. 25	450
14305	Mar. 5	800	7.40	S16512	Mar. 8	600
14420	Mar. 20	1,000	7.45	S16818	Mar. 15	350
				S17503	Mar. 29	620

Date	Purchase Order No.	Quantity Received	Unit Cost	Sales Order No.	Quantity Sold	Quantity Remaining
1/10/90	13501	500	7.35			900
1/27/90				S15211	600	300
1/28/90				S15269	150	150

Specific Identification

At the end of the year, and sometimes more frequently, accountants must actually count all inventory items in company warehouses to make certain that the remaining quantities of each item as shown on the inventory records agree with the number that are on hand in the warehouses. Referring to the inventory record in Figure 20.1 as an example, company accountants must make certain that there are 2,200 units of 24/8 oz SJ Tomatoes in the **ending inventory** (the inventory remaining at the end of the accounting period).

Also, the accountants must determine the value of the ending inventory. If the four different orders of tomatoes are kept separate from each other, we would know the **specific identification** of the 2,200 cases that are left over at the end of the year. We might know, for example, that they are part of the 2,500 order (Purchase

Order 15798, at $8.35 each). Correspondingly, we would know that the value of the ending inventory for this one item (24/8 oz SJ Tomatoes) is $18,370:

$$2{,}200 \text{ units} \times \$8.35 \text{ each} = \$18{,}370$$

Most businesses that use the specific identification method, however, do so for high-cost items such as stereos, refrigerators, automobiles, and machinery, and not for low-cost items such as canned tomatoes.

Some businesses value their ending inventory at cost or market—whichever is lower. The **cost** of an inventoried (stored) product is either (1) the amount of money that it cost the business to produce the item or (2) the price that the business paid another company to buy the item for resale. **Market** is the replacement value of the product—the amount of money that it would cost the business to produce or buy the product at today's prices.

Assume, for example, that a grocer has 1,000 cases of 24/15 oz tomato sauce on hand at the end of the year. Although the grocer paid the canning company $4.95 for each case of tomato sauce, the market price (the price he would have to pay today for the same item) is $5.25. Therefore, the grocer would place an ending inventory value of $4,950.00 on the remaining 1,000 cases of tomato sauce:

Quantity	Item	Cost	Market	Value
1,000	24/15 oz tomato sauce	$4.95	$5.25	$4,950.00

Because cost is lower than market, we multiply the number of cases on hand (1,000) by cost ($4.95). If the market (replacement) price had been lower than cost, on the other hand, we would have multiplied the number of cases on hand by the market price of $5.25.

Self-Check 20B Specific Identification

1. Six refrigerators are left unsold at the end of the month—one that the company purchased at a cost of $350 and five at a cost of $425 each. What is the value of the ending inventory of this item?

2. If a grocer has 500 cases of 24/16 oz applesauce in inventory at the end of the month, for which he had paid $5.20 per case, what value will he place on the 500 cases if today's price for this product is $5.10 and if he used the lower of cost or market?

3. Determine the total value of the following items on the basis of cost or market, whichever is lower:

Units	Cost	Market
365	$12.15	$13.25
410	6.85	6.50
281	15.12	15.10
618	13.11	13.25

Average Cost

Many businesses use the **average-cost method** to compute the value of their ending inventory, by multiplying the number of units on hand times the average cost of the items. Again using the inventory record in Figure 20.1, we find that the business received four separate orders of 24/8 oz SJ Tomatoes during the period covered, each at a different price:

Quantity received	×	Unit cost	=	Total cost
3,000	×	$8.00	=	$24,000
2,000	×	8.20	=	16,400
3,500	×	8.30	=	29,050
2,500	×	8.35	=	20,875
11,000				$90,325

By multiplying the quantities of tomatoes received by their unit cost (price paid for them), we find that the total dollar cost of all 11,000 cases of tomatoes is $90,325. We then find the average cost per case by dividing the total cost by the number of cases received:

$$\frac{\text{Total}}{\text{cost}} \div \frac{\text{Quantity}}{\text{received}} = \frac{\text{Average}}{\text{cost}}$$

$$\$90,325 \div 11,000 = \$8.21 \text{ per case}$$

Finally, we multiply the quantity remaining (the 2,200 cases of tomatoes that are still in the warehouse) by their average cost per case ($8.21):

$$\frac{\text{Quantity}}{\text{remaining}} \times \frac{\text{Average}}{\text{cost}} = \frac{\text{Ending}}{\text{inventory}}$$

$$2,200 \times \$8.21 = \$18,062$$

Using the average-cost method, therefore, the value of the ending inventory of 2,200 cases of 24/8 oz SJ Tomatoes is $18,062.

---

1. If an appliance store receives six microwave ovens from the manufacturer on January 6, for which it paid $550 each, and a second shipment of ten ovens on January 21 at $525 each, what was the average cost of the ovens?

2. If the store has four of the ovens remaining unsold at the end of the month, what is the ending inventory (value in dollars and cents) for the month, based on average cost?

3. Using the average-cost method of inventory valuation, determine the value of 310 units remaining in stock from the following shipments received. (Round the average price to the cents position.)

Units	Price
331	$23.18
225	16.85
150	10.35
315	12.12

FIFO and LIFO

FIFO stands for **first in, first out,** and **LIFO** means **last in, first out.** The following diagram of the inventory record helps illustrate these terms:

Received Jan. 5	Received Mar. 15	Received Aug. 15	Received Nov. 18
3,000 cases	2,000 cases	3,500 cases	2,500 cases
$8.00 ea.	$8.20 ea.	$8.30 ea.	$8.35 ea.
First in			Last in

Most businesses would sell the canned tomatoes received in January before starting to sell those received in March. They would then sell the March tomatoes before selling those received in August, and so on. Correspondingly, the January tomatoes (the first in) would be sold first (first out). Therefore, if the earlier orders have already been sold, the 2,200 cases remaining in inventory at the end of the year are part of the latest order received (the one received in November at $8.35 per case). Accordingly, the value of ending inventory is $18,370.

$$\begin{array}{c} \text{Quantity} \\ \text{remaining} \end{array} \times \begin{array}{c} \text{Most recent} \\ \text{price paid} \end{array} = \begin{array}{c} \text{Ending} \\ \text{inventory} \end{array}$$

$$2{,}200 \quad \times \quad \$8.35 \quad = \quad \$18{,}370$$

Instead of 2,200 cases of 24/8 oz SJ Tomatoes remaining in inventory at the end of the year, assume that 2,700 cases remain unsold in the warehouse. Under the FIFO method of inventory valuation, 2,500 of the 2,700 cases are from the latest order received (the one received in November at $8.35 per case), and 200 cases are from the next-to-last order received (the one received in August at $8.30 per case), giving us an ending inventory of $22,535:

$$\begin{array}{c} \text{Quantity} \\ \text{remaining} \end{array} \times \begin{array}{c} \text{Most recent} \\ \text{price paid} \end{array} = \begin{array}{c} \text{Ending} \\ \text{inventory} \end{array}$$

2,500	×	$8.35	=	$20,875
200	×	8.30	=	1,660
2,700				$22,535

Under the LIFO (last in, first out) method, the opposite situation prevails. We assume that the most recent order (last in) is the first to be sold (first out). Correspondingly, we pretend that the most recent orders received have been sold and that the 2,200 cases remaining at the end of the year are from the earlier order (the one received in January at $8.00 per case). Using the LIFO method of inventory valuation, therefore, we value the 2,200 cases remaining in inventory at the end of the year at $17,600:

$$\begin{array}{c} \text{Quantity} \\ \text{remaining} \end{array} \times \begin{array}{c} \text{Earliest} \\ \text{price paid} \end{array} = \begin{array}{c} \text{Ending} \\ \text{inventory} \end{array}$$

$$2{,}200 \quad \times \quad \$8.00 \quad = \quad \$17{,}600$$

The word *pretend* is accurate because businesses do not actually treat their inventories in this manner; they use the LIFO method only on paper as a way of legally reducing the taxes that they pay the federal and state governments. During times of inflation, LIFO reduces the value of ending inventories. This reduction, in turn, increases the stated costs of the goods that businesses make or buy (cost of goods sold), thus reducing the reported profits on which they must pay tax.

Instead of 2,200 cases of 24/8 oz SJ Tomatoes remaining in inventory at the end of the year, assume that 3,500 cases remain unsold in the warehouse. Under the LIFO method of inventory valuation, we pretend that 3,000 of the 3,500 cases are from the earliest order (the one received in January at $8.00 per case) and that 500 cases are from the next earliest order (the one received in March at $8.20 per case), giving us an ending inventory of $28,100.

$$\begin{array}{c} \text{Quantity} \\ \text{remaining} \end{array} \times \begin{array}{c} \text{Earliest} \\ \text{price paid} \end{array} = \begin{array}{c} \text{Ending} \\ \text{inventory} \end{array}$$

3,000	×	$8.00	=	$24,000
500	×	8.20	=	4,100
3,500				$28,100

Self-Check 20D   FIFO and LIFO

---

1. A business bought 1,000 units in January for $14 each, 1,500 units in June for $14.50 each, and 1,200 units in December for $14.75 each. Using the FIFO method of inventory valuation, what is the value of an ending inventory of 600 units?

2. Using the LIFO method, instead, what is the ending inventory for 1,200 units remaining unsold in the warehouse?

3. For 1,120 units remaining of the following items received, which method results in the higher value, FIFO or LIFO?

Date	Units	Cost
3/12	1,600	$2.32
4/15	1,000	2.38
6/21	1,200	2.41
8/13	1,200	2.44
10/12	800	2.48

Summary of the Four Methods of Inventory Valuation

Specific Identification

Use when the exact order and cost of the remaining inventory is known.

Average Cost

The ending inventory is multiplied by the average cost of all goods received during the period, giving us a weighted average.

First In, First Out

Assumes that the ending inventory is part of the most recent goods received at the warehouse.

Last In, First Out

Assumes that the ending inventory is part of the earliest goods received at the warehouse.

Answers to Self-Checks

Self-Check 20A

2/5/90: 14210; 1,000; 7.40; 1,150
2/25/90: S16101; 450; 700
3/5/90: 14305; 800; 7.40; 1,500
3/8/90: S16512; 600; 900
3/15/90: S16818; 350; 550
3/20/90: 14420; 1,000; 7.45; 1,550
3/29/90: S17503; 620; 930

Self-Check 20B

1. $2,475

2. $2,550

3. $19,444.83

Self-Check 20C

1. $534.38

2. $2,137.52

3. $5,111.90

Self-Check 20D

1. $8,850

2. $16,900

3. FIFO is higher by $166.40

Name _____

Inventory Valuation

Score _____

1. Inventory records (50 points each)

Using the following transactional data, complete the inventory record for 24/20 oz Crushed Pineapple (Item No. L92105) at Harbor Warehouse in San Pedro, California:

2,500 units remain in inventory on January 1, 1990
January 15 sold 500 units on Sales Order 16177
February 2 sold 750 units on Sales Order 16210
March 1 sold 500 units on Sales Order 17001
March 10 bought 2,000 units for $10.80 each on Purchase Order 69702
March 28 sold 750 units on Sales Order 18361
April 2 sold 1,000 units on Sales Order 18116
April 15 bought 1,500 units for $10.80 each on Purchase Order 70113
April 25 sold 250 units on Sales Order 18772
May 10 sold 300 units on Sales Order 18991
May 19 sold 450 units on Sales Order 19430
May 25 sold 500 units on Sales Order 19659
May 26 bought 1,500 units for $10.90 each on Purchase Order 70810

Inventory Record						
Item Number _____			Warehouse _____			
Description _____			City _____			
Date	Purchase Order No.	Quantity Received	Unit Cost	Sales Order No.	Quantity Sold	Quantity Remaining

1. Lower of cost or market (each of the five sections 10 points)

Using the lower of cost or market, calculate the value of the ending inventory for the following items.

Quantity	Item Description	Cost	Market	Value
145	210 DREM DRILL PRESS	$ 13.31	$ 13.42	
2065	223 DREM UNIVERSAL STAND	8.64	8.75	
188	280 DREM MOTO TOOL	26.65	26.50	
210	380 DREM MOTO TOOL	33.32	33.32	
2015	483 DREM 1/32 IN CHCK COLET	0.50	0.51	
11	85625 DREM ACC MERCHANDISER	165.92	171.36	
			Total	
1500	12/15 CORN BREAD MIX	3.12	3.09	
2104	24/8 CORN MUFFIN MIX	4.08	4.15	
1622	12/14 GINGERBREAD MIX	5.76	5.70	
150	12/14 GINGERBREAD MIX	4.92	5.00	
1742	12/12 CHOC CHIP COOKIE MIX	9.00	9.10	
1003	12/12 SUGAR COOKIE MIX	9.00	8.75	
242	12/12 BUTTER COOKIE MIX	9.08	9.10	
114	12/18 OATMEAL COOKIE MIX	7.92	7.90	
			Total	
16	120 VAC NO SWITCHES	85.80	86.10	
21	120 VAC ONE AUX SWITCH	98.05	98.00	
12	120 VAC TWO AUX SWITCHES	108.95	108.95	
31	24 VAC NO SWITCHES	85.80	85.50	
20	24 VAC ONE AUX SWITCH	98.05	98.90	
27	24 VAC TWO AUX SWITCHES	108.95	108.00	
			Total	
1200	12/22 PIE CRUST STICKS	9.24	9.30	
1750	12/14 CREAMY FUDGE FROSTING	5.52	5.00	
2009	12/14 CREAMY WHITE FROSTING	5.52	5.00	
1620	12/14 CREAMY WHITE FROSTING	8.40	8.55	
3500	12/10 COCO PECAN FROSTING MIX	9.00	9.10	
1321	12/10 WHIPPED VANILLA FROSTING	8.40	8.40	
1611	12/10 STRAWBERRY WHIPPED FROSTING	8.40	8.55	
520	12/16 BUTTER PECAN FROSTING	9.60	9.50	
			Total	
25	4/7 CUP DRIP COFFEE MAKER	17.16	17.26	
42	3/2 QUART WHISTLING TEA KETTLE	8.25	8.65	
60	4/5 CUP PERCOLATOR	13.00	13.05	
24	6/10 INCH TEFLON FRYPAN	16.50	16.25	
35	6-5/8 CAST IRON SKILLET	12.54	12.50	
39	8-1/8 CAST IRON SKILLET	22.96	23.10	
			Total	

	Inventory Record						

| Item Number   T12125 | | | Warehouse   City Center Storage | | | | |
| Description   Drill Press | | | City   Chicago | | | | |

Date	Purchase Order No.	Quantity Received	Unit Cost	Sales Order No.	Quantity Shipped	Quantity Remaining
9/14/90	P16125	2,000	12.50			3,300
9/28/90				W42012	500	2,800
10/1/90				W45168	1,100	1,700
10/15/90	P17214	3,000	12.60			4,700
11/2/90				W51001	850	3,850
11/28/90				W49021	1,500	2,350
12/5/90	P17902	2,500	12.90			4,850
12/5/90				W43110	1,000	3,850
12/16/90				W46000	1,200	2,650
12/29/90	P18027	2,500	13.10			5,150

1. Average-cost method (10 points each)

a. What is the number of and total value (based on cost) of all units purchased during September, October, November, and December?

b. What is the average per-unit cost of the items purchased?

c. Based on the average-cost method of inventory valuation, what is the end-of-year value of the 5,150 drill presses that remain in inventory?

d. If 8,500 units had remained in inventory instead, what would the total end-of-year value have been?

Summary of Orders Received			
Date	Purchase Order No.	Quantity Received	Unit Cost
1/15/90	13790	1,100	8.40
3/10/90	20241	1,000	8.45
5/5/90	29423	1,500	8.75
7/13/90	31516	1,000	9.10
9/25/90	40008	1,500	9.12
11/13/90	45169	1,000	9.40

2. First in, first out (FIFO) (10 points each)

a. Refer to the summary of orders received and compute the value of ending inventory for 823 units remaining unsold at the end of the month, using the FIFO method of inventory valuation.

b. Assume instead that 1,216 of the items remain unsold at the end of the month; what is the end-of-month valuation under the FIFO method?

3. Last in, first out (LIFO) (10 points each)

a. Refer to the summary of orders received and compute the value of ending inventory for 850 units remaining unsold at the end of the year, using the LIFO method of inventory valuation.

b. Assume instead that 1,216 of the items remain unsold at the end of the year. What is the end-of-year valuation under the LIFO method?

4. Average-cost method (20 points)

Refer to the summary of orders received and determine the value of 730 units in inventory at the end of the accounting period, using the average-cost method.

You may use this practice test to measure your preparation for the actual part test. Answers begin on page 417.

Mathematics of Accounting

1. Payroll records (10 points each)

a. If an employee's annual salary is $38,500, what is the biweekly gross pay?

b. If a salesperson receives a regular monthly salary of $1,200 plus $1\frac{1}{2}\%$ of sales during June totaling $145,218, what was the person's income for the one month?

c.

Over	But not over		Of excess over
$40	–$727	15%	–$40
$727	–$1,700	$102.98 + 28%	–$727
$1,700	–$3,905	$375.44 + 33%	–$1,700

After allowing for $75 (one withholding allowance) from a single employee's biweekly income, take the remainder of $1,500 to the above table and compute the amount of federal tax to be withheld.

2. Business taxes (10 points each)

a. Using a FICA rate of 7.51%, what is the total contribution of employer and employee on an employee's gross income of $2,240?

b. With a FUT rate of 0.8% and a SUT rate of 5.4%, what amount must the employer pay for these two tax obligations on an employee's gross pay of $1,500, assuming that this payment brings the employee's yearly income to $7,100 ($100 more than the $7,000 limit)?

c. Using the following schedule of corporate tax rates, compute the income tax to be paid on net income (profits) of $110,000.

$0	to	$50,000	15%
$50,001	to	$75,000	25%
$75,001	to	$100,000	34%
$100,001	to	$335,000	39%

$335,000 and over — a flat rate of 34%

3. Depreciation schedules (30 points)

Complete a 10-year, straight-line depreciation schedule for an asset valued at $120,000.

Year	Depreciation	Book Value
1		
2		
3		
4		
5		
6		
7		
8		
9		
10		
11		

Show your first-year computations in the following space.

4. Inventory valuation (10 points each)

Summary of Orders Received			
Date	Purchase order no.	Quantity received	Unit cost
3/3/90	15212	800	$23.10
6/13/90	17313	1,000	23.50
9/1/90	16918	850	23.50
10/14/90	17223	1,000	23.75
12/5/90	18111	750	23.90

a. Using the first in, first out (FIFO) method of inventory valuation, determine the value of 1,000 units remaining in inventory at the end of the accounting period.

b. Using the last in, first out (LIFO) method of inventory valuation, determine the value of 750 units remaining in inventory.

PART
6

Mathematics of Finance

21. Income Statements

Main Categories

Net Sales and Cost of Goods Sold

Comparative Income Statements

Percent of Increase or Decrease

22. Balance Sheets

Main Categories

Expanded Balance Sheet

Comparative Balance Sheets

23. Financial Ratios

Liquidity Ratios

Leverage Ratios

Activity Ratios

Profit Ratios

24. Costs, Profits, and Dividends

Distributing Costs

Dividing Profits

Computing Dividends

25. Stocks and Bonds

Interpreting Stock Quotations

Interpreting Bond Quotations

Prorating Bond Interest

Computing Gains and Losses

CHAPTER 21

Income Statements

After reading Chapter 21, you will be able to

- Explain the purpose of income statements.
- Describe the main categories of an income statement.
- Calculate net sales and cost of goods sold.
- Prepare comparative income statements.
- Determine the percent of increase or decrease in each income statement entry.

Key Terms

income statement	beginning inventory
gross profits	cost of goods sold
net income	comparative income statement
gross sales	ending inventory
net sales	

A company's performance must be evaluated regularly to provide answers to questions such as, How profitable is the operation? How much profit or loss has the business sustained during the accounting period (month, quarter, or year)? How secure is the future of the business? Are all aspects of the business being operated efficiently? How do outsiders view the business?

Outsiders? Yes, many people other than the owners are interested in the performance of a business. Before bankers loan money to businesses, they want some indication of profitability, some assurance that enough funds will be generated to enable the repayment of loans. Similarly, a business can buy supplies on credit only when the means of payment seems apparent. Potential investors in companies also have questions about the performance of a business. Is the firm efficiently managed? How much of the firm's value is represented by debt? What are the prospects for future income and growth? How secure is the investment?

Businesses rely mainly on two financial statements to answer such questions: income statements and balance sheets. The arrangement of these two statements tends to be standardized throughout the business world; if you can understand the financial statements of one company, you can interpret the statements of other companies. This chapter examines income statements; balance sheets are discussed in Chapter 22.

Main Categories

The **income statement** covers a specific period of time (a week, a month, a year). It relates incoming dollars (sales) to outgoing dollars (costs and expenses) and reflects the resulting profit or loss. To illustrate the income statement, assume that a business collects $80,000 from the sale of products during January. Assume further that it cost the company $26,500 to manufacture the products sold and an additional $21,000 for related expenses (showroom, salaries, office supplies, and so forth). Subtracting costs and expenses from sales, we find the net income (profits before taxes are paid) to be $32,500.

	Sales	$80,000
−	Cost of goods sold	26,500
=	Gross profit	$53,500
−	Expenses	21,000
=	Net income	$32,500

Notice that **gross profits** include profits before expenses have been deducted and that **net income** consists of the money remaining after expenses are subtracted from gross profits.

Self-Check 21A   Main Categories

---

1. If sales are $150,000 and the cost of goods sold is $110,000, what is the gross profit?

2. If expenses are $20,000, what is net income?

3. If expenses are $44,532; cost of goods sold, $108,980; and net sales, $213,512, what is net income?

4. If net income is $144,567; cost of goods sold, $798,925; and expenses, $376,118, what are net sales?

Net Sales and Cost of Goods Sold

A distinction is made between gross sales and net sales. **Gross sales** include every item sold by the business; however, some of the items sold may not please customers. **Net sales** are the revenues (incoming money) that remains after deducting customer refunds from gross sales.

$$\text{Gross sales} - \text{Returns} = \text{Net sales}$$

Businesses have a cost for every product they sell, either the cost of manufacturing the product or the cost of buying it from another company for resale. Business people refer to this cost as **cost of goods sold.** If a business has a beginning inventory (January 1) of $50,000, purchases $300,000 of goods during the year for resale, and has ending inventory (December 31) of $10,000, the cost of goods sold for the year is $340,000:

Beginning inventory	**$ 50,000**
+ Purchases	**300,000**
= Available for sale	**$350,000**
− Ending inventory	**10,000**
= Cost of goods sold	**$340,000**

Beginning inventory consists of products in storage that remain unsold from the preceding accounting period, and **ending inventory** includes items that remain unsold at the end of the current accounting period.

―――――――――― **Self-Check 21B**   Net Sales and Cost of Goods Sold ――――――――――

1. If a business realizes $215,000 from all sales during the month, $15,000 of which was returned to the store for refunds, what were the net sales for the month?

2. If beginning inventory is $500, ending inventory $1,000, and purchases during the month are $30,000, what is the cost of goods sold?

3. If beginning inventory was $98,605 and goods available for sale totaled $850,955, what was the dollar value of goods purchased during the accounting period?

4. Continuing with Problem 3, what was the cost of goods sold, provided that ending inventory was $112,313?

Comparative Income Statements

A more complete income statement is illustrated in Figure 21.1. Although more entries are included than in the preceding example, you will find that you are already acquainted with the main segments of the statement: sales, net sales, cost of goods sold, gross profit, expenses, and net income. From this statement, we can see that after costs and expenses have been deducted from incoming sales revenues, $111,500 of net income remains.

```
┌─────────────────────────────────────────────────────┐
│              ARROW ELECTRONICS                       │
│                                                      │
│              Income Statement                        │
│                                                      │
│          Year Ended December 31, 1990                │
│                                                      │
│  Sales revenues:        $323,426                     │
│    Returns                 4,426                     │
│    Net sales                           $319,000      │
│                                                      │
│  Cost of goods sold:                                 │
│    Beginning inventory  $ 14,500                     │
│    Goods purchased       130,000                     │
│    Goods available       144,500                     │
│    Ending inventory       15,000                     │
│    Cost of goods sold                  $129,500      │
│  Gross profit                          $189,500      │
│                                                      │
│  Expenses                                            │
│    Wages and salaries   $ 56,000                     │
│    Utilities              11,000                     │
│    Interest on loan        2,000                     │
│    Mortgage interest       6,000                     │
│    Depreciation expense    3,000                     │
│    Total expenses                      $ 78,000      │
│  Net income                            $111,500      │
└─────────────────────────────────────────────────────┘
```

Figure 21.1 Income Statement

A **comparative income statement,** like the one illustrated in Figure 21.2, provides a clearer picture by placing all entries alongside those for the preceding year and stating each entry as a percent of net sales.

We divide each item for 1990 by net sales for that year. On the first line, for example, we find that sales revenues are 101.4 percent of net sales:

$$\frac{\text{Sales}}{\text{revenues}} \div \frac{\text{Net}}{\text{sales}} = \frac{\text{Sales as a \%}}{\text{of net sales}}$$

$$323{,}426 \div 319{,}000 = 1.0138746$$

We then convert the answer to a percent (see % sign at top of the column) by moving the decimal two places to the right and rounding to the tenths position, giving us 101.4.

After following the same procedure for the 1989 figures, we may compare percents for the two years. We can see, for instance, that gross profit as a percent of sales declined from 61.1 percent in 1989 to 59.4 percent in 1990. Net income declined from 36.9 percent of sales in 1989 to 35.0 percent in 1990, with corresponding increases in costs and expenses.

ARROW ELECTRONICS

Comparative Income Statement

December 31, 1990 and 1989

	1990		1989	
	Amount	% of Sales	Amount	% of Sales
Sales revenues	$323,426	101.4	$290,221	100.7
Returns	4,426	1.4	2,110	0.7
Net sales	319,000	100.0	288,111	100.0
Cost of goods sold: Beginning inventory	14,500	4.5	15,609	5.4
Goods purchased	130,000	40.8	110,901	38.5
Goods available	144,500	45.3	126,510	43.9
Ending inventory	15,000	4.7	14,500	5.0
Cost of goods sold	129,500	40.6	112,010	38.9
Gross profit	189,500	59.4	176,101	61.1
Expenses: Wages and salaries	56,000	17.6	49,900	17.3
Utilities	11,000	3.4	9,002	3.1
Interest on loan	2,000	0.6	2,500	0.9
Mortgage	6,000	1.9	6,000	2.1
Depreciation	3,000	0.9	2,500	0.9
Total expenses	78,000	24.5	69,902	24.3
Net income	$111,500	35.0	$106,199	36.9

Figure 21.2 Comparative Income Statement (Percent of Net Sales)

─────────────── **Self-Check 21C** Comparative Income Statements ───────────────

Complete the following abbreviated income statement comparison and round the percent answers to tenths:

	1990		1989	
	Amount	% of Sales	Amount	% of Sales
Net sales	$245,000	100.0	$215.000	100.0
Cost of goods sold	190,000		172,000	
Gross profit				
Expenses	45,000		26,000	
Net income				

Percent of Increase or Decrease

We may also compare income statements for two years, as illustrated in Figure 21.3, by computing the amount and percent of increase or decrease from one year to the next.

We first subtract amounts for the earlier year from amounts for the more recent year. Then, to find the percent of increase or decrease, we divide the difference by the amount for the earlier year. To illustrate, sales revenues are compared as follows:

$$\frac{1990 \text{ amount} - 1989 \text{ amount}}{1989 \text{ amount}} =$$

$$\frac{323{,}426 - 290{,}221}{290{,}221} = \frac{33{,}205}{290{,}221} = 0.114 = 11.4\%$$

ARROW ELECTRONICS

Comparative Income Statement

For year ended December 31, 1990 and 1989

	1990	1989	Increase (Decrease) Amount	%
Sales revenues	$323,426	$290,221	$33,205	11.4
Returns	4,426	2,110	2,316	109.8
Net sales	319,000	288,111	30,889	10.7
Cost of goods sold: Beginning inventory	14,500	15,609	(1,109)	(7.1)
Goods purchased	130,000	110,901	19,099	17.2
Goods available	144,500	126,510	17,990	14.2
Ending inventory	15,000	14,500	500	3.4
Cost of goods sold	129,500	112,010	17,490	15.6
Gross profit	189,500	176,101	13,399	7.6
Expenses: Wages and salaries	56,000	49,900	6,100	12.2
Utilities	11,000	9,002	1,998	22.2
Interest on loan	2,000	2,500	(500)	(20.0)
Mortgage	6,000	6,000	—	—
Depreciation	3,000	2,500	500	20.0
Total expenses	78,000	69,902	8,098	11.6
Net income	$111,500	$106,199	$ 5,301	5.0

Figure 21.3   Comparative Income Statement (Amount and Percent of Change)

We move the decimal two places to the right, but, because the percent sign is shown at the top of the column in the comparative income statement, we do not enter the percent sign with the newly found percent.

The same procedure works for decreases, as in *beginning inventory*.

$$\frac{14,500 - 15,609}{15,609} = \frac{-1,109}{15,609} = -0.071 = (7.1\%)$$

The company has 7.1 percent fewer dollars tied up in inventory at the beginning of 1990 than at the beginning of 1989. Accountants commonly use parentheses to show that there has been a decrease, as is done here.

Self-Check 21D   Percent of Increase or Decrease

Complete the following comparative income statement and round the percent answers to tenths:

	1990	1989	Increase (Decrease) Amount	Percent
Net sales	$950,217	$895,310	$54,907	6.1
Cost of goods sold	737,800	712,111		
Expenses	196,212	156,212		
Net income	$ 16,205	$ 26,987		

Answers to Self-Checks

Self-Check 21A

1. $40,000

2. $20,000

3. $60,000

4. $1,319,610

Self-Check 21B

1. $200,000

2. $29,500

3. $752,350

4. $738,642

Self-Check 21C

Cost of goods sold: 77.6%; 80.0%
Gross profit: $55,000; 22.4%; $43,000; 20.0%
Expenses: 18.4%; 12.1%
Net income: $10,000; 4.1%; $17,000; 7.9%

Self-Check 21D

$25,689	3.6%
$40,000	25.6%
($10,782)	(40.0)

1. Income statement (5 points each)

a. If sales are $80,000 and the cost of goods sold is $65,000, what is the gross profit?

b. In Problem 1.a, what is the net income if expenses are $10,000?

c. If the net income is $65,000 and the gross profit is $125,000, what are the expenses?

d. If net income is $14,520, expenses $39,110, and cost of goods sold $158,210, what was sales?

e. If a business sells $295,000 of merchandise during the year and merchandise returns total $13,500, what was the amount of net sales?

f. During the year, a business purchased goods for resale totaling $280,300. If beginning inventory was $46,390 and ending inventory $55,934, what was the cost of goods sold?

g. If total sales were $185,000 and the cost of goods sold was $123,000, what percent of sales was the cost of goods sold?

h. If total expenses were $89,740 in 1989 and $97,403 in 1990, what was the amount of increase?

i. In Problem 1.h, what was the percent of increase?

j. If net income was $37,112 in 1990 and $48,650 in 1989, what was the percent of decrease?

2. Income statement analysis (50 points)

Complete the following income statement, showing each entry as a percent of net sales. Round to tenths of a percent.

S & J AUTO PARTS, INC.		
Income Statement		
December 31, 1990		
		% of Sales
SALES REVENUES	$1,209,009	
Returns	9,009	
Net sales	1,200,000	100.0
COST OF GOODS SOLD Beginning inventory	110,683	
Goods purchased	975,002	
Goods available	1,085,685	
Ending inventory	95,116	
Cost of goods sold	990,569	
GROSS PROFIT	209,431	
EXPENSES: Wages and salaries	126,332	
Utilities	8,764	
Interest on loan	1,263	
Mortgage	2,500	
Depreciation	1,200	
Total expenses	140,059	
NET INCOME	69,372	
Federal income tax	13,162	
AFTER-TAX INCOME	$ 56,210	

1. Comparative income statement (50 points)

Complete the following statement, rounding your answers to tenths of a percent so that net sales equal 100.0 percent.

	1990		1989	
	BIGELOW CORPORATION Comparative Income Statement 1990 and 1989			
Income:	Amount	Percent of Sales	Amount	Percent of Sales
Sales	$502,000		$468,960	
Returns	2,000		1,960	
Net sales	500,000	100.0	467,000	100.0
Cost of goods sold: Inventory January 1	45,000		38,750	
Produced during year	310,000		298,610	
Available for sale	355,000		337,360	
Inventory December 31	55,000		45,000	
Cost of goods sold	300,000		292,360	
Gross profit	200,000		174,640	
Operating expenses: Salaries	133,000		110,300	
Advertising	10,500		13,350	
Utilities	3,500		2,750	
Depreciation	3,000		3,000	
Property tax	1,000		1,000	
Interest	7,000		6,000	
Total expenses	158,000		136,400	
Net income	42,000		38,240	
Federal tax	6,300		5,736	
Net income after taxes	$ 35,700		$ 32,504	

2. Comparative income statement (50 points)

Complete the following statement, rounding your answers to tenths of a percent.

<table>
<tr><td colspan="5" align="center">BIGELOW CORPORATION
Comparative Income Statement
1990 and 1989</td></tr>
<tr><td></td><td></td><td></td><td colspan="2" align="center">Increase (Decrease)</td></tr>
<tr><td>Income:</td><td>1990</td><td>1989</td><td>Amount</td><td>%</td></tr>
<tr><td>Sales</td><td>$502,000</td><td>$468,960</td><td></td><td></td></tr>
<tr><td>Returns</td><td>2,000</td><td>1,960</td><td></td><td></td></tr>
<tr><td>Net sales</td><td>500,000</td><td>467,000</td><td></td><td></td></tr>
<tr><td>Cost of goods sold:
Inventory January 1</td><td>45,000</td><td>38,750</td><td></td><td></td></tr>
<tr><td>Produced during year</td><td>310,000</td><td>298,610</td><td></td><td></td></tr>
<tr><td>Available for sale</td><td>355,000</td><td>337,360</td><td></td><td></td></tr>
<tr><td>Inventory December 31</td><td>55,000</td><td>45,000</td><td></td><td></td></tr>
<tr><td>Cost of goods sold</td><td>300,000</td><td>292,360</td><td></td><td></td></tr>
<tr><td>Gross profit</td><td>200,000</td><td>174,640</td><td></td><td></td></tr>
<tr><td>Operating expenses:
Salaries</td><td>133,000</td><td>110,300</td><td></td><td></td></tr>
<tr><td>Advertising</td><td>10,500</td><td>13,350</td><td></td><td></td></tr>
<tr><td>Utilities</td><td>3,500</td><td>2,750</td><td></td><td></td></tr>
<tr><td>Depreciation</td><td>3,000</td><td>3,000</td><td></td><td></td></tr>
<tr><td>Property tax</td><td>1,000</td><td>1,000</td><td></td><td></td></tr>
<tr><td>Interest</td><td>7,000</td><td>6,000</td><td></td><td></td></tr>
<tr><td>Total expenses</td><td>158,000</td><td>136,400</td><td></td><td></td></tr>
<tr><td>Net income</td><td>42,000</td><td>38,240</td><td></td><td></td></tr>
<tr><td>Federal tax</td><td>6,300</td><td>5,736</td><td></td><td></td></tr>
<tr><td>Net income after taxes</td><td>$ 35,700</td><td>$ 32,504</td><td></td><td></td></tr>
</table>

CHAPTER

22

Balance Sheets

After reading Chapter 22, you will be able to

- Explain the purpose of balance sheets.
- Describe the main categories of balance sheets.
- Prepare comparative balance sheets.
- Determine the percent of increase or decrease of each balance sheet entry.

Unlike the income statement, which reflects incoming and outgoing dollars over a period of time, the **balance sheet** reveals the financial condition of a business at a specific moment. If the balance sheet is dated December 31, it reflects the condition of the business on that date only. The situation would have changed since November 30, and will soon change again. For this reason, the balance sheet is sometimes described as a "snapshot" of the business.

Main Categories

A balance sheet has three major segments: assets, liabilities, and ownership. An **asset** is anything that has economic value. One half of the balance sheet is a list of assets, and this list constitutes the value of the company. Assets *are* the company. A **liability** is a debt, an amount that is owed. **Ownership,** commonly referred to as "owners' net worth" and "owners' equity," equals the amount of money that owners have invested in the business. Owners share the business with creditors, therefore, in the sense that creditors have a claim on part of the business assets.

Because assets are the company and because liabilities and ownership represent claims on the company, it follows that the value of total assets must be equal to the sum of total liabilities and ownership. To illustrate, let's assume that a business has assets totaling $124,250, liabilities of $41,650, and ownership of $82,600:

$$\textbf{Assets} \ = \ \textbf{Liabilities} \ + \ \textbf{Ownership}$$
$$\$124,250 \ = \ \$ \ 41,650 \ + \ \ \$82,600$$
$$\$124,250 \ = \ \$124,250$$

Again, notice that total assets equal the sum of liabilities and ownership.

Self-Check 22A   Main Categories

1. Compute the balance of $21,949 in liabilities, $40,752 in assets, and $18,803 in ownership.

2. If ownership is $30,200 and assets are $40,156, what is the value of the company's debt?

3. If liabilities are $24,257 and ownership is $63,359, what is the value of total assets?

Expanded Balance Sheet

The balance sheet in Figure 22.1 consists of three categories just discussed (assets, liabilities, and ownership), except that more detail has been added.

Current assets are items of value that are usually consumed within one year, and **fixed assets** are those that last longer than one year. **Total assets,** which represent the recorded value of the company, are the sum of current and fixed assets.

Similarly, we add **current liabilities** (debts that come due within one year) and **long-term liabilities** (those that continue longer than one year) to derive total liabilities. Total liabilities are then added to total **capital** (ownership) to derive a grand total, a total that must agree with the figure for total assets ($383,747 = $383,747).

The word *capital* on a balance sheet signifies that the company is a *sole proprietorship* (owned by one person) or a *partnership* (owned by two or more persons). When a business is a *corporation* (owned by shareholders), ownership is referred to as **owners' equity,** which is the sum of the stock value and retained earnings. This point is explained further in Chapter 23.

ARROW ELECTRONICS

Balance Sheet

December 31, 1990

Current assets:		
Cash	$ 560	
Accounts receivable	20,187	
Inventory	15,000	
Short-term securities	6,000	
Total current assets		$ 41,747
Fixed assets:		
Equipment	$165,000	
Accumulated depreciation	36,000	
Net value of equipment	$129,000	
Buildings	213,000	
Total fixed assets		342,000
Total assets		$383,747
Current liabilities:		
Accounts payable	$ 14,331	
Income tax payable	2,110	
Wages payable	3,600	
Total current liabilities	$ 20,041	
Long-term liabilities:		
Bank loan	$ 14,600	
Mortgage	46,000	
Total long-term liabilities	$ 60,600	
Total liabilities		80,641
Total capital		303,106
Total liabilities and capital		$383,747

Figure 22.1 Balance Sheet

Self-Check 22B Expanded Balance Sheet

---

1. What are the five main categories on a balance sheet?

2. Under which heading would you place (a) inventories, (b) mortgage, and (c) accrued interest payable on a quarterly basis?

3. Why are accounts receivable placed under the heading "current assets"?

Comparative Balance Sheets

We may develop **comparative balance sheets** much as we prepared comparative income statements in Chapter 21. Using only the main elements of the Arrow Electronics balance sheet as an example in Figure 22.2, we may state each element as a percent of total assets.

	1990		1989	
	Amount	Percent of Assets	Amount	Percent of Assets
ASSETS: Current assets	$ 41,747	10.9	$ 38,616	10.8
Fixed assets	342,000	89.1	320,000	89.2
Total assets	383,747	100.0	358,616	100.0
LIABILITIES: Current liabilities	20,041	5.2	28,903	8.1
Long-term liabilities	60,600	15.8	48,600	13.6
Total liabilities	80,641	21.0	77,503	21.6
CAPITAL	303,106	79.0	281,113	78.4
Total liabilities and capital	$383,747	100.0	$358,616	100.0

Figure 22.2 Comparative Balance Sheet (Percent of Total Assets)

With total assets serving as the base, we divide each entry for 1990 by 383,747 and each entry for 1989 by 358,616.

This two-year comparison reveals that current liabilities declined as a percent of total assets, while ownership (capital) increased slightly. Accountants sometimes make such comparisons for several years of operations, rather than just the two years as shown here.

Self-Check 22C Comparative Balance Sheets

Complete this partial balance sheet, showing each entry as a percent of total assets and rounding your answers to tenths of a percent.

	1990		1989	
	Amount	Percent of Assets	Amount	Percent of Assets
CURRENT ASSETS:				
Cash	4,388		3,907	
Accounts receivable	33,062		28,631	
Inventories	72,358		65,730	
Prepaid expenses	5,401		4,812	
Total current assets	115,209		103,080	
FIXED ASSETS:				
Equipment	47,904		37,367	
Property	185,335		177,410	
Less accum. depreciation	−46,755		−35,825	
Total fixed assets	186,484		178,952	
Total assets	301,693		282,032	

Also, as illustrated in Figure 22.3, we may figure the amount of increase or decrease in each balance-sheet entry, much as we did with income statements in Chapter 21. As before, the difference between each pair of figures is divided by the figure for the earlier year, so that for *current assets* we have

$$\frac{\text{1990 figure} - \text{1989 figure}}{\text{1989 figure}} = \frac{41,747 - 38,616}{38,616}$$

$$= \frac{3,131}{38,616} = 8.1\%$$

From the comparative balance sheet in Figure 22.3, we can see that all items have increased substantially from one year to the next, except current liabilities, which decreased by a little more than 30 percent. As previously mentioned, a comparison of five or more years would have more meaning than this two-year comparison because it would enable us to identify trends in the financial condition of the business.

	1990	1989	Increase (Decrease) Amount	Increase (Decrease) Percent
ASSETS: Current assets	$ 41,747	$ 38,616	$ 3,131	8.1
Fixed assets	342,000	320,000	22,000	6.9
Total assets	383,747	358,616	25,131	7.0
LIABILITIES: Current liabilities	20,041	28,903	(8,862)	(30.7)
Long-term liabilities	60,600	48,600	12,000	24.7
Total liabilities	80,641	77,503	3,138	4.0
CAPITAL	303,106	281,113	21,993	7.8
Total liabilities and capital	$383,747	358,616	25,131	7.0

Figure 22.3   Comparative Balance Sheet (Amount and Percent of Change)

─────────── **Self-Check 22D**   Comparative Balance Sheet ───────────

Complete the following summary of business assets, rounding entries to tenths of a percent.

	1990 Amount	1990 %	1989 Amount	1989 %	Increase (Decrease) Amount	Increase (Decrease) %
Current assets	$25,904		$24,111			
Fixed assets	16,277		22,900			
Total assets	$42,181	100.0	$47,011	100.0		
Cur. liabilities	$ 7,682		$ 6,318			
L-T liabilities	12,153		11,591			
Capital	$22,346		$29,102			

Answers to Self-Checks

Self-Check 22A

1. $40,752

2. $9,956

3. $87,616

Self-Check 22B

1. Current assets
   Fixed assets
   Current liabilities
   Long-term liabilities
   Capital or equity

2. a. Current assets
   b. Long-term liabilities
   c. Current liabilities

3. Payments usually received
   within a short period of
   time — 10 to 90 days

Self-Check 22C

1990: 1.5, 11.0, 24.0, 1.8, 38.2
      15.9, 61.4, 15.5, 61.8, 100.0

1989: 1.4, 10.2, 23.3, 1.7, 36.5
      13.2, 62.9, 12.7, 63.5, 100.0

Self-Check 22D

Current assets: 61.4, 51.3, $1,793, 7.4
Fixed assets: 38.6, 48.7, (6,623), (28.9)
Total assets: ($4,830), (10.3)
Current liabilities: 18.2, 13.4, $1,364, 21.6
Long-term liabilities: 28.8, 24.7, 562, 4.8
Capital: 53.0, 61.9, ($6,756), (23.2)

1. **Balance sheet equation (round percent answers to tenths) (5 points each)**

a. What are total assets if liabilities are $460,000 and capital (ownership) is $375,000?

b. If total assets are $250,000 and total ownership is $216,000, what are total liabilities?

c. If total assets are $825,000 and liabilities are $413,000, what is the amount of ownership?

d. If current liabilities are $48,210, long-term liabilities are $128,500, and capital $245,000, what is the amount of total assets?

e. If current assets are $78,450 and total assets are $421,600, what percent is current assets of total assets?

f. If total liabilities are $98,480 and total assets are $875,100, what percent of total assets is total liabilities?

g. If total assets are $141,000 for the current year, compared with $127,300 for the last year, what was the amount of increase?

h. In Problem 1.g, what was the percent of increase?

i. If total liabilities for the current year are $678,208, compared with $721,446 for the previous year, what was the amount of decrease?

j. In Problem 1.i, what was the percent of decrease?

2. Balance sheet analysis (50 points)

Complete the following balance sheet analysis, showing each entry as a percent of total assets and rounding to tenths of a percent.

<table>
<tr><td colspan="3" align="center">S & J AUTO PARTS, INC.</td></tr>
<tr><td colspan="3" align="center">Balance Sheet</td></tr>
<tr><td colspan="3" align="center">December 31, 1990</td></tr>
<tr><td></td><td></td><td>Percent of Assets</td></tr>
<tr><td>Current assets:
Cash</td><td>$ 16,002</td><td></td></tr>
<tr><td>Accounts receivable</td><td>45,900</td><td></td></tr>
<tr><td>Inventory</td><td>95,116</td><td></td></tr>
<tr><td>Short-term securities</td><td>70,840</td><td></td></tr>
<tr><td>Total current assets</td><td>227,858</td><td></td></tr>
<tr><td>Fixed assets:
Equipment</td><td>422,142</td><td></td></tr>
<tr><td>Buildings</td><td>450,000</td><td></td></tr>
<tr><td>Total fixed assets</td><td>872,142</td><td></td></tr>
<tr><td>Total assets</td><td>$1,100,000</td><td>100.0</td></tr>
<tr><td>Current liabilities:
Accounts payable</td><td>65,010</td><td></td></tr>
<tr><td>Income tax payable</td><td>15,600</td><td></td></tr>
<tr><td>Wages payable</td><td>5,250</td><td></td></tr>
<tr><td>Total current liabilities</td><td>85,860</td><td></td></tr>
<tr><td>Long-term liabilities:
Bank loan</td><td>75,000</td><td></td></tr>
<tr><td>Mortgage</td><td>105,840</td><td></td></tr>
<tr><td>Total long-term liabilities</td><td>180,840</td><td></td></tr>
<tr><td>Total liabilities</td><td>$ 266,700</td><td></td></tr>
<tr><td>Owner's equity:
Common stock</td><td>500,000</td><td></td></tr>
<tr><td>Retained earnings</td><td>333,300</td><td></td></tr>
<tr><td>Total equity</td><td>833,300</td><td></td></tr>
<tr><td>Total liabilities and equity</td><td>$1,100,000</td><td></td></tr>
</table>

1. **Comparative balance sheet (50 points)**

Complete the following statement, rounding your entries to tenths of a percent.

	BIGELOW CORPORATION			
	Comparative Balance Sheet			
	December 31, 1990 and 1989			

	1990		1989	
	Amount	Percent of Assets	Amount	Percent of Assets
Current assets: Cash	$ 7,000		$ 8,500	
Short-term note	10,000		12,000	
Accounts receivable	13,000		12,500	
Merchandise inventory	55,000		45,000	
Total current assets	85,000		78,000	
Fixed assets: Buildings	200,000		200,000	
Equipment	215,000		200,000	
Accumulated depreciation	100,000		80,000	
Net fixed assets	315,000		320,000	
Total assets	$400,000	100.0	$398,000	100.0
Current liabilities: Accrued wages	$ 2,000		$ 3,000	
Accounts payable	14,000		9,250	
Notes payable	8,000		10,000	
Payroll taxes payable	1,000		900	
Total current liabilities	25,000		23,150	
Long-term liabilities: Notes payable	75,000		83,000	
Total liabilities	100,000		106,150	
Owner's equity: Common stock	200,000		200,000	
Preferred stock	25,000		25,000	
Retained earnings	75,000		66,850	
Total equity	300,000		291,850	
Total liabilities and equity	$400,000		$398,000	

2. Comparative balance sheet (50 points)

Complete the following statement, rounding percents to the tenths position.

<table>
<tr><td colspan="6" align="center">BIGELOW CORPORATION

Comparative Balance Sheet

December 31, 1990 and 1989</td></tr>
<tr><td rowspan="2"></td><td rowspan="2">1990</td><td rowspan="2">1989</td><td colspan="2">Increase (Decrease)</td></tr>
<tr><td>Amount</td><td>%</td></tr>
<tr><td>Current assets:
  Cash</td><td>$ 7,000</td><td>$ 8,500</td><td></td><td></td></tr>
<tr><td> Short-term note</td><td>10,000</td><td>12,000</td><td></td><td></td></tr>
<tr><td> Accounts receivable</td><td>13,000</td><td>12,500</td><td></td><td></td></tr>
<tr><td> Merchandise inventory</td><td>55,000</td><td>45,000</td><td></td><td></td></tr>
<tr><td> Total current assets</td><td>85,000</td><td>78,000</td><td></td><td></td></tr>
<tr><td>Fixed assets:
  Buildings</td><td>200,000</td><td>200,000</td><td></td><td></td></tr>
<tr><td> Equipment</td><td>215,000</td><td>200,000</td><td></td><td></td></tr>
<tr><td> Accumulated depreciation</td><td>100,000</td><td>80,000</td><td></td><td></td></tr>
<tr><td> Net fixed assets</td><td>315,000</td><td>320,000</td><td></td><td></td></tr>
<tr><td>Total assets</td><td>$400,000</td><td>$398,000</td><td></td><td></td></tr>
<tr><td>Current liabilities:
  Accrued wages</td><td>$ 2,000</td><td>$ 3,000</td><td></td><td></td></tr>
<tr><td> Accounts payable</td><td>14,000</td><td>9,250</td><td></td><td></td></tr>
<tr><td> Notes payable</td><td>8,000</td><td>10,000</td><td></td><td></td></tr>
<tr><td> Payroll taxes payable</td><td>1,000</td><td>900</td><td></td><td></td></tr>
<tr><td> Total current liabilities</td><td>25,000</td><td>23,150</td><td></td><td></td></tr>
<tr><td>Long-term liabilities:
  Notes payable</td><td>75,000</td><td>83,000</td><td></td><td></td></tr>
<tr><td> Total liabilities</td><td>100,000</td><td>106,150</td><td></td><td></td></tr>
<tr><td>Owner's equity:
  Common stock</td><td>200,000</td><td>200,000</td><td></td><td></td></tr>
<tr><td> Preferred stock</td><td>25,000</td><td>25,000</td><td></td><td></td></tr>
<tr><td> Retained earnings</td><td>75,000</td><td>66,850</td><td></td><td></td></tr>
<tr><td> Total equity</td><td>300,000</td><td>291,850</td><td></td><td></td></tr>
<tr><td>Total liabilities and equity</td><td>$400,000</td><td>$398,000</td><td></td><td></td></tr>
</table>

CHAPTER

23

Financial Ratios

After reading Chapter 23, you will be able to

- Judge the capacity of companies to pay bills promptly.
- Measure the qualifications of a company to repay short- and long-term loans.
- Assess the efficiency with which inventories are maintained and bills collected.
- Compute and compare the return on an investment with competing business opportunities.

Key Terms

liquidity
liquidity ratio
working capital
current assets
current liabilities
current ratio
quick ratio
acid test
leverage ratio
debt-to-total assets equation

debt-equity ratio
activity ratio
fixed-assets turnover
inventory turnover
receivables turnover
average collection period
profit ratio
sales margin
return on investment

Financial ratios provide a method of comparing two numbers in such a way that the relationship between those numbers is easy to comprehend. Rather than stating that short skirts outsold long skirts 824 to 103, for example, it is more effective to say that short skirts outsold long skirts by a ratio of 8 to 1:

$$824:103 = \frac{824}{103}:\frac{103}{103} = 8:1$$

We place both numbers side by side, and divide them both by the smaller of the two numbers. Because 103 is the smaller number, we divide 824 and 103 by 103, giving us 8 to 1.

Ratios that are commonly used for interpreting financial statements may be categorized as liquidity, leverage, activity, and profit ratios. The particular type of ratio that we rely on depends on whether we are creditors of the company, owners, or potential investors.

Liquidity Ratios

Liquidity in business is the amount of a firm's assets that can be converted to cash within the next few months, in relation to the amount of bills (debts) that must be paid during that time. **Liquidity ratios** provide business managers and their creditors with an indication of the company's ability to pay current bills promptly. To illustrate this concept, let's consider the income statement and balance sheet for Bigelow Corporation in Figures 23.1 and 23.2.

One measure of liquidity is **working capital,** which, although not technically a ratio, is the excess of **current assets** over **current liabilities.**

$$\frac{\text{Current}}{\text{assets}} - \frac{\text{Current}}{\text{liabilities}} = \frac{\text{Working}}{\text{capital}}$$

$$\$85,000 - \$25,000 = \$60,000$$

The difference of \$60,000 represents a significant degree of insurance against a possibility that the firm will run short of the amount of money that will be necessary to pay current bills as they come due.

The **current ratio** also relates current assets to current liabilities, but we divide instead of subtract:

$$\text{Current assets}:\text{Current liabilities}$$

$$\frac{\$85,000}{\$25,000}:\frac{\$25,000}{\$25,000}$$

$$3.4:1.0$$

BIGELOW CORPORATION

Income Statement

Year Ended December 31, 1990

Income:		
Sales	$502,000	
Returns	2,000	
Net sales		$500,000
Cost of goods sold:		
Inventory 1/1/90	$ 45,000	
Produced during year	310,000	
Available for sale	$355,000	
Inventory 12/31/90	55,000	
Cost of goods sold		300,000
Gross profit		$200,000
Operating expenses:		
Salaries	$133,000	
Advertising	10,500	
Utilities	3,500	
Depreciation	3,000	
Property tax	1,000	
Interest	7,000	
Total expenses		158,000
Net income		$ 42,000
Federal tax		6,300
Net income after taxes		$ 35,700

Figure 23.1   Income Statement

We divide current assets and current liabilities by current liabilities (the lower of the two figures), giving us 3.4 to 1. The value of current assets is almost $3\frac{1}{2}$ times the value of current liabilities. Assuming that a current ratio of 2 is common for the industry, creditors would view this ratio of 3.4 favorably because it indicates that the company has $3.40 in current assets for every $1.00 that it owes in current liabilities. From the owner's point of view, on the other hand, a high ratio of 3.4 may be an indication that the business has too much money tied up in current assets — money that could be invested and earning money.

The **quick ratio** (or **acid test,** as it is sometimes called) is the same as the current ratio, except that inventories are excluded from the computation:

$$\textbf{(Current assets − Inventories)}:\textbf{(Current liabilities)}$$

$$(\$85,000 − \$55,000):(\$25,000)$$

$$\$30,000:\$25,000$$

$$\frac{\$30,000}{\$25,000}:\frac{\$25,000}{\$25,000}$$

$$1.2:1.0$$

BIGELOW CORPORATION

Balance Sheet

December 31, 1990

Current assets:

Cash	$ 7,000	
Short-term notes	10,000	
Accounts receivable	13,000	
Merchandise inventory	55,000	
Total current assets		$ 85,000

Fixed assets:

Building	$200,000	
Equipment	215,000	
Accumulated depreciation	− 100,000	
Net fixed assets		315,000
Total assets		$400,000

Current liabilities:

Accrued wages	$ 2,000	
Accounts payable	14,000	
Notes payable	8,000	
Payroll taxes payable	1,000	
Total current liabilities		$ 25,000

Long-term liabilities:

Notes payable	$ 75,000	
Total long-term liabilities		75,000
Total liabilities		$100,000

Owners' equity:

Common stock	$200,000	
Preferred stock	25,000	
Retained earnings	75,000	
Total stockholder equity		300,000
Total liabilities and capital		$400,000

Figure 23.2 Balance Sheet

If creditors question the salability of the products in inventory, they may place a greater reliance on the quick ratio than on the current ratio. Because a 1:1 acid test ratio is generally considered to be the accepted standard in this industry, a ratio of 1.2:1 would appear favorable to short-term creditors. There are $1.20 of current assets, excluding inventory, for every $1.00 of current liabilities.

Self-Check 23A   Liquidity Ratios

---

1. If a company's current assets are $41,757 and current liabilities are $20,041, what is working capital?

2. In Problem 1, what is the current ratio?

3. If inventory is $15,000, what is the quick (acid test) ratio?

4. As a supplier who normally offers terms of 2/10, n/30, would you be inclined to make a credit sale to the company in Problems 2 and 3 — assuming the following industry averages?
   Current ratio: 2
     Quick ratio: 1

5. Using what might be described as common sense, what other factors would you consider when making the decision to offer credit to the company in Problem 1?

Leverage Ratios

Businesses and investors use **leverage ratios** to measure a company's borrowing power. Such ratios enable them to determine whether a company has borrowed too heavily or whether, instead, the company is in a position to borrow additional funds.

The **debt-to-total-assets equation** states outstanding debt as a percentage of total assets. To determine the percentage that total debt is of total assets, we divide total liabilities by total assets.

$$\frac{\text{Total liabilities}}{\text{Total assets}} = \frac{100,000}{400,000} = 25\%$$

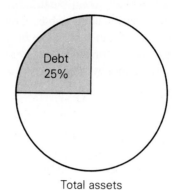

Total assets

Using the equation $BR = P$ (Base × Rate = Portion),

$$BR = P$$
$$400,000R = 100,000$$
$$R = 100,000 \div 400,000$$
$$R = 25\% \text{ or } 1/4$$

In effect, creditors have a claim to one-fourth of Bigelow Corporation. Because the creditors own one-fourth (25%) of the corporation, it follows that stockholders (owners of the corporation) have clear ownership to three-fourths (75%).

The **debt-equity ratio** expresses this relationship in a slightly different way. In dividing debt and equity by total debt (the lower of the two figures), we again find that creditors have claim to one-fourth of the company.

Debt:Equity

$$\$100,000 : \$300,000$$

$$\frac{\$100,000}{\$100,000} : \frac{\$300,000}{\$100,000}$$

$$1:3$$

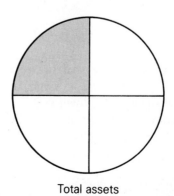

Total assets

Viewing the company as though it were a pie that has been divided into four pieces $(1 + 3 = 4)$, the creditors have claim to one piece $(\frac{1}{4})$ and the owners hold debt-free claim to the remaining three pieces $(\frac{3}{4})$. For every dollar that creditors have lent the firm, in other words, shareholders have contributed three dollars.

This situation is not necessarily undesirable. Creditors often have claim to 50 percent or more of a firm's assets. In fact, some business managers believe that they should continue adding to debt (borrowing) so long as they can earn a greater return by investing the borrowed money than it costs them in interest charges to borrow it.

Self-Check 23B   Leverage Ratios

---

1. If total liabilities are $175,000 and total assets are $525,000, what is the debt-to-total-assets percent?

2. If short-term liabilities are $75,000, long-term liabilities $326,000, and ownership $801,000, what is the debt-equity ratio?

3. Referring to Problem 2, would you, as a banker, be inclined to extend a long-term loan to this company on the basis of its debt-equity ratio—provided that most companies within the industry have a debt-equity ratio of $1:1$? Explain.

Activity Ratios

Activity ratios, which are related to time, measure the effectiveness with which the firm is using its resources. These ratios are of particular interest to managers, long-term creditors, and potential shareholders (owners).

The **fixed-assets turnover** measures the effectiveness with which business managers are utilizing their fixed assets (machinery, vehicles, buildings, and so forth) in relation to the amount of sales being realized.

$$\frac{\text{Net sales}}{\text{Fixed assets}} = \frac{500,000}{315,000} = 1.6 \text{ times}$$

If this turnover is high, compared with the average for the industry, we know that the business is getting a lot of use out of its fixed assets. If the ratio is comparatively low, instead, we know that the fixed assets are not being put to the best possible use.

The **inventory turnover** measures the number of times during the year that the merchandise in stock (inventory) has been sold and replenished.

$$\frac{\text{Cost of goods sold}}{\text{Average inventory}} = \frac{\$300,000}{\dfrac{\$45,000 + \$55,000}{2}}$$

$$= \frac{\$300,000}{\$50,000} = 6 \text{ times}$$

Average inventory was derived by adding beginning and ending inventories and dividing by 2. If we had three inventory figures for the year, including one for mid-year, we would add all three figures and divide by 3. If we had monthly figures, we would add them and divide by 12. The greater number of inventory figures we can average, the more accurate will be our results.

As with the other ratios, we may compare inventory turnover with those of our competitors within the industry. An inventory turnover that is too low indicates that we are carrying too much stock, generally resulting in excessive amounts of money being idle (not earning interest), higher insurance premiums, more pilferage, extra handling, and even obsolescence or spoilage. An inventory turnover that is relatively high, on the other hand, may indicate that we are sometimes short of stock, resulting in unfilled orders and lost customers.

The **receivables turnover** tells us how fast (or slow) the business is collecting money from credit customers. To determine the number of days that it takes us to collect for the products that we sell on credit, or the **average collection period,** we divide accounts receivable by the daily credit sales. Let's assume, for example, that 30 percent of our sales are for cash and that 70 percent are credit sales.

$$\frac{\text{Accounts receivable}}{\text{Credit sales}/360 \text{ days}} = \text{Average collection period}$$

$$\frac{\$13,000}{\dfrac{\$500,000 \times 0.70}{360}} = \frac{\$13,000}{\dfrac{\$350,000}{360}} = \frac{\$13,000}{972.2} = 13.4 \text{ days}$$

If our credit terms are for a period of 10 days, this average collection period of approximately 13 days is very good. Conversely, a long collection period would signal a need to tighten our credit approvals and improve our collection efforts.

Self-Check 23C Activity Ratios

---

1. If sales are $526,000 and returns are $10,500, what is the turnover of fixed assets totaling $350,000?

2. Beginning inventory was $44,600, midyear inventory was $59,260, and ending inventory was $49,445. If the cost of goods sold was $365,000, what was inventory turnover?

3. Fifty percent of all sales are made on credit, and total sales were $961,000. What was the receivables turnover if we have $21,214 in accounts receivable?

4. How do the preceding three ratios compare with the following industry averages?
   a. Fixed-assets turnover: 1.55 times
   b. Inventory turnover: 8.5 times
   c. Receivables turnover: 16 days

Profit Ratios

Owners, potential owners, and long-term creditors have a vital interest in **profit ratios,** which measure the profitability of a business. **Sales margin** is a common measure of profits, since it reveals the amount of profit realized from each incoming sales dollar.

$$\frac{\text{Net income after taxes}}{\text{Net sales}} = \frac{\$35,700}{\$500,000} = 0.0714$$
$$= 7.1\cent$$

Of each incoming sales dollar, a little more than 7 cents was after-tax profit, which means, of course, that the remaining 93 cents was used to pay costs and expenses incurred in earning the profit.

Return on investment, which states after-tax income as a percent of the investment, is a more reliable measure of profits in most situations and a measure with which you are probably familiar. If you are receiving $6\frac{1}{2}$ percent on the money you have deposited in a savings account, for example, you are realizing (after compounding quarterly) a return on investment of $6\frac{2}{3}$ percent.

The return on investment for Bigelow Corporation is 11.9 percent.

$$\frac{\text{Net income after taxes}}{\text{Ownership}} = \frac{\$35,700}{\$300,000} = 11.9\%$$

Ownership (equity) consists of the sum of common stock ($200,000), preferred stock ($25,000), and retained earnings ($75,000), giving us a total of $300,000 in stockholder equity. We should compare the 11.9 percent figure with the return on investment being realized by competing businesses and with other investment opportunities. If investment in Bigelow Corporation represents a high degree of risk, with respect to losing all or part of an investor's money, the investor might be better off to invest in another company or in government securities that represent a lower profit but also a lower risk.

Self-Check 23D   Profit Ratios

---

1. If net profit is $112,321, taxes are $47,414, and net sales are $2,163,567, what is the sales margin?

2. In Problem 1, what is the return on investment if the total value of the stock and retained earnings is $1,081,783?

3. Would you rather invest in the company discussed in Problems 1 and 2 or in another company with sales margin of 5¢ and a return on investment of 11%?

Summary of Financial Ratios

Liquidity ratios

$$\text{Working capital} = \text{Current assets} - \text{Current liabilities}$$

$$\text{Current ratio} = \frac{\text{Current assets}}{\text{Current liabilities}}$$

$$\text{Quick ratio} = \frac{\text{Current assets} - \text{Inventory}}{\text{Current liabilities}}$$

Leverage ratios

$$\text{Debt-to-total assets equation} = \frac{\text{Total liabilities}}{\text{Total assets}}$$

$$\text{Debt-equity ratio} = \frac{\text{Total liabilities and equity divided individually}}{\text{by the lower of the two figures}}$$

Activity ratios

$$\text{Fixed assets turnover} = \frac{\text{Net sales}}{\text{Fixed assets}}$$

$$\text{Inventory turnover (times a year)} = \frac{\text{Cost of goods sold}}{\text{Average inventory}}$$

$$\text{Receivables turnover (number of days)} = \frac{\text{Accounts receivable}}{\text{Credit sales} \div 360}$$

Profit ratios

$$\text{Sales margin} = \frac{\text{Net income after taxes}}{\text{Net sales}}$$

$$\text{Return on investment} = \frac{\text{Net income after taxes}}{\text{Owners' equity}}$$

─────────────────── **Answers to Self-Checks** ───────────────────

Self-Check 23A

1. $21,716

2. 2.1:1.0

3. 1.3:1.0

4. Yes

5. a. Payment record
   b. Value of the order

Self-Check 23B

1. $33\frac{1}{3}\%$

2. 1:2

3. Yes

Self-Check 23C

1. $1\frac{1}{2}$ times

2. 7.1 times

3. 15.9 days

4. a. Close to norm
   b. Relatively low
   c. Slightly lower

Self-Check 23D

1. 3¢

2. 6%

3. Inviting, but depends on risk factor

Using the following financial reports, compute the ratios. Round to tenths when appropriate (10 points each).

INCOME STATEMENT		
SALES REVENUES		$323,426
Returns		4,426
Net sales		$319,000
COST OF GOODS SOLD		
Beginning inventory	14,500	
Goods purchased	130,000	
Goods available	$144,500	
Ending inventory	15,000	
Cost of goods sold		$129,500
GROSS PROFIT		$189,500
EXPENSES		
Wages/salaries	56,000	
Utilities	11,000	
Interest on loan	500	
Mortgage	1,500	
Depreciation	3,000	
Total expenses		$ 72,000
NET INCOME		117,500
Federal income tax		69,900
AFTER-TAX INCOME		$ 47,600

BALANCE SHEET		
CURRENT ASSETS		
Cash	$ 560	
Accounts receivable	20,187	
Inventory	15,000	
Short-term securities	6,000	
Total current assets		$ 41,747
FIXED ASSETS		
Equipment	130,000	
Buildings	12,000	
Total fixed assets		$142,000
TOTAL ASSETS		$183,747
CURRENT LIABILITIES		
Accounts payable	$ 14,331	
Income tax payable	2,110	
Wages payable	3,600	
Total current liabilities		$ 20,041
LONG-TERM LIABILITIES		
Bank loan	$ 14,600	
Mortgage	46,000	
Total long-term liabilities		$ 60,600
TOTAL LIABILITIES		$ 80,641
OWNERS' EQUITY		
Common stock	$ 96,000	
Retained earnings	7,106	
Total owners' equity		$103,106
TOTAL LIABILITIES AND EQUITY		$183,747

a. Working capital

b.   Current ratio

c.   Quick (acid test) ratio

d.   Debt-to-total-assets

e.   Debt-equity ratio

f.   Fixed-asset turnover

g.   Inventory turnover

h.   Receivables turnover (75% of sales are on credit)

i.   Sales margin

j.   Return on investment

Using the following financial reports, compute the ratios. Round to tenths when appropriate (10 points each).

INCOME STATEMENT		
SALES REVENUE		$1,207,442
Returns		9,009
Net sales		$1,198,433
COST OF GOODS SOLD		
Beginning inventory		110,683
Goods purchased		975,002
Goods available		$1,085,685
Ending inventory		95,116
Cost of goods sold		$ 990,569
GROSS PROFIT		$ 207,864
EXPENSES		
Wages/salaries		$ 126,332
Utilities		8,764
Interest on loan		1,263
Mortgage		2,500
Depreciation		1,200
Total expenses		$ 140,059
NET INCOME		$ 67,805
Federal income tax		25,960
AFTER-TAX INCOME		$ 41,845

BALANCE SHEET		
CURRENT ASSETS		
Cash	$ 16,002	
Accounts receivable	45,900	
Inventory	95,116	
Short-term securities	10,000	$ 167,018
FIXED ASSETS		
Equipment	$422,142	
Buildings	450,000	872,142
TOTAL ASSETS		$1,039,160
CURRENT LIABILITIES		
Accounts payable	$ 65,010	
Income tax payable	15,600	
Wages payable	5,250	$ 85,860
LONG-TERM LIABILITIES		
Bank loan	$ 75,000	
Mortgage	45,000	120,000
TOTAL LIABILITIES		$ 205,860
OWNERS' EQUITY		
Common stock	$500,000	
Retained earnings	333,300	833,300
TOTAL LIABILITIES AND EQUITY		$1,039,160

a. Working capital

b. Current ratio

c. Quick (acid test) ratio

d. Debt-to-total-assets

e. Debt-equity ratio

f. Fixed-asset turnover

g. Inventory turnover

h. Receivables turnover (60% of sales are on credit)

i. Sales margin

j. Return on investment

Costs, Profits, and Dividends

After reading Chapter 24, you will be able to

- Distribute costs among the various divisions of a company on the basis of the amount of floor space or the number of employees in each area.
- Divide profits among the owners of a company, either equally or according to a predetermined formula.
- Compute the amount of profits to be "paid out" as dividends to the owners of common and preferred stock.

Key Terms

fixed ratio   common stock
dividend   preferred stock
shareholder   cumulative preferred stock

Business managers must establish guidelines for accountants to follow in charging each department a fair share of costs. Managers must also decide on an acceptable plan for dividing profits among the owners of the business.

Distributing Costs

To operate a business efficiently, managers must know whether a particular division or department of the company is profitable, and to what extent. They make this determination by identifying which costs are chargeable to each segment of the business.

Certain costs (such as wages, materials, and supplies) are chargeable to a certain department within the company. Some costs, however, do not belong to any one segment of the company. Because all operations within the business benefit from the services of the president, for example, each department must be charged a fair portion of his or her salary. The same statement is true with respect to such costs as insurance premiums, property taxes, air conditioning, custodial salaries, and office supplies.

Accountants may distribute (divide) such common costs among the various departments according to the number of employees. If a business has four departments, for example, accountants charge each department for part of a $5,000 insurance premium according to the percentage of total employees working within each department, as shown in Table 24.1.

Department	Employees	÷	Total	=	Percent
A	280	÷	1,400	=	20
B	490	÷	1,400	=	35
C	420	÷	1,400	=	30
D	210	÷	1,400	=	15
	1,400				100

Table 24.1 Percent of Employees in Each Department

To determine the percent of total employees working within each department, we divide the number of employees in each department by the total number of employees in the company (1,400). For example, we divide the 280 employees in Department A by the 1,400 people employed throughout the entire company and find that 20 percent of all employees work in Department A. We double-check our computations by making certain that the sum of employees in each department equals the total number of employees working for the company and that the sum of percents equals 100 percent.

Knowing the percent of employees in each department, we then distribute the $5,000 insurance premium among the departments, as shown in Table 24.2.

Department	Insurance Premium	×	Percent of Employees	=	Departmental Costs
A	$5,000	×	20	=	$1,000
B	5,000	×	35	=	1,750
C	5,000	×	30	=	1,500
D	5,000	×	15	=	750
					$5,000

Table 24.2   Distribution of Insurance Premium (By Percent of Employees in Each Department)

We double-check our computations by making certain that the total departmental costs equal the total cost that is being distributed, which in this case is a $5,000 insurance premium.

If, instead, costs are to be distributed on the basis of floor space, we begin by computing the square feet in each department as a percentage of total square feet in all departments, as shown in Table 24.3.

Department	Square Feet	÷	Total Footage	=	Percent
A	2,250	÷	10,000	=	22.5
B	3,250	÷	10,000	=	32.5
C	2,750	÷	10,000	=	27.5
D	1,750	÷	10,000	=	17.5
	10,000				100.0

Table 24.3   Percent of Square Feet in Each Department

We follow the same procedure as before. We divide the square feet in each department by the total square feet for all departments (10,000), giving us the percent of square feet for each department. And we double-check our accuracy by making certain that the sum of the square feet in each department equals the total square feet in all departments and that the sum of the percents equals 100 percent.

Knowing the percent of square feet in each department, we then distribute the $5,000 insurance premium among the departments as shown in Table 24.4.

Department	Insurance Premium	×	Percent of Total Area	=	Departmental Cost
A	$5,000	×	22.5	=	$1,125
B	5,000	×	32.5	=	1,625
C	5,000	×	27.5	=	1,375
D	5,000	×	17.5	=	875
					$5,000

Table 24.4   Distribution of Insurance Premium (By Percent of Square Footage in Each Department)

Again, we check to make certain that the sum of departmental costs is equal to the $5,000 insurance premium that is being distributed.

Self-Check 24A   Distributing Costs

---

1. Distribute a $1,868 electric bill among three departments on the basis of the following square footage:

   Dept. A: 2,160
   Dept. B: 954
   Dept. C: 2,250

2. Total company sales are $250,000, $37,500 of which were made by the Western Division. If overhead is distributed according to sales, how much of a $4,500 utility bill will be charged to the Western Division?

3. How much of the utility bill in Problem 2 will be charged to the Eastern Division, a division that generated $112,500 in sales?

Dividing Profits

When two or more persons enter into a partnership agreement to own a business, one of the first things that they should decide is how they are going to divide the profits — or the losses. If Smith, Jones, and Vacarro decide to divide everything equally, for example, each will receive one-third of the profits. Correspondingly, each partner will suffer one-third of any losses that the business may incur. Assuming an annual profit of $66,000, each partner will receive $22,000, as shown in Table 24.5.

Partner	Profit	×	Fraction	=	Share
Smith	$66,000	×	$\frac{1}{3}$	=	$22,000
Jones	66,000	×	$\frac{1}{3}$	=	22,000
Vacarro	66,000	×	$\frac{1}{3}$	=	22,000 $66,000

Table 24.5   Equal Distribution of Profits

The partners may alternatively decide to split their profits and losses according to a **fixed ratio,** with Smith receiving 3 parts, Vacarro 4 parts, and Jones 5 parts, as shown in Table 24.6.

Denominator of fraction

$$3 + 4 + 5 = 12$$

Partner	Profit	×	Fraction	=	Share
Smith	$66,000	×	$\dfrac{3}{12}$	=	$16,500
Vacarro	66,000	×	$\dfrac{4}{12}$	=	22,000
Jones	66,000	×	$\dfrac{5}{12}$	=	27,500
					$66,000

Table 24.6 Fixed Ratio Distribution of Profits

We begin by adding the three parts (3, 4, and 5), giving us a denominator of 12; and each of the three parts serves as a numerator. Smith receives 3/12 of the profits, Vacarro receives 4/12, and Jones receives 5/12. We double-check our computation by making certain that the sum of the individual shares equals the total profits to be distributed—in this case, $66,000.

It is also common practice for partners to divide their profits and losses according to the amount of money invested in the business. If Smith has $60,000 invested, Vacarro $90,000, and Jones $100,000, they divide the $66,000 as shown in Table 24.7.

Denominator of fraction

$$60,000 + 90,000 + 100,000 = 250,000$$

Partner	Profit	×	Fraction	=	Share
Smith	$66,000	×	$\dfrac{60,000}{250,000}$	=	$15,840
Vacarro	66,000	×	$\dfrac{90,000}{250,000}$	=	23,760
Jones	66,000	×	$\dfrac{100,000}{250,000}$	=	26,400
					$66,000

Table 24.7 Distribution of Profits (According to Amount Invested)

Note that this method is identical to the division of profits according to a fixed ratio. The sum of the investments becomes the denominator in our fraction, and the individual investments the numerators. We double-check our computations, as before, by making certain that the sum of the individual shares equals the total amount of profits to be distributed among the partners, $66,000.

Self-Check 24B Dividing Profits

---

1. If four partners agree to divide profits and losses equally, how much money will each partner receive from profits totaling $83,554?

2. How much of $65,112 profits would Mike James receive if he is entitled to 3 parts compared with 2 parts each for the other two partners?

3. How much of the $15,000 profits would Susan Hanson receive if the distribution is based on her investment of $5,000, which is part of a total investment of $95,000?

Computing Dividends

Unlike partnerships, in which relatively few owners divide profits and losses among themselves, the managers of corporations must determine each year the amount of **dividends** (share of profits) that is to be divided among many shareholders. The owners of corporations are called **shareholders** (or *stockholders*) because they own stock (shares of ownership) issued by the corporation. Shares of **common stock** are the main form of partial ownership in a corporation.

The amount of dividends (if any) that a corporation pays to an owner of common stock depends on the amount of profits that the company is distributing (paying to owners) and the number of shares held by the owner. If a company has $250,000 profits to be divided among 500,000 shareholders, a shareholder who owns 100 shares of common stock will receive $50:

$$\frac{\text{Total dividend}}{\text{Number of shares}} = \frac{\$250,000}{500,000} = 0.50 \text{ Dividend per share}$$

$$\frac{\text{Number of}}{\text{shares held}} \times \frac{\text{Dividend}}{\text{per share}} = \frac{\text{Dividend}}{\text{payment}}$$

$$100 \quad \times \quad \$0.50 \quad = \quad \$50.00$$

By dividing the total amount of dividends to be paid by the total number of shares, we find that each share is entitled to 50 cents. Therefore, the owner of 100 shares of common stock receives 50 cents for each share, or $50.

Businesses sometimes issue **preferred stock.** "Preferred" does not mean that the stock is better than common stock; it is simply different in several ways. One way that preferred stock differs from common stock is that preferred stock usually has preference to dividends. Having preference to dividends dictates that the business pay a specified amount of dividends to the owners of preferred stock before they pay any dividends at all to the owners of common stock.

To illustrate, assume that a company has issued 50,000 shares of a 6 percent preferred stock with a declared value of $10 per share. Before the business can pay dividends to the owners of common stock, a dividend of 60 cents per share must be paid to owners of preferred stock ($10 × 0.06 = 60¢).

Assume further that the directors of this company have just decided to pay an annual dividend totaling $250,000 to the 50,000 shares of preferred stock and to the 400,000 shares of common stock.

$$\frac{\text{Preferred}}{\text{stock}} \times \frac{\text{Dividend}}{\text{per share}} = \frac{\text{Pay out to}}{\text{preferred}}$$

$$50,000 \times \$0.60 = \$30,000$$

$$\frac{\text{Total}}{\text{dividend}} - \frac{\text{Payout to}}{\text{preferred}} = \frac{\text{Payout to}}{\text{common}}$$

$$\$250,000 - 30,000 = \$220,000$$

$$\frac{\text{Dividends}}{\text{to common}} \div \frac{\text{Number of}}{\text{common shares}} = \frac{\text{Dividend per}}{\text{share of common}}$$

$$\$220,000 \div 400,000 = 55¢$$

After computing the amount of dividends to be paid to preferred stock at 60 cents per share ($30,000), we subtract that amount from the total funds available for the payment of dividends ($250,000). The amount remaining ($220,000) is then divided by the total shares of common stock (400,000), resulting in a dividend to common stock of 55 cents per share.

An investor who owns 100 shares of preferred stock and 150 shares of common stock will receive dividends totaling $142.50.

	$\frac{\text{Number of}}{\text{shares}}$	×	$\frac{\text{Dividend}}{\text{per share}}$	=	$\frac{\text{Dividend}}{\text{payment}}$
Preferred	100	×	$0.60	=	$ 60.00
Common	150	×	$0.55	=	82.50
					$142.50

Some preferred stocks are **cumulative,** which means that if the business does not pay dividends for one or more years, the fixed dividend on preferred stocks accumulates until dividends are paid. At the time of payment, the business must pay dividends to the owners of preferred stock for the current year and for the years that were skipped before they can legally pay any dividends to the owners of common stock. The owners of preferred stock have certain disadvantages, however, such as not participating in company earnings beyond a fixed amount and not having a vote in company affairs.

──────────────── **Self-Check 24C**   Computing Dividends ────────────────

1. If a business has 160,000 shares of common stock outstanding, what is the dividend per share on a distribution of $80,000 in dividends?

2. If a business has 10,000 shares of 5% preferred stock with a declared value of $100, what amount of dividends will be paid for each share?

3. Regarding Problem 2, what is the dividend per share for common stock if a total of $190,000 is available for the payment of dividends and if there are 700,000 shares of common stock outstanding?

──────────────── **Answers to Self-Checks** ────────────────

Self-Check 24A	**Self-Check 24B**	**Self-Check 24C**
1. $752.21	1. $20,888.50	1. 50¢
$332.23		
$783.56	2. $27,905.14	2. $5
2. $675	3. $789.47	3. 20¢
3. $2,025		

ASSIGNMENT 24A

Name _____

Costs, Profits, and Dividends

Score _____

1. Distributing costs (5 points each)

a. Rickter Company has two departments. Department A has 2,142 square feet, and Department B has 3,500 square feet. Department A contains what percent of the total footage?

b. In Problem 1.a, Department B contains what percent of the total footage?

c. If the total number of employees at the Seaside Cannery Company is 2,300, 1,600 of whom work in the packing department, what percent of total employees work in the packing department? Round answer to the tenths position.

d. In Problem 1.c, if administrative costs of $15,000 are to be distributed among the different departments at Seaside Cannery on the basis of the number of employees working in each department, how much of $15,000 in overhead costs will be charged to the packing department?

e. Referring to Problem 1.c, if the shipping department at Seaside Cannery employs 65 workers, how much of the $15,000 should be charged to that department?

2. Dividing profits (5 points each)

a. If a partnership has profits of $126,000, how much will each of the three partners receive if they have agreed to divide their profits and losses equally?

b. Assuming, instead, that the partners in Problem 2.a have agreed to divide profits on the basis of a fixed ratio of 1:6:5, how much of $126,000 in profits will each of the three partners receive?

c. If James Ingram has $78,000 invested in a partnership, compared with his partner's investment of $46,000, how much of $26,000 profits will James receive if they divide the profits according to the amount of money each partner has invested in the company?

d. In Problem 2.c, how much money will James's partner receive?

3. Computing dividends (5 points each)

a. If Ace Distributors has set aside $128,000 to distribute as dividends among the owners of 400,000 shares of common stock, what will be the amount of dividends paid for each share?

b. In Problem 3.a, if you own 200 shares of Ace's common stock, what amount of dividends do you expect to receive?

c. If Reliable Carpet Mills has 20,000 shares of $5\frac{1}{2}\%$ preferred stock outstanding, with a declared value of $50 per share, what is the normal dividend per share that might be expected by owners of the preferred stock?

d. If Reliable Carpet in Problem 3.c pays out $150,000 in dividends this year, how much will Jean Simmons receive for the 100 shares of preferred stock that she holds?

e. Referring to Problems 3.c and 3.d, how much of a dividend will the holders of common stock receive per share, assuming that 250,000 shares of common stock are outstanding?

4. Distributing costs (30 points)

Jansens Department Store has four main department categories, with floor areas as shown in the following table. Distribute the monthly rent of $15,000 among the departments on the basis of floor space within each department. Double-check your totals.

Department	Floor Area	Percent of Overhead	Monthly Rent	Share of Rent
Clothing	2,600			
Furniture	4,500			
Housewares	1,150			
Appliances	1,750			
Totals				

Name _____

Costs, Profits, and Dividends   Score _____

1. Distributing costs (5 points each)

a. Southwest Paper Products has three divisions. The Western region has 310 employees, the Rocky Mountain region has 318, and the Eastern region has 372. What percent of total company works in each division?

b. In Problem 1.a, distribute total overhead of $95,310 among the divisions according to the number of employees in each division.

c. If the institutional division of a manufacturing company has a total working area of 6,500 square feet, out of a total company area of 500,000 square feet, how much of $126,000 in overhead costs are chargeable to this one division?

d. Groceries Unlimited operates a chain of 12 grocery stores. As manager of one of the stores, how much of a total overhead charge of $144,000 is chargeable to your store on the basis of floor space, if your store has a total of 12,300 square feet compared with a total of 125,000 square feet for all 12 stores?

e. In Problem 1.d, how much of the $144,000 in overhead costs would be chargeable to your store on the basis of employees, if only 75 of the 1,200 company employees work in your store?

2. Dividing profits (5 points each)

a. Divide $65,250.20 among three partners. One partner is to receive 1/2 of the profits, with the balance to be split evenly between the other two partners.

b. Distribute $150,225.50 among four partners according to a ratio of 3:5:7:2.

c. How much of a $7,500 loss should Wilma Prouse assume if profits and losses are shared on the basis of investment? Wilma has $74,750 invested, and total investment is $325,000.

d. What percent of profits will each partner receive on the basis of individual investments by Jon of $50,000, Joyce $25,000, and Thomas $35,000? (Round answers to tenths.)

e. If, in Problem 2.d, total company profits are $8,200, how much does Jon receive?

3. Computing dividends (5 points each)

a. How much money is required to pay the full dividend to holders of 20,000 shares of 6% preferred stock that has a $100 declared value?

b. Gemcor Corporation has set aside $129,000 of earnings for the payment of dividends. Gemcor has 300,000 shares of common stock outstanding and no preferred stock. What amount of dividends will Bob Rice receive for his 300 shares of common stock?

c. United Tube Corporation plans to distribute dividends totaling $78,000 among holders of both common and preferred stock. Common stock totals 175,000 shares, and preferred (5%, $25 par) stock totals 7,000 shares. What is the dividend per share for common stock? Round answer to even cents.

d. In Problem 3.c, if you own 1,000 shares of United Tube common stock, what amount of dividends do you expect to receive?

4. Distributing costs (30 points)

Distribute $66,000 in property taxes among the following departments on the basis of floor area.

Department	Floor Area	Percent of Overhead	Property Tax	Share of Tax
A	3,600			
B	3,000			
C	3,750			
D	2,100			
E	2,550			
Totals				

CHAPTER 25

Stocks and Bonds

After reading Chapter 25, you will be able to

- Interpret stock and bond quotations.
- Prorate interest equitably between the buyers and sellers of bonds.
- Compute gains and losses realized through the purchase and sale of securities.

Corporations raise money from people and organizations outside the company by either selling stock (shares of the company) or by issuing bonds (borrowing). Let's consider some of the detail that is involved in buying and selling both stocks and bonds.

Interpreting Stock Quotations

Stock quotations and **bond quotations** are listed in several publications, including *The Wall Street Journal* (a weekday newspaper), *Barrons* (a weekly newspaper), and most city newspapers. The following stock quotation is typical.

| 52 weeks | | | | Yld. | P-E | Sales | | | | Net |
High	Low	Stock	Div.	%	Ratio	100s	High	Low	Close	Chg.
$39\frac{7}{8}$	$29\frac{3}{4}$	Alcoa	1.20	3.6	17	2133	34	$33\frac{1}{8}$	$33\frac{3}{4}$	$-\frac{1}{2}$
A	B	C	D	E	F	G	H	I	J	K

The headings above the figures appear at the top of each column of quotations in the newspaper, whereas the letters below the figures are added here to help explain each entry.

A. $39.875 was the highest price this stock has sold for during the past year. You will recall from earlier chapters that we convert 7/8 to its decimal equivalent by dividing 7 by 8 (7 ÷ 8 = 0.875).

B. $29.75 is the lowest price the stock has sold for during the past year.

C. Alcoa is an abbreviation for the company name, Aluminum Company of America.

D. $1.20 is the annual dividend per share paid to stockholders.

E. The current **dividend** (payout), as related to the current price (**close**), represents a 3.6 percent annual **yield** or return on investment (1.20 ÷ 33.75 = 3.6%).

F. A **price-earnings (P-E) ratio** of 17 means that the current price exceeds company earnings per share by 17 times. A P-E ratio of 10 (price being 10 times earnings) is considered the norm, suggesting that this stock is overpriced in relation to company earnings. Notice that this figure is always listed in whole numbers.

G. 213,300 shares changed hands (were bought and sold) during this one trading day (2133 + 00 = 213,300), which is referred to as the volume for the day.

H. $34.00 is the highest price this stock sold for during this one trading day.

I. $33.125 is the lowest price of the day.

J. $33.75 was the price of the last transaction of the day — the **closing price.**

K. The stock lost one-half of a point (50¢) during the one trading day; that is, from the closing price the preceding trading day to today's closing price.

Self-Check 25A Interpreting Stock Quotations

Respond to the following questions relating to this quotation for International Business Machines (IBM).

52 weeks		Stock	Div.	Yld. %	P-E Ratio	Sales 100s	High	Low	Close	Net Chg.
High	Low									
$138\frac{1}{4}$	$102\frac{3}{4}$	IBM	4.40	3.6	12	17530	$123\frac{3}{8}$	$121\frac{1}{4}$	122	$+1\frac{1}{4}$

1. What was the highest price that IBM sold for on this trading day?

2. What was the lowest price during the past year?

3. What was the volume for the day?

4. How was a yield of 3.6 computed?

5. How much value did the stock gain per share during this one day?

6. Explain the *12* entry.

Interpreting Bond Quotations

Unlike stock, which represents ownership in a corporation, **bonds** represent debt to the issuing company. A bond is a kind of IOU that the corporation gives a bondholder, a promise to repay a borrowed sum of money. Bond quotations differ materially from stock quotations, as illustrated in the following quotation.

Bonds		Cur. Yld	Vol.	Close	Net Chg.
Alcoa	7.45s96	9.9	25	$75\frac{1}{8}$	$-1\frac{1}{4}$
A	B	C	D	E	F

A. Alcoa is the name of the company, Aluminum Company of America.

B. 7.45 is the annual percent of interest (paid semiannually) on this $1,000 bond, which amounts to $74.50 a year $(1,000 \times 0.0745 = 74.50)$. (Most corporate bonds are issued in denominations of $1,000.)

The letter *s* has no meaning other than to separate the interest rate from the maturity date and is not used when the rate contains a fraction $(7\frac{1}{8}96)$ rather than a decimal. Think of *s* as standing for *space*.

96 specifies that the bond matures (is payable by the company at the face value of $1,000) in 1996.

C. **Current yield** (return on investment) if purchased at today's closing price is 9.9 percent.

$$\frac{\text{Interest on face value}}{\text{Closing price}} = \frac{\$1,000 \times 0.0745 \times 1}{\$751.25}$$

$$= \frac{\$74.50}{\$751.25} = 0.9916 = 9.9\%$$

D. The volume is 25, meaning that 25 $1,000 bonds exchanged hands on this one trading day.

E. The closing price on the one trading day was $751.25,

$$75\frac{1}{8} = 75.125\%$$
$$0.75125 \times \$1,000 = \$751.25$$

F. Today's closing price declined by $1\frac{1}{4}$ $(1\frac{1}{4}\%)$ from the closing price of the preceding trading day, resulting in a net change of $12.50.

$$0.0125 \times \$1,000 = \$12.50$$

The interest rate of not quite $7\frac{1}{2}$ percent is much lower than the rates on newly issued bonds at this particular time, making it necessary for any bondholder wanting to sell to do so at a $250 discount $(\$1,000.00 - \$751.25 = \$248.75)$. When the interest on a bond is higher than current rates, on the other hand, a bondholder may sell at a premium, as illustrated in the following self-check.

Self-Check 25B   Interpreting Bond Quotations

Respond to the following questions relating to this quotation for a bond that was issued by Citicorp, a banking institution.

Bonds		Cur. Yld	Vol.	Close	Net Chg.
Citicorp	$11\frac{1}{4}98$	10.9	100	$102\frac{3}{4}$	$-\frac{3}{4}$

1. How much did the purchaser of the last sale of the day pay for this $1,000 bond?

2. How much interest does the bondholder receive every 6 months?

3. How was the yield of 10.9% computed?

4. The ownership changed hands for how many Citicorp bonds on this one trading day?

5. What is the year of maturity?

6. How much money will the owners of one of these bonds receive from Citicorp on the maturity date?

7. How much value (in dollars and cents) did this bond lose from yesterday's close to today's close?

Prorating Bond Interest

Investors generally employ the services of stockbrokers when buying and selling securities; and when investors buy and sell bonds, brokers must prorate the **bond interest.** In addition to the selling price of the bond, sellers expect to receive any interest that the bond has earned—less the broker's commissions, of course:

$$\text{Amount seller receives} = \text{Selling price} + \text{Accrued interest} - \text{Broker's commission}$$

Interest is figured from the last payment date (usually January 1 or July 1) to the **settlement date** (the date that the seller is credited and the buyer charged).

We compute the amount to be paid by the buyer in the same way, except that the broker's commission is added rather than subtracted.

$$\text{Amount buyer pays} = \text{Selling price} + \text{Accrued interest} + \text{Broker's commission}$$

To illustrate such a transaction, assume that you sell at 97 one $1,000 bond that pays 11 percent interest, with April 1 being the settlement date. Assume further that the broker's commission is $5 per bond:

$$\text{Selling price} = \$1,000 \times 0.97 = \$970$$

$$\text{Accrued interest} = \$1,000 \times 0.11 \times \frac{90}{360} = \$27.50$$

$$\text{Amount seller receives} = \$970.00 + \$27.50 - \$5.00$$

$$= \$992.50$$

Buyers of bonds have five trading days (not including Saturdays, Sundays, or holidays) to pay for their purchases, with the fifth day being the settlement date. The buyer pays for the value of the bond or bonds and any interest that the seller has already earned, as well as a broker's commission.

$$\text{Amount buyer pays} = \$970.00 + \$27.50 + \$5.00 = \$1,002.50$$

The $27.50 interest that the buyer pays the seller will be reimbursed, in effect, when the buyer receives the six-month interest payment from the issuing corporation. The related dates are as follows:

January 1

Last interest payment received by seller from the corporation.

April 1

Settlement date for the exchange, at which time the buyer pays the seller interest for the three-month period from January 1 to April 1.

July 1

Buyer collects interest from the corporation for six-month period from January 1 to July 1.

Self-Check 25C   Prorating Bond Interest
---

1. What will be the total cost to the buyer of ten $1,000 bonds that earn interest of 12% and sold for 113, if the broker's buying commission is $5 per bond and 30 days have passed since the last payment?

2. How much money will the seller receive if the broker's selling commission is also $5?

3. If the buyer holds the bonds until the next interest payment is due, how much money will be received from the corporation?

4. What size payment will the buyer receive from the corporation at the date of maturity?

Computing Gains and Losses

A **capital gain** (or **loss**) is a gain (or loss) that corporations and individuals realize from the sale of such properties as stocks, bonds, vehicles, machinery, and buildings. When investors sell stocks, they deduct the amount that they originally paid for the stock (including buying and selling commissions) to determine their capital gain or capital loss.

Selling value
- __Broker's commission__
= __Net value__
- __Purchase price (including commission)__
= Capital gain or loss

If you purchased 300 shares of stock for $10,000, plus broker's commission of $150, and sold them for $15,000, less broker's commissions of $175, you have a capital gain of $4,675:

$15,000 Selling value
-     175 Selling commissions
= $14,825 Net value
- 10,150 Purchase price (including commission)
= $ 4,675 Capital gain

Until recently, investors received special tax treatment on capital gains from the sale of securities that they had owned for longer than six months. Currently, however, 100 percent of all capital gains are taxable.

Self-Check 25D Computing Gains and Losses

---

1. You have just learned from your broker that 200 shares of Goodyear stock has been purchased at your request at a quote of $52\frac{3}{4}$. What will be the amount of your check to the broker—assuming a buying commission of $131.88 and a transaction tax of $6.15?

2. If you sell 150 shares of IBM for $18,300, with a broker's commission of $65 and a transaction tax of $2.35, what should be the amount of the check that the broker issues to you?

3. If you purchased 10 bonds at a price of $870 each and sold them 5 years later at a price of $910 each, what is the taxable gain? Assume a broker's commission of $7 per bond on both the purchase and the sale and ignore any state and local taxes that might prevail.

—————————————————————— **Answers to Self-Checks** ——————————————————————

Self-Check 25A

1. $123.375

2. $102.75

3. 1,753,000

4. $\dfrac{4.40}{122.0} = 3.6\%$

5. $1.25

6. Only slightly above the norm

Self-Check 25B

1. $1,027.50

2. $56.25

3. $\dfrac{112.50}{1,027.50} = 10.9\%$

4. 100

5. 1998

6. $1,000

7. $7.50

Self-Check 25C

1. $11,450

2. $11,350

3. $600

4. $10,000

Self-Check 25D

1. $10,688.03

2. $18,232.65

3. $260

ASSIGNMENT 25A   Name _____

Stocks and Bonds   Score _____

1. **Interpreting stock quotations (5 points each)**

| 52 Weeks | | Stock | Div. | P-E Ratio | Yld. % | Sales 100s | High | Low | Close | Net Chg. |
High	Low									
$37\frac{1}{2}$	$26\frac{1}{4}$	JB Ind	.75	12	2.3	20	$33\frac{3}{4}$	$32\frac{1}{2}$	$33\frac{1}{8}$	$+\frac{3}{4}$

a. In this stock quotation, what is the highest price in dollars and cents that the stock sold for on this one trading day?

b. What was the highest price (in dollars and cents) that the stock has sold for during the past 12-month period?

c. How many shares exchanged hands on this one trading day?

d. In dollars and cents, what was the closing price of the stock? (Round answer to tenths of a cent.)

e. In dollars and cents, how much higher is the closing price than the closing price for the preceding day?

2. **Interpreting bond quotations (5 points each)**

Bonds	Cur. Yld.	Vol.	Close	Net Chg.
AAirl 11s98	14.3	4	77	+1

a. In this bond quotation for American Airlines, what is the closing price?

b. How many American Airlines bonds were bought and sold on this one trading day?

c. If you bought one or more of these bonds at the closing price, what would be your annual return on investment?

d. What is the rate of interest on these bonds?

e. In dollars and cents, how much did the price for American Airlines bonds increase since the closing price for the preceding day?

3.   **Prorating bond interest (5 points each)**

a.   If you buy a $1,000, 15% bond, how much interest will you have to pay the seller if interest was last paid 30 days before the settlement date?

b.   What will be your total cost for the bond in Problem 3.a, excluding broker's commissions and taxes, if the bond is bought at a price of 98?

c.   How much money will the seller receive if commissions are $7 and taxes are $1?

d.   Find the total cost for the purchase of five $1,000, 9 percent bonds quoted at $85\frac{1}{2}$, if commissions are $7.50 per bond and interest is payable on January 1 and July 1 and the settlement date is July 15.

e.   In Problem 3.d, how much money will the seller receive, assuming a selling commission of $7 per bond?

4.   **Computing gains and losses (5 points each)**

a.   If Jean Simes sells her 100 shares of TWA stock today for $9\frac{1}{4}$, which she had purchased approximately 2 years ago at $12\frac{1}{2}$, what is her gain or loss? She paid $42 in commissions when she bought the stock and $36 in commissions at the time of the sale.

b.   If you sell 300 shares of Shell Oil stock for $71\frac{1}{8}$ and the broker's selling commission is $265, how much money will you receive from the transaction?

c.   In Problem 4.b, if you originally paid $65\frac{1}{4}$ for the stock (plus $250 commission) and held it for 12 months before selling, what would be your gain?

d.   Amanda Morris bought 5 Cities Service $1,000 bonds at a quotation of $102\frac{7}{8}$ and paid a broker's commission of $6.50 per bond. How much money did she have to send to the broker, ignoring any interest payments?

e.   If Amanda sells the 5 bonds about 3 months later, what is her taxable gain, assuming a selling price of $1,075 and a commission of $7 per bond?

1. **Interpreting stock quotations (5 points each)**

52 weeks		Stock	Div.	P-E Ratio	Yld. %	Sales 100s	High	Low	Close	Net Chg.
High	Low									
$66\frac{1}{4}$	$33\frac{5}{8}$	Boeing	1.60	2.5	18	4279	$65\frac{1}{4}$	$64\frac{5}{8}$	65	$+\frac{5}{8}$

a. What is the lowest price in dollars and cents that the stock sold for during the last year?

b. In dollars and cents, what was the highest price the stock sold for on this one trading day?

c. What amount of quarterly dividend may be expected per share?

d. How many shares exchanged hands on this one trading day?

e. Assuming a commission charge of $96.93 and a related tax of $16.15, what amount must the buyer of 100 shares of Boeing pay? Use the lowest price of the day.

2. **Prorating bond interest (5 points each)**

a. If you buy a $1,000, 7% bond on December 18 at a quotation of 96, what is the total cost, not including interest or commissions?

b. In Problem 2.a, how much interest must you pay the seller for the bond, assuming that interest payments are made on January 15 and July 15?

c. If you sell ten $1,000, 7% bonds on July 15, how much interest will you receive since the last interest payment on June 30?

d. What amount of interest will the holder of a $1,000, 7% bond be paid on January 15 if the closing quotation is 84 and the payment dates are January 15 and July 15?

e. If the closing quotation of a $1,000 bond is $95\frac{1}{2}$, on which interest of $8\frac{1}{2}$ percent is paid, what is the yield? (Round answer to tenths of a percent.)

3. Interpreting bond quotations (5 points each)

Bonds	Cur. Yld.	Vol.	Close	Net Chg.
Exxon $6\frac{1}{2}98$	7.7	15	84	$\frac{1}{8}$

a. In this bond quotation, what is the closing price?

b. What is the semiannual interest payment on just one bond?

c. How many Exxon bonds were bought and sold on this one trading day?

d. Enter the equation that is required to compute the current yield of 7.7 percent.

e. What does the number *98* designate?

4. Computing gains and losses (5 points each)

a. If Frank Osborne bought 100 shares of Chevron stock last year at $38\frac{1}{4}$ and sells it today at $46\frac{3}{4}$, what is his gain?

b. In Problem 4.a, what amount will Frank receive from the broker for this one transaction, assuming a selling commission of $58, and a tax of $3?

c. Rhonda bought five $1,000 bonds 5 years ago when they were selling at $77\frac{1}{2}$. Ignoring interest and commissions, what was her capital gain when she sold them at $88\frac{3}{4}$?

d. In Problem 4.c, how much interest did Rhonda receive from the buyer if the transaction was made exactly 45 days since the last interest payment, assuming an interest rate of $9\frac{5}{8}$?

e. What was the amount of the check received by Rhonda, assuming a broker's selling commission of $5 per bond and a transaction tax of $3.16?

Mathematics of Finance

1. **Income statement (20 points)**

   Complete the following comparative income statement, showing each entry as a percentage of net sales (round percents to tenths position).

Comparative Income Statement	1990 Amount	1990 % of Sales	1989 Amount	1989 % of Sales
Net sales	500,000		450,000	
Cost of goods sold	375,000			
Gross profit			135,000	
Expenses	115,000			
Net income			36,000	

2. **Balance sheet (20 points)**

   Complete the following comparative balance sheet, showing the increase (decrease) and percentage of increase (decrease) (round percents to tenths position).

Comparative Balance Sheet	December 31 1990	December 31 1989	Increase (decrease) Amount	Increase (decrease) Percent
Current assets	50,000			
Fixed assets		140,000		
Total assets	200,000	185,000		
Current liabilities	32,000			
Long-term liabilities	80,000	75,000		
Ownership		75,000		
Total		185,000		

3. **Financial ratios (10 points each)**

   a. Using the data in Problem 2, compute the current ratio for 1990 (round answer to tenths).

   b. Using the data in Problem 2, compute the debt-equity ratio for 1990 (round answer to tenths).

4. Costs, profits, and dividends (20 points)

Distribute $10,000 of overhead expenses among the departments of Westbrook Company on the basis of square footage, as shown in the following table:

Department	Square Feet
A	1,300
B	1,500
C	1,200
D	2,000

5. Stock and bond quotations (5 points each)

52 weeks High	52 weeks Low	Stock	Div.	P-E Ratio	Sales 100s	High	Low	Close	Net Chg.
30	$25\frac{3}{4}$	Texaco	2	8	1221	$26\frac{1}{2}$	$26\frac{1}{8}$	$26\frac{3}{8}$	$+\frac{1}{8}$

a. If you buy 100 shares at the highest price of the day, how much do you have to pay, not including broker's commission?

b. If your broker sells 100 shares of this stock for you at the closing price, stock which you bought 2 years ago at a price of $24\frac{1}{2}$, what is your taxable gain? (Ignore commissions).

Bonds	Cur. Yld.	Vol.	Close	Net Chg.
Exxon 6s97	7.2	3	$83\frac{7}{8}$	$+\frac{1}{8}$

c. If you bought 5 bonds at the closing price, how much did it cost you, not including commissions, taxes, or interest?

d. In Problem 5.c, if the settlement date is 30 days following the last payment of interest, how much interest must you (the buyer) pay the seller?

APPENDIX

Answers to Selected Assignment Problems

Assignment 1A

1. 20,779   18,068   17,540   12,349   55.86   3,396.54   15,304.74   202.631
2. **a.** $2,705.83   **c.** 556 gal
3. 277   453   −73   345   661   514   164   161   59.25   438.707
4. **a.** $1,274.40   **c.** $10,309   **e.** $142.28

Assignment 1B

1. 19,890   19,188   14,760   490,960   325,800   2,058.4   148.80   2.5864
2. **a.** $133.13   **c.** $2.60
3. 5.70   16.4   252   212.4316   18.5
4. 1,680   3,438   266   5.26   390,000
5. **a.** $370   **c.** $687.50

Assignment 2A

1. $\frac{13}{4}$ $\frac{63}{5}$ $\frac{37}{5}$ $\frac{35}{8}$ $\frac{65}{3}$

2. $1\frac{1}{3}$ $11\frac{3}{8}$ $2\frac{1}{3}$ $8\frac{5}{7}$ 3

3. 21   24   168   350   72

4. $\frac{1}{2}$ $\frac{1}{3}$ $\frac{1}{4}$ $\frac{2}{5}$ $\frac{2}{3}$

5. 1 $1\frac{3}{16}$ $15\frac{7}{8}$

6. $\frac{5}{8}$ $3\frac{1}{15}$ $4\frac{17}{35}$

7. a. $33\frac{17}{20}$ lb   **c.** $24\frac{5}{24}$

Assignment 2B

1. $\frac{1}{2}$ $\frac{3}{11}$ $\frac{7}{18}$ $\frac{1}{4}$ $\frac{5}{33}$ $\frac{1}{24}$

2. a. $\frac{3}{32}$ **c.** \$2,000

3. $\frac{2}{3}$ 12 $\frac{12}{49}$ $2\frac{1}{6}$ $\frac{5}{18}$ $3\frac{1}{2}$

4. a. 15   **c.** 160

Assignment 3A

1. 0.4   0.025   1.5   0.00026   0.25   0.0016   0.0367   2   0.002   0.5
2. 50%   75%   99%   0.5%   33.3%   0.25%   16.5%   975%   100%   110%
3. a. 0.143
4. 0.4   1   0.75   0.375   0.167   0.833   0.25   0.75   1.1   7.04
5. $\frac{2}{5}$ $\frac{1}{2}$ $\frac{31}{50}$ $\frac{11}{50}$ $\frac{7}{8}$ $2\frac{1}{5}$ $\frac{3}{10}$ $\frac{1}{8}$ $\frac{4}{5}$ $\frac{3}{5}$
6. a. 37.5%

Assignment 3B

1. 0.04   0.0125   2.33   0.0075   2   0.00125   0.172   0.1   26   0.0012
2. 180%   210%   300%   12.5%   150%   1,250%   2,500%   125%   200%   0.1%
3. a. \$5.89
4. 0.25   0.32   2.125   0.8   0.55   0.4   0.45   8.6   0.28   0.48
5. $\frac{4}{5}$ $1\frac{1}{4}$ $\frac{1}{5}$ $\frac{81}{100}$ $\frac{5}{8}$ $\frac{1}{200}$ $1\frac{3}{5}$ $\frac{7}{10}$ $\frac{22}{125}$ $5\frac{3}{4}$
6. a. 0.875

Assignment 4A

1. -1 35   2   17 -14 74   1 -34 1   2
2. 28   48 -16 40   28   18   27 -120 30 -48
3. 3 -4 9   0.3 -3 35   6 -4 -1 1
4. 5   10   9   10 -3 12   2 -3 5   4

Assignment 4B

1. a. \$1,600   **c.** \$1,625.50   **e.** 60
2. a. \$8.80   **c.** 40   **e.** 10,350 gal

Practice test 1

1. 10,150   57.19   3,406.13   8,783.23 -8
2. 104,092   273.210   41   421   41.2
3. 27/8   39/4   57/8   100/3   3 3/4   5 2/3   6 1/3
   3 2/5   6/13   1/5   3/16   4/9

4. 8/15   3 32/35   7/8   3 7/8   1/4   1/20   1 11/24   10
5. 0.65   0.015   0.005   0.5%   350%   26%
6. 0.875   0.6   0.75   3/10   3/1,000   17/100
7. 3   −13   3   2.5
8. a. 20 million   **b.** 1,550

Assignment 5A

1. $34.56   **3.** $324   **5.** $9.05   **7.** $403.50   **9.** 44¢   **11.** $21\frac{1}{2}$¢
13. 3¢ per oz   **15.** $2.88   **17.** $30,500   **19.** $1,375

Assignment 5B

1. $17.39   **3.** $6.50 (no savings)   **5.** 405 sq ft   **7.** 1,481 cu yd   **9.** 27.5
13. Denver, 10.00 A.M.; Dallas, 11:00 A.M.; Philadelphia, 12 noon   **15.** 3 hours   **17.** $1,750
19. 350

Assignment 6A

1. 165.60   **3.** 11,520   **5.** 4,300   **7.** 36.4% increase   **9.** 8 1/2%   **11.** 13.3%
13. $1,541.25   **15.** 68%   **17.** 24,960   **19.** 323%

Assignment 6B

1. 1,533   **3.** 360   **5.** 5% increase   **7.** $400   **9.** $42,500   **11.** $48.75
13. 8% increase   **15.** $2,750   **17.** (2.7%)   **19.** $275,324

Assignment 7A

1. a. $16,686.50   **c.** Mean, $615.33; median, $605   **e.** $548.40
2. a. 118.2% increase   **3. a.** $4.88   **c.** $2.50

Assignment 7B

1. a. $1,016.67   **c.** $500   **e.** $22,500
2. $780.60   **3. a.** 53.3%

Assignment 8A

c. 40%, 35%, 25%

Assignment 8B

3. a. Department A   **c.** Department B
4. a. coal   **c.** $255,000   **e.** 14.3%

Practice test 2

1. a. 55¢   **b.** 2.2¢ oz   **c.** 20¢   **d.** 33 1/3 sq yd   **e.** 5 A.M. California time
2. a. 6,875   **b.** $9.53   **c.** 16%   **d.** 42%   **e.** $220,000   **f.** 160
    g. 10.5%   **h.** $179.25   **3. a.** $76,456   **b.** $22.23

Assignment 9A

1. **a.** $75.45   **c.** $250   **e.** $87.51   **g.** $4.30   **i.** 10 1/2%
2. **a.** $18,737.50   **c.** 1 1/4 years   **e.** $1,045

Assignment 9B

1. **a.** $2,000   **c.** $1,348.50   **e.** 8 1/2%   **g.** $5,107.40   **i.** $979.17
2. **a.** 9 1/2%   **c.** $3,200   **e.** $11,540

Assignment 10A

1. $46.88   **2. a.** $1,160 balance   **3. a.** $83.08   **4. a.** $797.31

Assignment 10B

1. $1,000   **2. a.** $3,548.08   **c.** $2,702.48   **3. a.** $13.46   **4. a.** 16.8%
   c. None   **e.** $1.19

Assignment 11A

2. Final balance, $289.38

Assignment 11B

1. Balance figure, $347.45   **3.** $1.61

Assignment 12A

1. **a.** $47,875   **c.** $50,000   **e.** $682.50   **g.** $24,300   **i.** 9.9%   **k.** $21,276.60
   m. $1,276.60   **o.** $32,508.83   **q.** $850   **s.** $877.50

Assignment 12B

1. **a.** $525   **c.** $26.25   **e.** $525
2. **a.** $18   **c.** $19 (from our company)   **e.** $731.25
3. **a.** $337.50   **c.** $45.71   **e.** $47.50   **g.** $6,495.50   **i.** $104.50

Assignment 13A

1. **a.** $627.20   **c.** $1,503.66   **e.** $262.73   **g.** $507.54   **i.** $1,591.35
2. **a.** $\% = 6, n = 30$ **c.** $\% = 6, n = 20$ **e.** $\% = 5\frac{1}{2}, n = 3$
3. **a.** $1,499.35   **c.** $5.69   **e.** $2,031.58

Assignment 13B

1. **a.** $2,344.96   **c.** $6,437   **e.** $7,060.95   **g.** $1,557.12   **i.** $111,555
2. **a.** 5, 20, compound amount   **c.** 6, 30, present value   **e.** 5, 28, compound amount
   g. 3, 20, present value   **i.** 4, 16, compound amount

Practice test 3

1. **a.** $4.44   **b.** 3 years   **c.** $722   **d.** 11.25%
2. $186.43   **3.** $204.57
4. **a.** $26,315.79   **b.** $10,139.79
5. **a.** $7,878.56   **b.** 8, 20, compound amount   **c.** 12, 15, sinking fund
   d. 3, 20, compound amount   **e.** 1 1/2, 60 amortization   **f.** 4, 24, present value

Assignment 14A

1. **a.** $87.75   **c.** $270   **e.** $233.75   **2. a.** $22.50   **c.** $42   **e.** $12
3. **a.** $73.72   **c.** $19.80   **e.** $593.64   **4. a.** 7.9%   **c.** 14.3%   **e.** No difference

Assignment 14B

1. **a.** $490   **c.** $275.50   **e.** $25.50   **g.** $223.96   **i.** October 25
2. **a.** $900   **c.** $3.50   **3. a.** $97.96   **c.** $510.20   **4. a.** $292.89

Assignment 15A

1. **a.** $303.75   **c.** $6.84   **e.** $6,773.03   **g.** $24,437.60
2. **a.** $118.75   **c.** $2,256.25   **e.** $67.69

Assignment 15B

1. Total amount, $723.38   **2.** Total, $18,742.50

Assignment 16A

1. **a.** $280   **c.** $78.72   **2. a.** $68   **c.** $500
3. **a.** $30.60   **c.** 51¢   **4. a.** $86.67   **c.** $1.04   **e.** $1,307.69
   g. $71.25   **i.** $23.22   **k.** 15%

Assignment 16B

1. **a.** 98%   **c.** 11.1%   **2. a.** $104.17   **c.** $15.00
3. **a.** $52.94   **c.** $35.11   **4. a.** $12   **c.** $12.50   **e.** 20.83%   **g.** $1.70
   i. $16.63   **k.** 40¢

Practice test 4

1. **a.** $14.26   **b.** $3.52   **c.** 14 1/2%   **d.** $2,462.50   **e.** $1,484.77
2. **a.** $21   **b.** $25   **c.** none   **d.** $2,131.25   **e.** $60
3. **a.** $19.77   **b.** $5.52   **c.** $1.74   **d.** $18.75   **e.** 27.3%   **f.** 37.5%
   g. $2,000   **h.** $63.24   **i.** 52.4%   **j.** 110%

Assignment 17A

1. **a.** $443   **c.** $21,320   **e.** $21.60
2. **a.** $45   **c.** $36.29   **e.** $633.01
3. Total net pay is $2,635.69

Assignment 17B

1. **a.** $942.31 **c.** $16,120 **e.** $313.60
2. **a.** $31 **c.** $34.92 **e.** $371.94
3. Total net pay is $3,790.88

Assignment 18A

1. **a.** $67.59 **c.** $55.80 **e.** $864.20
2. **a.** $560 **c.** $45,000 **e.** $220
3. **a.** $3,033.30 **c.** $425,112.88 **e.** $27.8%
4. **a.** $493.60 **c.** $444.52 **e.** $18,956.21

Assignment 18B

1. **a.** $21.18 **c.** $116.40 **e.** $28.08
2. **a.** $25 **c.** $0.18 **e.** $3,750
3. **a.** $357,000 **c.** $6,976.67 **e.** $32,000
4. **a.** $1,687.50 **c.** $1,093.75 **e.** $593.13

Assignment 19A

1. **a.** $5,000 **c.** $45,000 **2. a.** $3,571.43
3. **a.** $4,700 **c.** $7,520 **e.** $1,282,500
4. Yearly depreciation, $12,466.80; first year depreciation, $6,233.40; book value, $118,434.60

Assignment 19B

1. **a.** $1,250 **c.** $8,750 **2. a.** $23,863.67
3. **a.** $350 **c.** $560 **e.** $106,837.50
4. First-year depreciation, $8,420; book value, $75,780

Assignment 20A

1. Ending quantity, 2,500 **2.** Totals: $34,583.37, $50,754.93, $12,265.70, $104,559.80, $3,278.44

Assignment 20B

1. **a.** 10,000 and $127,800 **c.** $65,817 **2. a.** $7,736.20 **3. a.** $7,140
4. $8.87, $6,475.10

Practice test 5

1. **a.** $1,480.77 **b.** $3,378.27 **c.** $298.42
2. **a.** $336.44 **b.** $86.80 **c.** $26,150
3. Yearly depreciation, $12,000; first-year depreciation, $6,000
4. **a.** $23,862.50 **b.** $17,325

Assignment 21A

1. **a.** $15,000 **c.** $60,000 **e.** $281,500 **g.** $66\frac{1}{2}\%$ **i.** $8\frac{1}{2}\%$
2. Sales revenues, 100.8; cost of goods sold, 82.5; total expenses, 11.7; net income after taxes, 4.7

Assignment 21B

1. Cost of goods sold, 60.0 and 62.6; gross profit, 40.0 and 37.4; total expenses, 31.6 and 29.2; net income after taxes, 7.2 and 7.0
2. Net sales, 33,000 and 7.1; cost of goods sold, 7,640 and 2.6; total expenses, 21,600 and 15.8; net income after taxes, 3,196 and 9.8

Assignment 22A

1. **a.** $835,000   **c.** $412,000   **e.** 18.6%   **g.** $13,700   **i.** ($43,238)
2. Total current assets, 20.7; total fixed assets, 79.3; total current liabilities, 7.8; total long-term liabilities, 16.4; total equity, 75.8

Assignment 22B

1. Total current assets, 21.3 and 19.6; net fixed assets, 78.8 and 80.4; total current liabilities, 6.3 and 5.8; total liabilities, 25.0 and 26.7; total equity, 75.0 and 73.3
2. Total current assets, 7,000 and 9.0; net fixed assets, (5,000) and (1.6); total current liabilities, 1,850 and 8.0; total liabilities, (6,150) and (5.8); total equity, 8,150 and 2.8

Assignment 23A

a. $21,706   **c.** 1.3:1.0   **e.** 1.0:1.3   **g.** 8.8 times   **i.** 14.9% or 14.9¢

Assignment 23B

a. $81,158   **c.** 1.0:1.2   **e.** 1:4   **g.** 9.6 times   **i.** 3.5% or 3.5¢

Assignment 24A

1. **a.** 38%   **c.** 69.6%   **e.** $420   **2. a.** $42,000   **c.** $16,354.84
3. **a.** 32¢   **c.** $2.75   **e.** 38¢   **4.** Share of rent: 3,900; 6,750; 1,725; and 2,625

Assignment 24B

1. **a.** Western: 31.0%, Rocky Mountain: 31.8%, Eastern: 37.2%   **c.** $1,638
   e. $9,000   **2. a.** $65,250.20   **c.** $1,725   **e.** $3,731
3. **a.** $120,000   **c.** 40¢   **4.** A: 15,840; B: 13,200; C: 16,500; D: 9,240; E: 11,220

Assignment 25A

1. **a.** $33.75   **c.** 2,000   **e.** 75¢
2. **a.** $770   **c.** 14.3%   **e.** $10
3. **a.** $12.50   **c.** $984.50   **e.** $4,257.50
4. **a.** $403 loss   **c.** $1,247.50   **e.** $163.75

Assignment 25B

1. **a.** $33.625   **c.** 40¢   **e.** $6,575.58
2. **a.** $960   **c.** $29.20   **e.** 8.9%
3. **a.** $840   **c.** 15   **e.** 1998
4. **a.** $850   **c.** $562.50   **e.** $4,469.49

Practice test 6

1. Cost of goods sold: 375,000; 75.0; 315,000; 70.0
   Gross profit: 125,000; 25.0; 135,000; 30.0
   Expenses: 115,000; 23.0; 99,000; 22.0
   Net income: 10,000; 2.0; 36,000; 8.0
2. Current assets: 50,000; 45,000; 5,000; 11.1
   Fixed assets: 150,000; 140,000; 10,000; 7.1
   Total assets: 200,000; 185,000; 15,000; 8.1
   Current liabilities: 32,000; 35,000; (3,000); (8.6)
   Long-term liabilities: 80,000; 75,000; 5,000; 6.7
   Ownership: 88,000; 75,000; 13,000; 17.3
   Total: 200,000; 185,000; 15,000; 8.1
3. **a.** 1.6:1.0 **b.** 1.3:1.0
4. 2,170; 2,500; 2,000; 3,330; $10,000
5. **a.** $2,650 **b.** $187.50 **c.** $4,193.75 **d.** $25